Studies in Chinese Folklore

INDIANA UNIVERSITY FOLKLORE INSTITUTE
MONOGRAPH SERIES, VOL. 23

Bloomington, 1970

Wolfram Eberhard

Studies
in Chinese Folklore
and Related Essays

Published by
INDIANA UNIVERSITY RESEARCH CENTER
FOR THE LANGUAGE SCIENCES, BLOOMINGTON
Mouton & Co., The Hague, The Netherlands

INDIANA UNIVERSITY PUBLICATIONS

FOLKLORE INSTITUTE MONOGRAPH SERIES

Publications Committee

The Indiana University Folklore Series was founded in 1939
for the publication of occasional papers and monographs.

Standard Book Number 87750-147-5

Library of Congress Catalog Number: 79-630297

Orders for the U.S.A. and Canada should be
placed with Humanities Press, Inc., 303
Park Avenue South, New York, N.Y. 10010

Orders from all other countries should be sent to
Mouton & Company, Publishers, The Hague, The Netherlands.

Printed in the United States of America

FOREWORD

With the exception of two articles, all of these essays have been previously published in various journals over the course of the last thirty-five years. Several reasons have convinced me that an edition now in book form would be of value. Most of these studies were published in German before World War II, and consequently never enjoyed a wide distribution, while others appeared in print in English, but in hard-to-locate small journals in a number of different countries. The original Chinese manuscripts for most of the essays in Parts I and II were in my possession, but these manuscripts were deposited in the Berlin Anthropological Museum and were destroyed during the War. Even more importantly, my decision was influenced by the observation that there is little hope today that contemporary China will provide us with folkloristic data comparable to that collected before World War II. The times have changed, and the interests of Chinese folklorists have changed with them. There is, then, a basic scarcity of reliable materials on Chinese folklore. It is my hope that this small book to a modest degree, will help to remedy this situation.

These studies do not contain much in the way of "folkloristic theory," although they have served as building blocks for theories in my own work. I have attempted to show, principally in the articles brought together in Part I, that folktales should not be studied in isolation, separated from other aspects of the culture, since they are often closely connected with festivals, ceremonies, rituals, or ethnic traditions.

Secondly, I have tried to demonstrate that, in a literate society, contemporary folklore should be studied together with the historical data, since it is quite possible for folktales or folk paintings to be related thematically to classical folk novels or folk plays, all of which have their own history, often going back many centuries. In some cases we are able to establish changes in themes or motifs. In many instances, such modifications in the text may be associated with changes in the environing society, so that we have ample reason to initiate research linking folklore with sociology.

Thirdly, and in a similar manner, by comparing Chinese tales with their Near Eastern counterparts, and by stressing the differences between both versions of the same folktale, it becomes possible to point to corresponding differences in the respective social and cultural structures underlying the tales. Work along such lines may someday lead to a clearer theory of the transmission of folktales, a theory which would also encompass the storytellers and their audiences, and/or their readers. Most of my present work on Chinese folklore deals with this problem of transmission and change, and is being pursued in connection with the elaboration of a more general sociological theory of development and change.

Lastly, and most importantly, the data in these essays have served as building blocks in my attempt to reconstruct "local cultures" in China, and to propose a hypothesis concerning the origin of what is now called "Chinese society" or "Chinese culture" on the basis of the existence, distribution, and cultural characteristics of these "local cultures." In point of fact, this work, subsequently published in my *Kultur und Siedlung der Randvölker Chinas* (Leiden, 1942),[1] and in *Lokalkulturen im alten China,*[2] was initially stimulated by the folkloristic research which I undertook in China in 1934-35, and again in 1937. For this reason, the main "theory" behind these essays is the hypothesis of the existence of local cultures in China, and their later coalescence into a Chinese culture in which, even today, we can still discern the remnants of the early local cultures.

I am grateful to my Chinese folkloristic colleagues for much of the material contained in these papers. Their names are found throughout the book; unfortunately, conditions at this time make it impossible for me to thank each of them personally. Without their stimulation and help, I would often have been unable to collect the data.

I decided, after re-reading the essays, to leave them basically unchanged, but to add certain explanatory information such as would contribute to a better understanding of the material. Many of these new additions are the result of research done in more recent years. The essays brought together here are, therefore, more or less "up-to-date" as far as content is concerned, while their original form has generally been preserved.

Finally, I wish to express my special thanks to Mr. William Templer, who carefully translated the German essays into English, and who edited the other papers. I also want to thank Professor Richard M. Dorson, who first encouraged me to bring out these essays in book form, and who has aided me in their publication.

TABLE OF CONTENTS

ILLUSTRATIONS

INTRODUCTION

THE USE OF FOLKLORE IN CHINA*

1. *Definition of Folklore*

Folklore belongs to the social sciences, but it is probably the least developed part of the social sciences. In only a few countries is folklore regarded as an independent field of specialization. Folklore is often treated as a part of anthropology, or, perhaps even more commonly, as a branch of linguistics, or the national philologies (Germanistics, English studies, Romanistics). This is, at least in part, the result of a lack of clarity in the definition of the field. In general, we find two definitions of folklore. According to the Anglo-American definition, folklore is limited to the oral traditions or oral literature of a society. It therefore encompasses folktales, fairy tales, epics, folksongs, riddles, proverbs, proverbial sayings, and even folk novels, if it can be assumed that they were a product of oral tradition and were printed only at a later stage. The continental European definition of the scope of folklore is wider, and includes, in addition to the areas I have just mentioned, folk dance, folk costume, folk medicine, folk beliefs, folk religion, and even folk housing. In this definition, folklore is "folk culture," and is thus quite close to culture anthropology in substantive scope. The principal difference is that conventional anthropology formerly did not study advanced societies, and that folklore formerly did not concern itself with the culture of the "primitives," merely because in simple societies there is no "common man" such as we find in more developed societies. In terms of the British definition, even primitive societies can have folklore, and perhaps they have only folklore and nothing else in the field of the arts. On the other hand, anthropology has always regarded the study of oral literature of simple societies as its own field. In both cases, then the concept of folklore is not clearly defined. For a long time, therefore, folklorists have limited themselves to the collection of data in developed societies, simply because anthropologists were not particularly interested in this kind of material. The

*Based on a lecture given at the University of Kansas, April, 1965, and published here for the first time.

discipline of folklore, however, has also attempted to become a comparative science, and has tried to develop its own methods of comparison and its own theories regarding the origin, distribution, and change of elements of folk culture. Because the material for which these theories were deveoped was often highly complex, the theories have frequently attempted to be more exact than analogous anthropological theories which were formulated principally on the basis of the study of relatively simple material objects.

The basic concept of the "folk" has remained crucial throughout the entire development of folklore as a field of study. The first beginnings of scientific folklore in Europe date back to the early nineteenth century, to the time of the Grimm brothers in Germany and the Romantic movement, though the term "folklore" was coined several decades later. In central Europe, the early nineteenth century was the time in which the Romanticists were attempting to establish what was "truly" German, Swiss, French, and so on. Their ultimate, and often perhaps unconscious, aim was to find an ideological basis for the newly created or planned national states, such as the German Empire or the Third Empire in France. They made use of two different approaches. On the one hand, they went back into history and studied the earliest existing remnants of "Germanic" culture in the hope of finding those elements which, consciously or unconsciously, were common to all Germans. On the other hand, they ventured out of the cities into the rural milieu of the "simple man," the "folk," in the hope that there they might discover that which was truly German, Swiss, or French in language and culture, still undisturbed and unaltered by the influence of Latin or French, the main languages of the educated upper classes in Europe at that time. They hoped to find customs which were still uncorrupted by the fashions of the courts and the cities, customs which were thus still "natural," "simple," and "good." Looking at folklore from this point of view, it was, from its very beginnings, a "political science," a field of study closely connected to the rise of the nationalistic political ideologies. In point of fact, the development of folkloristics in the European countries was parallel with the evolution of the national states. Perhaps most typical is the case of Finland, a country which even today is still among the ranks of the leaders in folklore studies. Finnish folklorists collected old songs, ballads, and epic fragments, and since they believed that the Finns, like the Germans, French, British, and Scandinavians, must have had a national epic, they put these fragments together and thus created a national epic, the *Kalevala*. Although this folk epic probably never existed in this form, in the twentieth century it gradually became *the* national epic of the Finnish nation.

We could cite many more such examples from our own time and century. The process which took place in Europe during the nineteenth century is now taking place in the developing nations of Africa and Asia. The state of Israel, a country with a deep interest in folklore and much scholarly activity in the field, is another typical recent example.

I hope that this brief analysis of the situation of folklore studies in the West may prove useful for an understanding of what has happened in China.

2. *Origins of Folklore Studies in China*

The onset of Chinese folklore studies was in the period from 1917-1919, those years which, as we now know, were so crucial for the entire development of modern China, and years for which the "Fourth of May Movement" became the symbol. While the events of May fourth were of political importance as the first nationalistic student rebellion against a regime which could not represent China and which had tried to sell China out to Japan, the other aspect of this movement was the so-called "literary revolution." This revolution, like the political revolt, was also led by students from the very same National Peking University.

Seen from the outside, this "literary revolution" appears as a reaction to the impact of Western literature in China. The Chinese had been translating books of a scientific and technical nature from the European languages into Chinese since the late nineteenth century. They had also begun to translate literary works into Chinese. These translations opened up a whole new world to the Chinese. One should remember that at that time European literatures were in the age of Naturalism and Realism. No Chinese writer had ever attempted to describe the world in which his heroes lived in the most minute detail. They had never tried to describe men as individuals, possessed and often torn by contradictory traits of character, nor had they sought to depict their actions, even the most trivial and unimportant ones, in every detail, or ventured to describe sex as it really is. No Chinese writer had taken the trouble to study in detail the man on the street, the poor, the peasant, nor had they ever been made the hero of a novel. No Chinese writer had yet attempted to write the way the common man speaks, with all his colloquialisms and dialect expressions. The traditional writer made use of a literary style which was incomprehensible to the common man, a style which was often so complicated and refined that only a select few of the writer's friends and colleagues could fully understand the depths of his thoughts and the beauty of his allusions — a situation, I might add, quite similar to the esoteric manner characteristic of some of our modern Western poets. In the course of time, many different literary styles were developed in China, but all of these were used only *by* scholars, and only *for* scholars. The same held true for the lyric poem: there were several different types of poems, but they all used rules and rhyme schemes which were more than a thousand years old. In fact, frequently the words no longer rhymed in their modern pronunciation, and it was necessary to know the historical pronunciation in order to appreciate the poem. Moreover, all ordinary and "profane" words were tabooed, and an idea, if possible, was to be expressed in quotations and allusions drawn from earlier poems. Starting in the thirteenth century, a special style for novels had developed, and at the time of its development this style had been very close to the ordinary language. But novels were regarded by the educated elite as a kind of "kitsch," low-class products for low-class people, and even this vernacular style had, in the meantime, become separated from the daily language. Under these conditions, the translation of novels, poems and short stories from nineteenth century Europe proved to be extremely difficult, because the problem was not simply that of translating from one language into another, but from a European everyday idiom into Chinese literary language and style. The literary language of traditional China was not equipped for this task.

This is the point at which the "literary revolution" set in. Young Chinese who had studied abroad, men like Hu Shih and others, or men who had become acquainted with Western literature through translations (often translations into Japanese — Lu Hsün is now the most famous man of this group), turned against the literary language and began to use the language of the people in their works. This led to two developments, just as it had done in Europe in the early nineteenth century. One group occupied itself with a study of the Chinese past. Under the leadership of Hu Shih and his friends, these men tried to show that the literary use of popular language was not un-Chinese, and certainly not new. They stated that some authors had used colloquial language right from the early literary periods on, and that this had been especially true in the very earliest stages of the literature. But again and again, in the course of time, this colloquial language had been refined and had developed into the literary language of the scholars. Books like Hu Shih's *Pai-hua wen-hsüeh shih (History of Literature in Colloquial Language)* contain very valuable compilations of texts and textual fragments of the early Chinese literature written in colloquial language. Moreover, this group also worked out a new theory about the origin and development of specific styles and forms of Chinese poetry, especially the *tz'u* poetry of the third century B. C. Thus, they found in the old literature, and especially in the early poetry, models which could serve for a rejuvenation and transformation of present-day literature. They regarded the classical novels of China as the most suitable model for prose literature, and many of the early literary products of this group followed the novel style quite closely. The advocates of this school, then, were of the opinion that modern Chinese literature should not have to imitate the Western models, and should not of necessity have to break with all indigenous literary traditions, but should rather set about to develop trends already present in the corpus of classical Chinese literature. In one of my last talks with Hu Shih, he was very outspoken on this point. One can regard such a position as "reactionary," and the members of this group have indeed been accused of harboring reactionary attitudes by those of the other group. But we may also consider this to be a nationalistic attitude, since, in practice, a total break with Chinese traditions had to lead to an imitation of European developments. It is, therefore, quite significant that the representatives of this school were, politically and ideologically, bourgeois liberals or liberal nationalists. And it is understandable that this school later found its refuge and protection in Taiwan under the regime of Chiang Kai-shek. Hu Shih, who was the leader of this group from its very inception, died just a few years ago as president of the Academica Sinica.

The second group struck out in the opposite direction, a path which had also been travelled in nineteenth century Europe. They proclaimed that the true way to create a new, popular, and generally understandable literature, a literature in which everything that the common man says and thinks can be written down, is to go to the common man and to study his language. This group, which soon came under the leadership of Lu Hsün, led logically to the development of Chinese folklore studies. Its first leaders were Lu Hsün and Ku Chieh-kang (the latter scholar is still alive). Its center was the National Peking University, the place where the entire literary and political movement had originated. Folklore (in its British meaning) was to point the way for a new literature. Because young Chinese scholars had always had special enthusiasm for poetry, the students of National Peking University first went out to collect folksongs — although, unfortunately, they collected the texts but not the music. In a few years, more than ten thousand songs from all parts of China had been collected and stored in the archives. Many of the (usually short-lived) literary and folkloristic magazines which appeared in those years published selected folksongs. Later some larger collections were published in book form. But, even today, only a small percentage of the archival folksong material has appeared in print.

The collection of folktales began a little later. The purely linguistic and stylistic aspects were never particularly important to the tale collectors, so that, even today, we have few tale texts which give us the feeling that they report exactly the words of the original storyteller. Professional folklorists today require a high degree of fidelity in the recording of texts. The majority of tales are presented in the language of the writer himself, who tried to remain faithful to the words of his storyteller informant, but also wanted to write "beautifully." The "editing" of these texts is clearly recognizable in the emendation of all vulgar or obscene expressions, as well as in the change of all purely dialectical and local expressions. The collectors of tales who worked in the 1920's were interested mainly in folktales, legends, sagas, and anecdotes, because this popular literature described situations and topics which the classical literature had never described. In common with European folklorists of the late nineteenth century, they also believed that tales, legends, and sagas contained survivals of China's oldest traditions. By comparing modern tales and legends collected in the field with similar tales reported briefly in the classical literature, they felt they would be able to show to what extent and for what reasons the literati had falsified and changed folk traditions. Under the leadership of Ku Chieh-kang, this group came to the conclusion that most of the reports about the earliest history of China were historicized legends and tales, and were not true historical accounts. Thus, some two thousand years of so-called "Chinese history" had to be crossed out as merely legendary, and the documented history of China thus did not begin until about 1500 B. C.

This had two immediate consequences. The reduction of China's history deeply offended Chinese nationalists and conservatives. They argued that according to this interpretation China had been inferior to the West right from its very beginning, since China had become civilized only after the Western world had already had a civilization for thousands of years, a period during which China had languished in barbarism.

On the other hand, however, if through the use of folklore materials it might be possible to unmask the venerable traditional history of ancient China, with all its wise emperors, as pure legend, then a reinterpretation of China's earliest history according to other principles could be attempted. We have to bear in mind that this "literary revolution" took place at the same time as the Russian Revolution, a time in which so many hoped to see a new world and a new concept of the world emerging. It is thus understandable that Chinese communists and fellow-travellers accepted this new school of interpretation of Chinese history, because now a new interpretation along the "scientific" lines of Marxism seemed to be both possible and justified.

This is not the only branch of folklore studies which soon veered strongly in the direction of Communism and Socialism. The idea that the common man — the simple, unperverted man of the street — is a better, more honest and moral man than his refined city bourgeois counterpart, is a typical by-product of nineteenth century European Romanticism, and was an element underlying the thought of Karl Marx. According to this concept, the literary products of the common man, his folksongs, ballads, folktales and other folk stories, express the true and genuine values of the society, as opposed to the artificial, over-refined, dead values of the upper classes. Thus, under Lu Hsün's leadership, the collectors of folksongs and ballads evinced tendencies toward Socialism right from the very beginning. In Communist China today, Lu Hsün has posthumously become the leader of the "Literary Revolution" as well as a leading figure in Communist poetry and prose. We should also note that Mao Tse-tung likewise participated in this movement while serving as a young library assistant at National Peking University, although in more recent years he has returned to classical literary Chinese for his own poetry.

Although folklore became a tool of liberal nationalism and nourished the ideology of the national states in nineteenth-century Europe, and although it proved exceedingly useful to twentieth-century European ideologies of National Socialism and Communism, the liberal nationalists in China never took to folklore. Perhaps this is because they saw only too clearly the possible dangers involved in this. The folklore movement, it should be remembered, arose during the period of the warlords who often had relations with foreign powers. These liberal nationalists may have reasoned that if folklorists were then beginning to record the songs and tales of one particular part of China, taking note of the local dialect and local expressions, their works could easily become tools for separatist movements.

From these considerations, I think it is thus quite understandable that the regime of Chiang expressed little sympathy for folklore studies as soon as Chiang controlled larger areas of China (i.e., after 1928). He regarded the study of folk traditions and tales as dangerous because he thought that this would lead to a destruction of the traditional and glorious history of ancient China. He was against all other folkloristic activity because he felt it could be used by separatist movements. And because Chiang had identified with the liberal, rational, and evolutionary currents in Western thought, he also regarded folklore studies as reactionary, because they tended to glorify ancient superstitions and traditions, instead of helping to replace superstition by modern science. For this reason, Chinese folklore studies, which had developed rapidly in the years between 1919 and 1928, and had witnessed the creation of a number of active folklore societies throughout the country, became less and less popular and started to die out in the years after 1934.

There can be little doubt that one of the principal reasons why Chinese folklore studies were not able to escape an entanglement with prevailing ideologies is the widespread lack of training in methods of fieldwork and meager knowledge of folkloristic theory. None of the prominent folklorists of the time really knew the methods and theories of Western folkloristics as they had developed after 1900. Not until the late 1920's were there translations into Chinese of a general introduction to folklore by Charlotte Burne (*The Handbook of Folklore*) and Arnold van Gennep's *Le Folklore*. The publications of Finnish, German, Swiss and Russian folklorists remained totally unknown. I should perhaps add that even today the situation is not much better. The main works of modern Western folklorists are still unknown in both Chinas. I am familiar with one folklorist in Taiwan who has recently begun to analyze Chinese tales as reported in the classical literature along lines which have been developed by one branch of American Folklore studies, but he has taken his methods from the anthropological, rather than the folkloristic literature. In Communist China I am familiar with the case of a folklore teacher who got himself into great trouble as a result of his trying to apply the system of the tale and motif-index as developed by Finnish and American scholars.

3. *Folklore in Taiwan*

Since 1948 we have had *de facto* two Chinas. Both claim to rely upon the ideology of Sun Yatsen (Sun is regarded by one group as a liberal Nationalist, and by the other as a Communist, and both camps can cite appropriate statements of Sun, who was never quite clear and knew comparatively little about Western thought, in defense of their positions). Both Chinas regard the "Movement of the Fourth of May" and the Literary Revolution as their own. Indeed, many of the leaders in the two Chinas are former students of National Peking University.

Officially, Taiwan still does not recognize folklore as an independent field of study. Anthropologists collect the traditions and oral literature of the remaining non-Chinese aborigines of Taiwan, following earlier anthropological and particularly Japanese traditions of research. A few folklorists active in the 1920's have done little more than to reprint their old books. Some have collected a few more tales from Mainland Chinese immigrants or Taiwan-Chinese. In recent years, a group of scholars has formed who are interested in the customs of the Taiwan-Chinese, and they have also begun to collect the oral literature of the Taiwan-Chinese. It is understandable (if only because of the difficulty of the Taiwanese dialects) that these men should be native Taiwan-Chinese who are quite proud of their own past. These men, however, are not simply nationalistic Taiwanese whose political ideal is a Taiwanese state, since by recording the traditions of their own group, they supply, at the same time, some insight into the culture of the provinces of Fukien and Kuangtung, those parts of China from which they originally came. From a political point of view, therefore, this activity has a certain value, since the materials collected have been used for radio propaganda beamed toward Mainland China – another utilitarian "use of folklore." We should, however, add that this small group of folklorists has, in most instances, a good training in anthropology, and can therefore remain more objective than their earlier colleagues.

4. *Folklore in Mainland China*

In contrast to the situation in Taiwan, folkloristic activities in Mainland China have shown considerably greater progress. Their folklorists are not better trained than the Taiwanese, and most of them are ignorant of the new methods in the field. But the government is very much in favor of folklore. We can compare this with the case of Soviet Russia, which witnessed a great spurt in folkloristic research after the Revolution, although this activity came to an end in the 1930's. It is significant that modern Chinese publications appear to show the same characteristics as Russian publications before 1930.

Let me give a brief sketch of the state of research in the various subfields of folklore. In the area of folksong, we can report that large collections of songs have been published, including songs from different parts of the country as well as songs from different sectors of the population. This activity is an aspect of a more general interest in encouraging the making of poetry in Communist China. There appear to be two reasons for this programmatic stimulation of popular poetic creativity. In former times, writing poetry was the status symbol of the gentry. Poems were made when scholars sat together at a party; poetry was part of entertaining among the elite. In order to make a poem, one had to have extensive education and knowledge, and no common man was able to make a poem or understand one. The new Communist regime has certainly tried to obliterate this status symbol and to give every citizen the feeling that he too can create poems. Since the modern poem has done away with rhyme, and has also generally given up rhythm as well, the composing of poems is now a relatively simple task, and millions of poems have been made, poetry contests have been organized, and many of these poems have even been published as "folksongs." These songs either glorify the achievements of the new regime, or dramatize the evils of an older time. They thus have a certain value as propaganda, and are, at the same time, a harmless and simple way to give vent to tensions of a nonpolitical character.

Many of these songs have been published as "folksongs" in various folksong collections, although they are brand new and have been composed by authors who are known. Here again we have a question of definitions: Western folklorists generally consider a folksong to be a song which had a definite author, although his name is often forgotten and not recorded, which has spread widely in oral tradition, and (this is the decisive point) which is found in different variant forms. Russian and Chinese Communists, on the other hand, consider a folksong to be any song which is composed and liked by the "people," and which expresses the feelings of the common man, or at least what the party conceives those feelings should be. Thus, while we do not regard worksongs, labor songs, political songs, or songs of protest as folksongs in the strict sense of the term (even though we may collect and study them), such songs are considered to be folksongs in China and Russia, and are included as such in the collections. This constitutes a problem for the folklorist, since collections will thus contain both genuine and spurious folksong material. Only by carefully comparing the modern collections with pre-1948 or Taiwanese songs can we decide whether a song in a Mainland collection is indeed a genuine folksong. However, since only a few thousand genuine songs have been published, it is often impossible to say whether a song recorded in a Communist collection is a hitherto unknown form of a genuine folksong, or a fake song of modern provenience. Even more important is the fact that genuine folksongs do have variants. If we come across a variant form of a known folksong in a Communist collection, it is often impossible to say whether this is a genuine variant, widely known and liked in a particular part of the country, or a fake variant, altered for purposes of political propaganda. It might be possible to decide this question if we had complete collections of the total repertory of a single folksinger, or complete collections of the songs from one area, but none of the published collections fulfills these conditions. All of them contain "selected" examples, and if variants are given, we find only one or two "suitable" variants, and nothing else. The principle of selection is the "beauty" of the song (i.e., the degree to which the song expresses those items which the regime wants to have expressed). Thus, the Mainland collections include many songs in which women deplore the hard life of oppression they suffered in an earlier period, and in which they curse their parents who forced them to marry an unloved and bad husband. But such collections contain few songs in which women sing about their love for their husband, except in the case of songs which do not state how the marriage was concluded. In such instances, the reader can get the impression that a modern type of marriage for love is meant — and this was most certainly not the case.

The situation is very similar in the field of folktale, legend and saga. Here too, many collections have been published, usually arranged according to provinces. In no instance has the attempt been made to collect this kind of oral literature completely for a single area, including all existing variants, or even to collect all the tales a specific storyteller had to tell. Again, only certain "representative" tales are published. Usually, the kind of contextual information which we now generally try to furnish, such as: who told the tale, when, where, who wrote it down, what was the occasion at which the tale was told, and what kind of audience was present? — is completely missing. Sometimes the name of a storyteller is noted along with a very general placename, but we do not learn what his occupation was, how much education he had, how old he was, and so on. Occasionally the additional remark is made: "edited by XYZ." We should be very grateful for this brief indication, since this means that the original text has been greatly altered, and that we should exercise extreme caution in using it as scholarly information.

In two instances, the same tales have been published both in Hong Kong and Peking. A comparison of the different editions shows that (a) the

Hong Kong edition still contains a number of local expressions which the Peking edition has emended; (b) stories of religious content have been included in the Peking edition only if the deities mentioned are ridiculous, or can be regarded as negative, but powerless phantoms; (c) stories in which the heroes are of the upper class and are of good character are not included in the Peking edition, but all stories in which (1) the heroes are women and are depicted as better and more modern than men, (2) the heroes are farmers or members of the lower class and are positive characters, (3) members of the upper class are described as mean, shrewd, evil, or greedy, have all been included in the collection; and finally, (d) the Hong Kong edition gives some information about the ethnic group in cases of stories from Chinese ethnic minorities, but the Peking edition attempts to lump all minorities together into a very few large groups, and suppresses the names of tribes. Even worse, in its collection of Yünnan tales, the Peking edition contains some stories not present in the Hong Kong edition. Furthermore, these stories are not known from any other reliable collection of tales from China, but are indeed well known from the Indian collections. Now, no information is given as to whether the story was told by a Yünnanese, or whether perhaps the story was heard by a Yünnanese from Yünnanese, or from an Indian soldier. I regard it as highly likely that stories from India which express well what the regime wants to have stressed are published as Chinese tales.

Since I have in my possession a collection of more than three thousand modern Chinese folktales, all collected before 1940, and another collection of tales culled from earlier Chinese literature, I am often in a position to push the analysis still further. If we compare a tale from a Communist collection with a version of the tale collected at an earlier time, we can see that the tenor and content of the tales has been purposely changed. Wherever we find a landowner or landlord in a genuine text, he is sometimes depicted as good, and sometimes as neutral. But in the Communist text he receives as many negative traits as possible. His appearance is either repellent or ridiculous, and his manners are repulsive or mean. Any artisan or farmer, conversely, is automatically depicted as a positive figure, even if the original text described him in neutral or slightly negative terms: he looks wonderful, and he is open, honest, simple and proud; he invariably wants the best, but is cheated, made fun of and exploited by the bad landlords and officials. The motive of economic exploitation is never left out. Even the environment of the common man is always described in a positive manner: he lives simply, and is clean and frugal, earning his living by hard work. Episodes in the genuine texts in which deities, ghosts, and spirits occur are often omitted, and the mutilated text sometimes becomes unintelligible. Such supernatural beings are retained in the Communist text only if, by forcing the text, they can be described as cruel, stupid, mean, or powerless.

There are several publications and a number of essays in which editors or writers indicate why they publish folktales. They usually state that "tremendous masses of tales" have already been collected.[1] The writer then explains that he has published only those stories which best exemplify the spirit of the people, and which, for this reason, might serve as cultural documentation. In addition, the editors aver, these publications should stimulate the writers, since they can find therein motifs and topics which are truly popular, and by using these topics and themes they should be able to write good literature. Folktales thus are, in their view, both the raw materials and the models for the creative Chinese writer.

I have not seen any large collections of riddles and proverbs, although this does not mean such collections do not exist. Communist speakers love to quote proverbs, but most of these are derived from the classical novels, such as the *Shui-hu chuan*, and some are from the native locale of the speakers (i.e., they are proverbs which the speaker learned as a child). Riddles are completely devoid of any value from the stand point of Communist ideology, and proverbs often contain rules which may conflict with the rules of the regime. Nevertheless, I believe that a systematic study of those proverbs which are used by Mao Tse-tung and his colleages might well yield some interesting insights into his thought and politics, as would a careful study of the quotations from classical literature which he employs.

The greatest activity of the regime up until the summer of 1964 has been in the field of folk theater. Collections of two to three volumes, often containing more than a thousand pages, have been published, so that we now have the local folk plays for many of the provinces of China. This material is of especial interest to us. We were aware that, apart from the official Peking and other drama, there were several forms of folk opera and drama in existence. But none of the pre-war Chinese folklorists paid any attention to such forms. I know of only one book containing resumés of folk dramas from Hunan province, and only one collection of fully reported texts from Hopei province, but this was a collection of a special type of drama, the so-called *yang-ko*. I think that this failure on the part of Chinese folklorists was simply due to a lack of sufficient research funds. One can hardly expect that a group of actors will dictate a play slowly, word by word, without receiving a handsome remuneration in return, and the publication of such plays would also cost money. Pre-war folklore organizations, even when connected with universities, were extremely weak financially. It is also quite possible, and even likely, that the actors were not willing to have their plays written down, and had to be forced to do so. Only the modern regime is in a position to exert such force. The collection of *yang-ko* mentioned above was published by a community development agency which had some money at its disposal, and which had gained the confidence of the people over years of collaboration.

For this reason, the new opera texts are of great interest for us. We hear of new styles, their distribution and spread, and sometimes even learn about their historical origin, and we are provided with the full texts. Unfortunately, we are once again bitterly disappointed, because these texts are also so unreliable that they can hardly be used for scholarly purposes. As in the case of folksongs, these collections have likewise included brand-new plays specifically written for purposes of propaganda, even though they are labelled as "folk plays." It is usually quite simple to single out such plays, because the topics are typical: husband and wife co-operate in the building of a dam, or the good girl sacrifices her finest dress to protect some sacks of cement against the rain.

In some cases we find a helpful introductory remark by the editors which may state that the play was related by XYZ and edited by ABC. For us, this serves as a warning that the play has undergone extensive alterations. In a few cases, the kind of change is even indicated, by statements such as: "We omitted a number of unimportant persons in the drama in order to make the character of the action clearer," or "This play had some purely mythological sections which we have omitted." Unfortunately, in such cases we only know that the texts have been tampered with, but we do not know how they were in their real and original form. We are, however, not at a complete loss. The overwhelming number of folk plays are based on plays of the city theater, or have their parallels in the classical dramatic tradition. In other cases, they are based on short stories or parts of novels which we know. Equipped with a good knowledge of the official, "classical" drama, the short story, and novelistic literature, it is often possible to compare the two versions and to establish the nature of the falsifications. If all the differences between the folk and classical forms of the drama lie in a specific direction (i.e., if they coincide with the official Party doctrine, we can generally spot the differences and reconstruct the probably true form of the drama). As far as I have been able to ascertain (and my study is not yet completed), the changes in the folk drama are similar to those in the tales: members of the upper class receive negative attributes as far as is possible without destroying the meaning of the play; members of the lower class are always given positive traits; women are always depicted as heroines and as strong personalities, while the men with whom they fall in love are often portrayed as ridiculous weaklings; and mythological and religious scenes are deleted if they cannot be transformed into ridiculous scenes. In addition, probably for purposes of practicality, the number of secondary characters has been drastically reduced. For instance, although the classical drama typically has a maiden accompany the heroine, or a servant who helps the hero (and the hero then has sexual rights over the servant girl), the Communist texts leave these servants out if they cannot make use of them as comic figures. Finally, we do not have a single complete collection of plays, so that we have no idea whether the published plays are truly representative for a certain area of China or not. I have the impression that they are not representative in our sense, and do not want to be representative. They are published in order to provide professional and amateur actors in China with texts and music which are locally known and loved, but which are (or are made to be) "educational" in the Communist sense. Since the summer of 1964, the regime has turned against classical Chinese drama and its topics, and sponsors plays which have been written very recently, and which glorify the achievements of the new era while depicting the horrors of the old. A similar evolution is known to have taken place in the Soviet Union, and represents a second stage in the use of theater as propaganda. We can, therefore, expect that little more will be published in the field of folk theater in China.

As far as I am able to ascertain, no texts of the marionette, puppet, and shadow play have been collected and published by the new regime. All these popular forms of theater did exist and have enjoyed a long tradition. The neglect probably stems from the notion that with the spread of motion picture theaters, it is no longer important to preserve these popular dramatic arts. Already prior to the revolution they had lost much of their traditional appeal. Unfortunately, only a few shadow play texts, and virtually no marionette or puppet play texts have ever been collected, although they all still can be seen in Taiwan.

Folk dance was never very popular in China. Two thousand years of Confucianism have almost succeeded in killing off what was once a lively folk art. In order to create something to countervail the wave of foreign dances and dance music penetrating China, the regime elevated the above-mentioned *yang-ko* to the level of a national dance, adopting some of the ideas of men associated with the community development project of 1930. Otherwise, the regime attempts to show dances taken from non-Chinese minorities or dances which are not folk dances at all, but which derive from the tradition of the classical opera. Unfortunately, there are no pre-war collections of dance tunes. Judging from records and movies, folk tunes have been "adapted" in a manner quite similar to the way in which the Russians appropriated and changed Central Asian folk tunes by the use of modern, or even foreign instruments, and by straightening out and otherwise "correcting" the rhythms.

Those additional areas of folklore included in the Continental European definition, such as folk religion, folk custom, folk dress, superstition, folk housing, folk festivals, and folk medicine, did not arouse much interest in China before the Revolution, with perhaps the exception of folk festivals and folk religion. Communist China has likewise not shown any interest in these subfields, except for the area of folk medicine. Here, too, there has been a good deal of field collecting, and dozens of thick volumes have been published. I do not personally feel competent enough to evaluate the worth of these collections. As a matter of fact, no foreign scholar has, to my knowledge, paid any attention to these collections, although it might well profit scholarship to do so.

We do, however, have a good idea as to the reasons for this folk medical activity. Since about 1920 there has been a battle waging between modern, Western-trained doctors and traditional Chinese doctors. Each group regarded itself as superior, and the defence of the traditional practitioners was strengthened when, in the 1920's, Western chemists analyzed traditional Chinese remedies and isolated some important and now commonly used chemical drugs. The new regime exploited this struggle for its own purposes. It needed many more doctors for its medical programs than were readily available. By requiring the modern doctors to take courses in traditional medicine, the regime gained the confidence of the Chinese doctors, and could then induce them in turn to learn at least the fundamentals of modern hygiene, so that they could be pressed into service as long as there were an insufficient number of modern doctors. The collection of folk medicines and prescriptions had three principal aims. First of all, modern Chinese chemists obtained many new drugs and remedies not formerly known to modern science, and it was hoped that out of this fund of traditional remedies certain new and modern drugs could be developed. Secondly, as long as the Chinese chemical industry was unable to produce enough modern drugs, some of the old remedies could be used in their stead. Formerly it was the common practice for a traditional Chinese healer to keep his prescriptions secret so that his competitors could not copy them, and so that he could retain a monopoly on certain cures. Now, this monopoly has been broken: the Chinese practitioner has been granted the honor of having his remedies appear in print, but now all doctors can know what was once his private property, so that his stronghold is broken. Finally, the publication of these materials is supposed to demonstrate to the outside world the high stage of development of ancient Chinese medicine, and thus to satisfy the national pride — one of the most glaring characteristics of the new regime.

5. Conclusions

I hope I have been sufficiently able to show that folklore studies, even at their inception in China, were a tool for other movements, and not an independent scholarly field. This, of course, was also the case with folklore in Europe during the nineteenth century, and in Soviet Russia in the 1920's. We could also cite parallel cases from the present-day situation in other new and developing national states. I am reminded of the instance of Turkey, where in the 1930's the totalitarian party then in power did exactly the same sort of thing as was done in China and the Soviet Union, and where, at a later stage, folklore was subsequently rejected as a political tool. The uses to which folklore has been subjected in Communist China have prevented the development of a truly scholarly field of study on the Mainland, although in Taiwan such a discipline seems to be emerging. We have a considerable amount of new material from Red China, but because of its blatantly political character, most of it remains scientifically worthless, or can be used only after we have resorted to complicated methods of comparison and other precautions. On the other hand, these so-called folkloristic materials can be used by us as sources for the study of the aims of politicians, as sources for the methods and uses of indoctrination under a Communist regime. This is another field which I cannot go into, but which some other scholars should certainly explore.

PART ONE / *Essays on the Folklore of Chêkiang, China*

ON THE FOLKLORE OF CHÊKIANG*

I
The Tree Temples of Chin-hua (Chêkiang)[1]
1.
by Feng Hui-t'ien

The practice of naming temples after trees is common only in the district around the city of Chin-hua in Chêkiang province. About one third of the approximately sixty temples in the district of Chin-hua are named after trees. This custom is not found in other neighboring areas, and there has been no lack of scholarly discussion and attempts to explain the reason for this peculiarity. These temples are distinguished from all others in that it is impossible to learn anything about the gods worshipped in them or their history. Usually such information is not difficult to obtain. To be sure, the chronicles pay careful attention to canonical sacrifices, but only give brief mention to the so-called "wild" or uncanonical sacrifices. The names of these district temples are not canonical, nor are their sacrifices considered classical, and they are therefore regarded as "wild" places of sacrifice and are not mentioned in historical works and chronicles. This naturally presents a great obstacle to the scholar who would investigate the origin of these temples. Moreover, the material that might be extracted from folk traditions is inconclusive, due to the age of the temples and the confusion of these traditions. For this reason, we can do no more than advance theories about this custom, as hypothetical and questionable as such theories may be.

If a temple is built in honor of a deity, then this deity must exist. However, whether this deity ever really existed, or whether it is just an invention, is not always absolutely clear. Thus sacrifices are made to Ch'en Tao in the Tsung-kuan temple[2] in Chin-hua, and to the brothers Chiang in the Kuang-fu temple. These personages exist, and their history is well-known. However, all that is known about the Tsung-lü Tree temple or the Date Palm temple is that "such-and-such a progenitor" is worshipped there. No-one knows his name or even his history. The progenitor is, however,

*This study was based upon a field trip undertaken in 1934-35 and supported by the Baessler Foundation. The original paper, "Zur Volkskunde von Chêkiang," appeared in *Zeitschrift für Ethnologie*, LXVII (1936), 248-265, and has been translated and revised for publication.

nothing more than the first ancestor, and the person who sacrifices to him must in fact therefore recognize the deity as his ancestor. Thus, the deities to which sacrifices are made in these temples are invented (i.e., deities who never actually existed). Nevertheless, the reason why sacrificial temples were built to them is the same as in the case of the other (real) gods. In both cases it is because of their deeds performed for the benefit of man. In my opinion, the real gods (i.e., those who really existed) are products of the imagination of individuals; the invented deities, however, are products of the folk. The real gods live on due to their services on behalf of mankind, the invented deities because of their services to heaven. Men consider the accidents of everyday life to be the work of the gods, and they make sacrifices to that god or deity which they associate with the image of this unforeseen event.

In some of the temples the sacrificial ritual is regulated by sacrificial books, but in others it has been created by the folk. The latter temples, in which sacrifices are made to deified human beings, tree gods, deities of mountains, rivers, earth, fire, and so on, were at first without any definite rules. The temple was initially built in recognition of what these deities had done for mankind, and afterward it was hoped that they would protect the district belonging to them. At times they were also named by the people as the masters of a particular district, thereby becoming the protectors of the population living in that district. In this way they received sacrifices and offerings of thanks, and were supplied with incense for time immemorial.

The area which a god controls is frequently named after the district. In ancient China this was known as *shê* or the "district of the earth god." This practice is found in cities as well as in rural localities. Thus, when people say the "hall of the local god," they mean the temple in which the respective district makes its sacrifices. The district god (this may be the ancient earth god) watches over life and death, joy and sorrow, happiness and misfortune, flood and drought, disease, plague, famine, fire and other troubles which may befall all the inhabitants of his district. This god is worshipped only by those people belonging to his district, never by outsiders. Thus, the Tsung-lü Tree temple is worshipped solely by the inhabitants of its district, and other districts show no interest. Whoever moves to a new district must accept the duties of the local cult, and whoever leaves a district is likewise relieved of any and all cult responsibilities. This is similar to the practice associated with movements in and out of government districts, but there the bonds are not as strict. Thus, a man standing in a particular relationship with a district deity may continue to sacrifice to him even after leaving his district.

The following story is related concerning the establishment of these tree temples: It seems that at one time under some dynasty the city was supposed to be destroyed, and the only favor that the highest official was able to obtain was that everything located three feet or more above ground might be saved. Thereupon, the entire populace climbed up trees, so as not to die. For this reason, the trees were later considered to be gods. Temples were built in their honor and sacrifices made. This story is not reported in any historical works, and is therefore not a trustworthy source. Modern sociology would probably explain the custom by associating it with totemism. This seems to be appropiate if one keeps in mind the object of the cult (a tree as progenitor) and its purpose (to promote happiness and good fortune). But the fact that a person changes his cult when moving to a new district does not accord with a totemistic hypothesis. Moreover, no additional evidence for totemism can be furnished.[3]

2.
by Wolfram Eberhard

Tree temples are, in fact, a phenomenon peculiar to Chin-hua.[4] I have not found any such temples even in the area surrounding the city proper, and have never encountered them in other parts of China. The temples are usually located right amidst the houses lining the street, generally have no courtyard or gate, and consist only of a single room containing one or two Taoistic deities, sometimes with attendant figures. I was unable to locate any dedication pillars which might have provided some information on the age of the temples. The local gazetteer likewise furnished no relevant data except for a listing of the names of each temple.[5] I am not familiar with any legends about the temples other than those given by Feng. These are also the only ones known to Ts'ao Sung-yeh, who collected all the folktales of the district.[6]

I believe that the question of the tree temples can be approached from another angle. The district of Chin-hua is distinguished by a large number of special customs, and stands apart from the other areas of Chêkiang province. This is, for example, the only district to preserve the bullfight, as well as certain types of folktales.[7] Likewise, there is only one cult peculiar to this area and the adjoining more southern parts of China, namely the cult of trees. The trees involved are generally large camphor trees. At any rate, these are the only kind of holy trees I have ever encountered. In Chin-hua, for example, I came across a holy tree, in front of which there were still some incense sticks and the remains of numerous prayer notes addressed to the "mother camphor tree." The people told me they chose the tree as the mother of a child, so that the child might grow strong as the tree. Sacrifices to the tree are made on the day of the winter solstice, during the Ch'ing-ming festival (occurring in late March, 105 days after winter solstice), and on the fifteenth day of the eighth month. A similar tree is found in Yün-ho, but there it is designated as "adopted father." The bark of this tree had been removed in many places. This bark is put in the children's clothes to make them stronger. In the fields near Li-shui there is an enormous camphor tree (illustration 1.) with a built-in niche containing incense cones and an earthenware dish for sacrifices. I also noticed a large number of prayer notes. The local inhabitants called the tree a *T'ui-ti P'u-sa* (i.e., an earth god). In Chin-yün I obtained one of these prayers from a holy camphor tree. The text, written on a piece of rough, red cloth, is as follows:

> With Reverence!
> In China, Chêkiang province, county of Ch'u-chou, district Chin-yün, in the south, in the village of Wu-ling, I, Yeh Kuan-chou, received a son by the name of Yün-ch'ing ("Cloud-blue"). Since I sorely fear that his life is in jeopardy and danger, I have reverently brought sacrifices and wine, and now bow down before the god of the camphor tree of the mountain of the earth god as his natural mother. I beseech the mother to protect Yün-ch'ing, so that he may grow strong and live long. On his birthday in one year I will again prepare sacrifices and wine and worship his natural mother, and I am not ungrateful for the kindness of the god.
>
> This is in the chrysanthemum month of the eighteenth year of the Republic (1929).

I have found very similar prayer notes in the temple of the city god of Chin-yün, with the same wishes directed to the city god, as well as in the Kuan-ti temple on Mt. Lion near Yün-ho, with the same request to the war god Kuan-ti. This information about the tree cult helps clarify matters. The trees are conceived of and actually worshiped as deities. They are, however, also designated as earth gods. Feng points out that all the tree temples in

1. Sacred camphor tree in Li-shui, Chêkiang, 1934.

Chin-hua are district temples, i.e., temples each meant for a specific group of families. In *Li-chi*[8] there is mention of the fact that every group of twenty-five families had its own earth-god temple. In *Shuo-wen* we find the same state of affairs, with the additional information that the altar of the earth god had trees.[9] References to trees on the altar of the earth god are very common in ancient literature.[10] This appears to have been a widespread practice common throughout ancient China, which later disappeared in some areas. Today, as a matter of fact, all Chinese temples are still distinguished by the presence of trees whose only apparent function is to provide shade and make one's stay pleasant. It is, in my opinion, highly probable that the tree-god temples of Chin-hua are a parallel to the ancient earth-god altars with trees (*shê*), since they are still bound in exactly the same way to definite groups of families and districts of settlement. I am, however, not in a position to decide whether we are dealing here with the survival of an ancient custom, in which case the holy trees of Chêkiang would represent a later variation on the temples, or whether, on the contrary, the tree temples perhaps developed out of the cult of the holy trees. Thus, the holy tree of Li-shui was surrounded by a small wall and contained a shrine, (i.e., the ostensible beginnings of a temple). Holy trees, after all, are worshiped far beyond the borders of Chêkiang to the south in Kuangtung and Kuanghsi. Viewed in this light, the similarity with the ancient earth-god altars would then only be some kind of convergence. This matter is particularly difficult to decide due to the fact that we have evidence for large settlements of Chinese in the Chin-hua area only after 800-900 A. D. The first settlement wave appears to have begun in the fifth century, but does not seem to have been extensive in scope. Before that time, remnants of the Yüeh tribes were still located in this area. Was the custom of the holy tree at the earth altar still so vigorous in the home areas of the settlers of Chin-hua, the provinces Kiangsu and Anhui, that they simply brought this custom along with them, or did they borrow the tree cult of the Yüeh, the previous inhabitants of the region, and then slowly adapt and transform it? Yüeh tribes were likewise present at an earlier period in Kuangtung and Kuanghsi provinces, and a tree cult can still be found in these areas today. Furthermore, it is of special interest that the tree is generally addressed as a female deity. The cult of female deities is particularly characteristic of southern Chêkiang province.

Let us return to the camphor trees. The camphor tree has given its name to the province of Kiangsi,[11] because it is a symbol of death and resurrection. The tree dries up and then becomes green again.[12] Camphor trees also supply the material for chests and drawers which keep textiles "alive," because of the smell which wards off insects and moths. Early and late texts refer to deified camphor trees, and apparently they too were usually of female sex.[13] Idols made of camphor wood can also exhibit magic

powers,[14] and a lamp made of camphor wood changed into a demon. [15]
The camphor tree is most typical for China south of Yang-tse and the areas
of Yüeh settlement. On the other hand, we know of numerous "unofficial"
temples, including tree temples, which have quite a different origin. As an
example, let me give a Sung-period story which comes from Shu
(Szuch'uan), but which could have easily occurred in Chêkiang as well. It
illustrates better than anything else the ways in which cults can arise and the
attitudes of scholars toward such cults:

> On the road to Shu was an old tree, one hundred years old. Its twigs
> and branches were dense, so that their shadow covered one *mou*
> (land). Therefore, travellers from East and West often rest under
> them and occasionally change their sandals there. Then, as a joke,
> they hang their old ones onto the branches. In the course of time,
> there were thousands of pairs hanging there. There were people who
> often asked the oracle about personal matters and they often had
> response, so that people thought the tree was holy. Once a scholar on
> the way to his examinations passed by, and there were no other
> people. So he took his knife and carved these words into the bark of
> the tree: "Great King Straw Shoe descended in such-and-such a year,
> in such-and-such a month." Nobody knew of this. When he returned
> to T'u, there was already a small temple with four columns there.
> The scholar laughed and didn't say anything. When he came there
> again, some three years later, there was a magnificent temple and also
> more than ten families living at its side. He was startled and
> questioned them, and they told him in detail about the efficiency of
> the deity. He remained there overnight, and asked the god: "The
> name of you, God, was a joke of mine. How is it that you became so
> flourishing? Who are you anyway?" During the night he dreamt that
> the god, dressed in purple bands, wanted to see him. He told him: "I
> lived nearby as an old gendarme. During my life I never dared to
> cheat. When I was sifted out, whenever I saw a man with a load so
> heavy that he could not go on, I accompanied him for five *li*, so that
> he could rest his shoulders. I have no other virtues. Shang-ti noted
> this work, but as I had no place and since you gave this name, I was
> enfeoffed with it, so that I could receive offerings." The scholar
> replied: "But how could you get magic powers?" The deity said: "I
> could not do this. In each case, when people pray for rain or
> sunshine or for good luck, this is reported to God. God, because of
> their earnest intentions, fulfills their wishes." The scholar said: "May
> I then ask about my future fate?" The god said: "Yes"....
>
> (*Lu-p'u pi-chi* IV, 4a; Sung)

II
The Night of Candles in Chin-hua (Chêkiang)
1.

by Ts'ao Sung yeh

There are differences in the way the Night of Candles is celebrated in the city and in the country. In the city of Chin-hua (Chêkiang) things are done according to the old style during the night of the twelfth day of the first month. Red candles are lit in the district temples all over the city. The candles are surrounded by dragon figures and sayings such as "May gold and jewels fill the house" or "Fame, glory, wealth and honor!" are written on them. Written vertically on the candle altar we find the words "Donated by X", as for example, "Reverently donated by Chang Chin-sheng," while horizontally we can read "May gold and jewels fill the house ! " The shape of the candelabra is approximately like this: ⧕ . The size of the candles is not uniform. In the city the largest ones weigh about 11-12 Chinese pounds, while in the country, in the village of Hsia-fang-fou, there are red candles weighing 80-100 pounds, which can burn for five days and nights. They stand in the middle of the incense hall. The incense hall is the hall of the god of the district temple of this village. But that is something unusual. In rural areas candleholders are generally made of bamboo, a point which I will discuss later on.

Only one candle is lit at a time. While the candles are being lit, incense is burned and one prays to the god of the temple. Only the families in which sons have been born may light the candles. The inhabitants of the same district, however, can obtain wine, meat or cake from the family in which a son has been born.

On the evening of the twelfth, each district provides a set of the usual musical instruments played by children (a gong, a drum, a large and small cymbal, and a large gong – the sounds of all these instruments don't go together). At the same time two adults take a red candle and go to each family in the district to "send masculine descendants" (similar to the practice of "sending children" of the deity Kuan-yin). Each family sets up a square table in front of their main hall, on top of which they place a candleholder, two still unlit red candles, and an incense tray. These persons going from house to house remove the red candle from the lantern and place it in the candleholder of the respective family. Then they light the candle belonging to the family, put it in the lantern and continue on their rounds. If a son is born to a family in the following year, then they must light the candles for a period of three years. The night of the twelfth is probably the liveliest. Activities in every district last until morning.

Every night about midnight in the district temple of Jade Spring Street (Kuan-ti is worshiped there), a man takes a large wax candle without a holder, and runs back and forth with it in the respective district street three times. This practice is known as candle-running. During the running all the stores and businesses along the street shoot off small rockets for amusement, and they also call out to the runner.

In the district temple of Leather Market the practice of candle-running is also known, but there the candleholder is included, and the stores along the street do not set off fireworks.

In the district temple of the Su family the candle-running takes place inside the temple, and the spectators throw the rockets at the head of the man carrying the candle.

The population of Chin-hua and its surroundings is divided into various districts of unequal size, each containing anywhere from a few to several dozen families.

In the countryside surrounding the city the time for the Night of Candles is not the same everywhere, but usually falls sometime between the ninth and fifteenth of the first month. The candles are sometimes similar in form to the cockscomb flower, and one can also compare them to an inverted trumpet. They are made of bamboo, mounted on the candleholder, and covered outside with red paper. Theater scenes or the image of the god of the district temple are painted on the paper, and one finds sayings such as "May the grain prosper." A piece of red cloth hangs down from the top of the candle.

The village inhabitants prepare pork and chicken during Candle Night, burn incense before the candle and pray. The various types of grain are then supposed to prosper, and people are supposed to be able to have sons.

On the following day the farmers carry the candle around the neighborhood, and all the families in which a son was born the previous year are expected to provide wine and food for the others. In I-tou even casual passers-by receive such food and drink.

The farmers trace the custom of carrying around the candles back to the fact that Liu Hsiu (Kuang-wu-ti of the Han dynasty, 25-57 A. D.) hid himself from his enemies here, and was later rescued.

In rural areas we find another type of wax candle or candleholder, which has six corners and stands about four feet high. It is made of wood and is carved in numerous patterns. A piece of wood similar in appearance to a writing brush is mounted in the center of the upper section. The village inhabitants cover the candles during the procession with a candle hat which has two sections, is white on the inside and red on the outside, and looks like a bushel basket. The red part is carved with a tendril design. When the candles are carried around, the candle cover is placed over the pointed, brush-like protuberance, and this is then placed in the lap of the women. After this they should be able to give birth to sons. The first candle-hood is supposed to be particularly auspicious.

In addition, the image of a deity is carried behind the candelabra, and the farmers naturally venerate the divine image and not the candle. This again appears to be a custom different from the one reported.

In primitive societies there is a so-called phallic cult, and the two rural customs reported above could perhaps be regarded as survivals of this cult, although the material here is insufficient to allow us to reach any conclusion.

2.
by Wolfram Eberhard

Ts'ao acquaints us here with a custom typical only of Chin-hua. The twelfth day of the first month is still a part of the New Year's festival, but in other parts of China no particular ceremony is performed. The closest parallel I know of is the ceremony called "fire festival," performed in Hopei province on that day. All old, unuseable shoes were burned on that day. The evening of that day was believed to be the wedding day of the rats.[16]

The candleholder which I saw in the city consisted of three vertically-mounted pieces of wood lacquered in red. The central piece was somewhat larger and longer than the two side pieces, which were mounted slanting toward the outside. Each of the pieces was fastened in the center and below by a cross-brace. The holder stood about forty centimeters high, and the name of the child born in the respective year was inscribed on the upper cross-brace. The same candlestick also stood as a temple candlestick in a tree temple known as the "Corn-Tree Ancestor Temple."

In the countryside, the candleholders described by Ts'ao stand over two meters high, and are made of tubes assembled from single bamboo rods which widen toward the top. The informants I questioned in the village of I-tou explained that the procession on the thirteenth day of the first month brings a good harvest and masculine descendants. This procession initiates the lantern festival, which reaches its peak on the fifteenth day of the first month and ends on the eighteenth day. The relation of the candlestick to the tree temples, as reported above, is also of interest in this connection, when one considers the role that the tree-gods play in protecting the children.

The possibility that we are dealing here with the survival of a phallic cult cannot be hastily dismissed. In some areas of China, even the lantern festival has a special significance for families in which a son has been born, and the associated customs are almost identical with those of the Candle Night in Chin-hua.[17] Related Japanese customs also come to mind. Nevertheless, I am still of the opinion that it is very risky to speak about "survivals" of a custom in China, since it is extremely likely that a more detailed study, particularly an historical one, will reveal that what we have here is nothing more than the illusion of a survival, and that the custom represents the final stage in a very different kind of development. The only other example of something resembling a phallic cult that I am familiar with in modern China is from the region of Yang-chou, where phallic representations are carried around during processions. It seems unwarranted to draw parallels here with the custom in Chin-hua. Ts'ao also considered a relationship between the two customs unlikely.

III.
The Rain Prayer Stele in the Temple of the City God of *Chin-yün (Chêkiang)*
by Wolfram Eberhard

The City God temple is by far the most famous temple in the small district city of Chin-yün in Chêkiang. Visitors come from distant points, particularly on the fourteenth and fifteenth days of the tenth month, when the god is carried around through the city and a great festival is held in his honor. This day is, most probably, the "birthday" of the deity. Each deity, it is believed, has its birthday which is celebrated by sacrifices, and often by processions and theatre performances in honor of the god. These days are not festival days in other parts of China, and are not part of a general festival. Across from the entrance there is a theater stage, as is so often the case in Chinese temples. At the entrance one finds several gate deities, with attendant deities at the sides of the courtyard. The punishments of hell are portrayed on tablets located in front of the main hall. The god himself stands accompanied by his personal staff in the main hall, and he is portrayed once more in the rear hall. A sideroom serves as his bedroom, and is furnished just like a real bedroom with a bed, tables and chests. His weapons are there too. Many pairs of shoes stand at the foot of the beds, and pieces of red cloth covered with prayers hang from the bedposts. This cloth has been donated by believers. Near the window one also finds a small altar with a statue of the deity and his wife, as well as some sacrificial offerings. The bedroom belonging to the wife of the deity and located to the right of the rear hall of the temple is not well preserved. Both rooms are occupied by people who desire to regain their health or are praying for a dream.

The famous stele stands in a sideroom of the temple. It is almost two meters high, and appears rather faded as a result of the many copies which are continually being cast from it. In Chin-yün the following story is related about this stele: Once, during the T'ang period, there was a great drought in Chin-yün. In spite of all the sacrifices, the rains refused to come. Then the mandarin Li said: "If you haven't brought any rain by tomorrow, I'll destroy your temple! "[18] After that it rained. But the prayer was engraved and kept sacrosanct. Later Li traveled down the river to Hang-chow and drowned somewhere in the rapids. Much later than this four students were on their

way to Hang-chou for an examination and spent the night in the Temple of
the City God in Chin-yün. There they had a dream in which the god told
them that if they were to carry a copy of the inscription on their person,
then they would not drown, but they would have to burn the copy before
they reached the rapids.[19] Moreover, two of the students would pass their
exams. Since they all had the same dream, they were very astonished. They
took along a copy of the inscription and were, in fact, spared from
drowning. Two of them also passed the exam. After that time the inscription
became famous, the copies were in great demand, so that even fake
reproductions were put in circulation. The inscription stele is therefore now
known as "the stele which holds the wind." It is also useful in storms at sea.

The text of the inscription is difficult for the present-day population to
read, since it is written in so-called seal-script. Nevertheless, it has also been
reproduced in the local gazatteer of Chin-yün, and here the text is easy to
identify. The fact that the stele text is difficult to decipher accounts for the
discrepancies between the modern legend and the content of the stele itself.
The text translates as follows:

> There are not city gods in the official rituals of sacrifice.[20] But
> they are found in Wu and Yüeh and it is customary to pray to them
> in times of flood, drought and disease. In 759 A. D. it did not rain
> during the seventh month. On the fifteenth day of the eighth month
> the governor of the Chin-yün district personally prayed to the deity
> and made the following condition: If it doesn't rain in five days, I'll
> burn down your temple. At the appointed time a great rain fell,
> enough for the entire district. To show their gratitude, the officials,
> the elders and all the officers moved the temple from the west valley
> to the top of the mountain.
>
> This is worthy of being passed on, of not being forgotten.
> —Secretary for the encouragement of agriculture Wu Yen-nien.

The district chronicle preserves the same text.[21] But elsewhere the
chronicle contains additional information about the stele. A portion of the
text of the stele, actually known as the "rain prayer stele," is already
mentioned as early as the Sung period in a work by Ou-yang Hsiu entitled
Chi-ku-lu. The beginning of the stele is repeated in particular, and he also
relates the event, but in his version the stipulated time is seven days. He also
tells about the moving of the temple.[22] The biography of Li Yang-ping
already attributes the inscription to him, and it also confirms that he was
governor of Chin-yün around the year 759 A. D.[23] The stele is also
mentioned by Chao Hsien in *Shih-mo-chien-hua*. Chao Hsien lived around
1580 A. D.[24] Of well-known scholars, the most recent to discuss the stele in
detail is Ch'ien Ta-yin in the *Ch'ien-yen-t'ang chin-shih-wen pa-wei*.[25] The
name "stele which holds the wind" is first mentioned in the literature by Li

Yü-sun in the *Kua-ts'ang Chin-shih-chih*.[26] Li lived around 1800.[27] It also indicates that the inscription is useful during storms at sea. He also believes that there are similar such stele effective against sea storms in the Yün-ho district and in other districts surrounding Chin-yün.

The exact age of the stele itself cannot be ascertained, since it is impossible to establish when a certain man Wu, who erected the stele, is supposed to have lived. Nevertheless, the text of the stele can, without a doubt, be traced back to the Sung period, and there is in fact no reason to doubt that the stele was actually erected as early as the eighth century.

This stele deserves particular attention due to the nature of the introductory portion of its text. It is stated there that the city gods are a custom of south China, and are not officially recognized. They had not yet received official recognition in the T'ang period. Various Chinese scholars have disagreed with this. Thus, the cult of the city god is traced back to the very beginning of Chinese history in the *Ch'un-ming yü-lu*.[28] Ch'ien Ta-yin[29] also attempts to find earlier stages of the contemporary cult of the city god in notes given in the *Tso-chuan*. Neither attempt seems convincing, but there is an important reference made by Ch'ien to the effect that the cult was known at least as early as the sixth century.[30] During the T'ang period it presumably continued to spread, in the Sung period it was widely known, and not until the Ming period in the fourteenth century did the city god receive official honorary titles and recognition. Thus, we are dealing here with a south Chinese cult, perhaps even borrowed from a non-Chinese segment of the population,[31] which gradually spread to the north and eventually achieved general recognition throughout China. Our rain-prayer stele is then one of the oldest monuments of this cult. In the eighth century the Chin-yün area had not been long settled, and it is probably not erroneous to assume that the Chinese settlers were greatly outnumbered by the non-Chinese at that time.

The transfer of the temple is still alive in contemporary folk tradition, and the following legend is related: The temple was originally located on the eastern mountain at the eastern gate. But the people at the western gate thought that the temple was situated too far away and that it certainly was not of much use to them. So one night after a snowfall, a man went backwards into the temple, removed the god, and then, walking back in his own footprints, proceeded on to the western mountain. Then he said he had dreamt that the god wanted to go to the western mountain. And they actually discovered the following morning that the god had apparently gone there by himself. Since then the temple has been standing on the western mountain. The statue is not made of clay, as is customary, but rather of wood. Moreover, it is movable, so that the god can actually walk. Movable statues of deities were not uncommon in China. Many statues were led around during processions, and the carriers hid under the dress of the deity. I have seen such movable statues in present-day Taiwan, though these were not the statues of city gods.

According to present-day tradition, the burial grounds of the Ch'en clan are supposed to have been located where the temple now stands. The grave had to be moved slightly to one side when the temple was transferred. But as late as twenty years ago, the sacrificial offerings for the dead, a part of the Ch'ing-ming festival, were not made at the grave but rather in the temple itself, since this was considered to be the actual burial grounds. This fact is recorded in the Ch'en register. This indicates a special relation of the Ch'en clan to the deity. It is possible that the god was a deified ancestor of the clan, although this is not reported. But even if not, we know that families may monopolize certain temples and operate them as a kind of business which may bring in money, but certainly does bring prestige to the family which operates such a temple. I could not clarify whether this was the case here in Chin-yün.

The chronicle does not relate this variant of the moving of the temple and gives only the version of the stele.[32] This legend, therefore, appears to be of a more recent date.

IV.
The Cult of Female Deities in Southern Chêkiang
by Wolfram Eberhard

When visiting in Yün-ho in southern Chêkiang, one is immediately struck by the prevalence of numerous temples for female deities. Although Yün-ho is small and has comparatively few temples, I saw a large temple of the dragon mother (Lung-mu), of the heavenly queen (T'ien-hou), as well as the temple of another female deity located on Mt. Horse Sattle right near the city. Temples for female deities are similarly common in Li-shui (=Ch'u-chou), but become less frequent to the north in Chin-yün, and there are almost no such temples in Chin-hua. The distribution of the cult of the goddesses is thus limited to the southernmost part of Chêkiang and diminishes as one travels northward. Buddhistic goddesses have naturally been excluded from this study. Other female deities of various kinds are worshiped throughout China, but their cult does not play as large a role as it does here. Moreover, these goddesses are venerated only for certain properties, such as effectiveness against smallpox or eye diseases.

The local gazetteer gives the following information about these goddesses:

> Liu Hsiang-feng reports: In the city there is the custom of receiving the goddess. The custom is undoubtedly an old one, since the wagon of the gods located at the west gate of the women's temple bears the inscription "Hung-chih 5" (1492 A. D.). We can therefore conclude that the custom probably originated during the Ming dynasty. The rite is as follows: on the first favorable day of the tenth month during a "wu-k'uei" year (i.e., one year in a cycle of sixty years), they remove the images of the women Ma, Ch'en and Liu together with twenty-four assistant gods and lead them around the city....Some say that these are non-canonical sacrifices and must be abolished. But I have personally witnessed processions in Li-yüan in honor of a certain women Yen, and have encountered sayings addressed to a woman Ch'ang in the western section of Li-shui. This information is not contained in the written reports, but all of the local people are familiar with it. In the provincial capital (i.e., in Li-shui) on Mt. Chiao there is a temple for the woman Ma, protectress of the empire, and in the village of T'ai-p'ing we find a woman of aid called Ch'en with her associated temple. In Wan-hsiang-shan, in a locality called Nan-yüan, there is a temple for a woman Lin who protects against smallpox. They all have definite times for sacrifice: on Mt. Chiao on the seventh day of the seventh month, in T'ai-p'ing on the fourteenth of the first month, and in Nan-yüan on the nineteenth of the ninth month. They all have processions with lamps. It's really like they say: 'The power of the gods in the world is like the water on the earth: you find it everywhere.' And the people of Yün-ho have enjoyed good fortune from the time the temple was erected during the Ming dynasty until today. That's a long time.

1.

Thus we find here reference to the women Ma, Ch'en, Lin. The only oral information I received about Ma is that she was a pious girl from Ching-ning. Her temple and many traces of her can be found there. Ching-ning is a district bordering on Fukien province, and is in fact ethnographically an integral part of Fukien. Nothing further can be done with the Ma legend. Her birthday is celebrated on the seventh day of the seventh month in the city of Yün-ho.

2.

The following legend is related concerning the woman Ch'en: She comes from the district of Ku-t'ien in Fukien province, and lived during the Sung period. Her older brother is called Fa-t'ung, her younger brother

Fa-ch'ing. People say they were all able to work magic and drive out evil spirits. The magic powers of the sister were greatest, followed in strength by those of her older brother Fa-t'ung. The powers of her youngest brother were the weakest. Present-day magician's boys generally trace their art back to Fa-ch'ing. Fa-ch'ing stuttered. The sister came only when needed (oral explanation: when Fa-ch'ing had called for her help by stuttering). In many respects it is black magic. In the lower street of Yün-ho there is a house which is supposed to be free from mosquitos on hot summer days. They say that during the Sung period Ch'en often came into the house to live or spend the night. But this rumor is not very certain.[34]

This legend is important for several reasons. It is a report about shamanism, a subject we will discuss later. In addition, it tells about stuttering during a shamanistic procedure. This technique was also known in ancient China. The legend of the house without mosquitos was related in Chin-yün[35] with reference to a magician called Chao Ping living in the later Han period.

3.

People appear to have associated the woman Lin with the queen of the heavens, since this queen always was a member of the family Lin in the source materials. The following legend is told about her: A small girl, while in a trance, was always saving the victims of shipwrecks. One day she saved her own father and her two brothers. But at this time she was lying completely lifeless at home, and her mother, who thought she must be dead, was crying. For this reason the girl uttered one word. After that she told how she had to open her mouth in order to speak, and that in this way she had lost her father, whom she was holding in her mouth. When her brothers returned home later they confirmed the story. The girl then became a nun, and later a goddess.[36] She has been mentioned in the literature since the Sung period. Her cult originated in Fukien and is still today most active there, although it has spread more-or-less throughout all of present-day China.

Lin's temple in Chin-yün, built in 1768, is connected with the clubhouse of the people of Fu-kien. The local gazetteer[37] indicates that she received official honorary names in 1123 A.D. The story in the chronicle concerning Lin's origin is somewhat simpler than the modern legend related above.

4.

Today one of the largest temples of the goddesses in Yün-ho is that of the dragon mother. I was told the following tale about this goddess: In the east street of Yün-ho the family had a daughter about sixteen or seventeen years old. One day she went with her sister-in-law to Hou-ch'i (one of the streams in Yün-ho) to do the wash. Suddenly she saw a wonderful egg slowly floating down the stream. When she saw it, she grabbed it immediately. But when her sister-in-law saw this, she wanted to take a look at the egg too, and stretched out her hand. The girl was afraid her sister-in-law wanted to take the egg away from her, and she put it quickly into her mouth. But the girl wasn't careful enough and the round thing suddenly slipped down right into her stomach. After that she became pregnant. The months passed quickly, and soon it was time for her delivery. But on this day her body was so painful that she fell unconscious. Later, when she awoke as if from a dream, she was well again, and had given birth to a child. But, strangely enough, it was impossible to see exactly what she had given birth to — only that at night something came and drank her milk. During the bright daylight there was nothing more to be seen. After some time the mother finally said: "My strange child! What in the heaven are you? Can't I get to see you? " The child said: "You must fast and purify yourself and burn incense. Tomorrow, after the sun has disappeared behind the mountains, I will reveal myself." And the next day it really appeared. But before it came there was a great storm, and after that it came. It then wound itself several times around a pillar of the house, and after a while it took its mother on its back and flew away. Do you know where the flew to? They flew to the Hsia-tung-t'ien (a mountain near Yün-ho). The country around there is simply beautiful. The mother became a deity there and today the people call her the Dragon Mother Saint.[38]

The chronicle[39] has a somewhat different version: "A woman from the Liu family[40] swallowed a dragon egg while washing clothes. The egg was unusual. She bore a strange child. After one month it got up one morning and said to the mother:'I'm going to go away with you in three days.' When they were underway there was rain and lightning. A dragon came, let them climb on, and flew off with them. They made an idol in Hsia-tung-t'ien, made sacrifices to the Dragon Mother and prayed successfully for rain."

The legend of the swallowed egg is also an ancient Chinese legend which appears very early in the literature.[41] There is also another dragon mother worshiped widely throughout China. She belongs to the Wen family and comes from the province of Kuangtung. The following legend is told about her: While washing in the river she found a large egg. She decided to keep it and put it in a pot. After a while animals similar to snakes emerged from the pot. They grew quickly and covered the water. Then she put them in the water and the animals began to catch fish for her. The people thought they were dragons. The emperor Shih-huang-ti (third century B. C.) ordered the girl to come to him, but the dragons appeared and pulled back her ship several times. When she died they buried her near the river, but during a large storm her grave was shifted to the other side of the river. She then received temples and is an effective deity.[42] The legend is mentioned in the literature from about 800 A. D. on. In the course of time her cult spreads out over a wide area. but is particularly popular today in Kuangtung near her home.[43]

This legend undoubtedly has certain similarities with our legend from Yün-ho. Nevertheless, there is no direct connection between them, but we should rather assume an inner connection of some sort.[44]

5.

The Chin-hua chronicle also tells of a woman named Chou, who had the power to cause rain,[45] but gives no information about her history.

6.

The stories of almost all these female deities show that they come from Fukien or Kuangtung. It is possible that immigrants from Fukien who colonized the southern parts of Chêkiang in the seventeenth century brought these stories with them. At least our first text, however, seems to indicate that the cults were known in Chêkiang as early as the Ming period. We think that such cults are part of a larger complex which centers around female cult leaders, or around a system of dual kingship or dual leadership, in which a woman is spiritual leader while her brother is political leader. This complex seems to have stretched from Kuangtung over Fukien and Chêkiang to the Ryukyu Islands and Japan. An almost perfect variant of the story of T'ien-hou (No. 3) has been found in the Ryukyu Islands.[46]

Furthermore, the legends almost all show some connection with shamanism. Now shamanism is, as a matter of fact, still widely encountered in central and southern Chêkiang. We have reports on female shamans and their activities from various areas. Male shamans also appear. In southern Chêkiang the influence of shamanism is still particularly pronounced. Apparently we are also dealing here with an influence from the coastal culture area. Since Professor Stübel is preparing a special study on the shamanism of Lung-ch'üan, located about fifty kilometers from Yün-ho, I will limit myself here only to a few notes on Yün-ho.[47]

The male and female shamans are said to dance on one leg during their performances. By doing this they are able to call forth a spirit who speaks through them. We already know through the work of Marcel Granet[48] that dancing on one leg was practiced in ancient China as a magical dance ("dance of Yü). The female shaman covers her eyes and face with a red kerchief, then places herself in a trance by dancing, and then the spirit also answers to questions speaking through her. The spirit is not always supposed to be the same one, and I was also informed that three sisters are called who are somehow connected with a grotto in Chin-hua. But this tradition was not completely certain. An inquiry in Chin-hua did not result in any information concerning the relation of the three sisters to the grotto. Otherwise the information on Chin-hua was confirmed. There too, female shamans rather than male shamans are generally the rule. The dance is supposed to symbolize the long journey of the shaman to the place where the event occurred about which she is being asked. In any case, the reference concerning the three sisters shows again, as in the legends cited above, the close relationship of shamanism to the cult of the female deities. We can therefore also assume that this form of shamanism came from Fukien. On the basis of a survey of the entire corpus of reports concerning modern shamanism, it appears likely that modern Chinese shamanism originated in the south. As early as the Han period, the shamans who were most famous and in greatest demand came from the southern state of Yüeh.[49]

7.

I was informed by Mr. Russenberger, the missionary in Yün-ho, that certain individuals there often allege that they see spirits, and found cults in their honor. We may assume that we are dealing in these cases with a shaman. Pictures, altars and the like are then set up in the house of such a man, amulets are distributed, and the relatives and neighbors admire the man. The ultimate success of the cult depends on his abilities. In such cases the missionary entered the houses in question, and subsequently removed and banned all cult objects. The people did not interfere with the missionaries, but said that punishment was certain. After the expected punishment failed to appear, the cult was finished, asserted the missionary.

This valuable material demonstrates that even today there is fertile soil for the birth of new cults. It seems highly probable that a large number of local cults, as well as those cults which were initially local and are now more widely spread, came about in a psychologically similar manner. The probability of this is enhanced by many legends, including those I have reported above.

2. TALES ABOUT COUNT HU*

I have brought with me from the field a number of folktales and texts collected in the area of Chin-hua in Chêkiang province[1] by Ts'ao Sung-yeh. This material includes a separate group of tales about Count Hu and the cult which worships him on Mt. Fang-yen near Yung-k'ang in Chêkiang province. This cult is one of the mountain cults typical of many areas of China. The best known of these cults is the cult of Pi-hsia yüan-chün on Mt. Miao-fêng near Peking, and the cult of the same Pi-hsia yüan-chün on Mt. T'ai located in Shantung province. These mountain cults, as far as we can at present ascertain, do not all derive from the same culture. The concept of the death mountain (i.e., a mountain to which the souls of the dead make their journey),[2] appears to have been typical of the northern area of ancient China. In Shantung province, however, there existed a special cult for eight deities, in which the cult of the "Navel of the Earth" (an artesian well near Chi-nan-fu, Shantung) occupied a central position, but in which mountains also played a role. Finally, we find that in ancient central China, mountains were associated with the concept of fertility. Here a young couple was pledged to a certain mountain, and after having been treated as deities for a year, they were then sacrificed. The concept of the mountain as a source of fertility was found not only in central China, but also in western and northwestern China in ancient times. In these areas, however there was no sacrifice.

I shall now present a number of texts which deal with the cult of the deity Hu on Mt. Fang-yen. The texts were written by schoolchildren at the request of Mr. Ts'ao. Since they were written by children, these texts are often not completely clear and contain stylistic errors, but are, for this very reason, all the more genuine in content.

1.

The given name of Count Hu is Tsê. During the Sung era he rose to the rank of a court assistant (*lang*). Afterwards a temple honoring him was erected in Yung-k'ang near Mt. Fang-yen. There he receives the veneration

*This translation is a revised version of "Die Geschichten vom Grafen Hu," *Zeitschrift für Ethnologie* LXXI (1940), 293-300.

and offerings of the people and is very effective. Every year at the beginning of the eighth month the gates of the temple are opened.[3] All of the pilgrims to Fang-yen fast and eat no meat. They are careful not to speak without first pondering their thoughts. They come with an honest, respectful heart to worship him, and along the way some stop to bow down every three steps in his honor. On the fifteenth day of the eighth month there is a great reception in Chin-hua, at which men strike gongs and beat drums. Standards and banners are carried aloft bearing the slogan: "He protects and helps the people." Others hang up long green streamers, because Count Hu is one of the five counts.[4] He is a deity who is loved by the people, who helps the people and protects them. He also protects the five kinds of grain and the six kinds of household animals.

(II, 30 — from Chin-hua)

2.

In my home village, people are very faithful in worshiping at Fang-yen. Young people between sixteen and twenty, and old people between fifty and sixty years of age, go without fail to Fang-yen to worship the Buddha. Before starting out on the pilgrimage, there is much to do. First everyone buys a lantern on which he writes his name. On the other side of the lantern he writes: "Pilgrim to Fang-yen." Then sacrificial paper, candles, incense and other things must be purchased. One day before, on the twelfth day of the eighth month (which is the set time every year), everyone washes himself and goes to the temple to pray to Buddha. At midnight one makes an offering to the heaven and earth, and sends greetings to the "Old Lord,"[5] Then they shoot off rockets to call together all the pilgrims from the immediate and neighboring villages. Everyone carries a basket or bundle containing food, clothing and the things for the offering.

The pilgrimage lasts from the twelfth to the twentieth day of the eighth month every year. While the pilgrims are underway, those who remained at home light candles, burn incense and sacrificial paper, and pray in the direction of Mt. Fang-yen. On the twentieth, the last day of the pilgrimage, the pilgrims buy many small trinkets such as miniature tigers, cakes, etc., and bring them back home. After their arrival, they go to the temple and pray to Buddha.[6] After returning to their homes, they pray to the heaven and earth, and to the "Old Lord," and shoot off rockets. Then they distribute the small trinkets which they have brought with them among the neighbors. The neighbors express their gratitude with such phrases as: "The Fang-yen pilgrim has returned. We thank you." The people of my village go only to Fang-yen to honor Count Hu, who has such great magic powers. Children go on the pilgrimage because they have made a vow during an illness, and the old people go because they wish to continue to have good fortune.

3.

My village is located in a secluded area, far from the main roads, so the majority of the villagers live only by farming. Aside from the thunder and lightning, they believe only in the Buddha.[7] Buddha is their sole belief, a belief even more powerful than that in lightning and thunder. Everyone believes that the Buddha has the power of a great spirit, and that it would be very dangerous to do anything against him. If anyone does displease him, then he must go in person and show that he has repented. Buddha can remove the sins of man and hears those who pray to him...[8]

For this reason, everyone upon reaching his sixteenth birthday must go once to Count Hu on Mt. Fang-yen. Poor people, who do not have the money for the long trip, go only to the Nine-Peak Crag which is located in our district. This is one of the local sights in our area. In a cave there one finds a picture of the great god Count Hu, and this cave is known as the "Holy Cave of the Nine Peaks." It is said that Count Hu never fails to appear here during the period from the seventeenth to the nineteenth of the eighth month, so it is just as good to go there as to Fang-yen. Otherwise one has to start out on the first day of the eighth month, either by land or by water. If a person travels by land he takes along dumplings for food, as well as sacrificial paper, incense sticks, candles and so forth. The parents advise their young not to say anything foolish. At home there is a three-day fast, and each morning and evening everyone bows towards the east, because the country of Count Hu lies to the east of my village. Those who go to Mt. Fang-yen always carry a lantern with them, on which their own name is written as well as the words: "Incense-bringer to Fang-yen." When the time for the return journey comes, the children along the roadside are filled with joy when they greet the traveller, because they know they will receive dolls and other toys from the pilgrims. During this time there is laughter in every village, joined with the quarreling of the children among themselves.

(III, 12 — from T'ang-ch'i)

4.

On a certain day every year in my village, we always shoot off rockets, buy pigs'-heads, chickens or ducks, and make offerings to heaven before the gates of the houses. It is as lively as it is at the New Year. What day is it? Why, it is the eighteenth day of the eighth month, the day the pilgrims return from their worship of Count Hu on Mt. Fang-yen. It is the day on which they wish to thank the Count for the good journey.

In our village, when a man becomes twenty years old, he always goes to the mountain, and even if he is working outside the village, he comes back to make the pilgrimage. In addition, more than thirty men from those who are thirty, forty, or fifty years old, go every year as well. Starting three days before the pilgrimage, one must eat nothing but vegetables. At the same time one must have a pure heart and should not speak any evil. Otherwise he will be punished by the great god Hu. Once there was a woman who wanted to go to Fang-yen. Now because she didn't want to carry such heavy kinds of food as dumplings, dried bean cheese and the like, she bought two pounds of Chinese dates and took them with her. But unfortunately Count Hu found out about this and said: "This person does not have the proper spirit. She is coming only in order to eat." To punish her he did not allow her to eat. After that the dates smelled very badly.

But when one is sincere, then Count Hu rewards this sincerity well. There was once a man who had promised his life to Count Hu three years before. When the third year came in which he was to make the promised pilgrimage, it so happened that the date chosen for his marriage[9] was the sixteenth day of the eighth month. Anyone else would have been very happy about this. He, however, paid no attention to the wedding preparations, but rather got his baggage ready, took some money, and prepared to start on the pilgrimage. His parents tried to persuade him not to go, as did everyone else, but he was determined to have his way. So he asked his sister to help him. Then something unusual happened. When the man got to Fang-yen, Count Hu already knew about him, so he changed himself into a monk and began to question the man. The man answered everything very truthfully. Then the monk said: "You are really an honest man, and I shall reward you for it." Then he took his holy whisk and shook it before his face. He raised up a black cloud and placed the man on top of it. The cloud flew off to the man's house and in a moment's time he was dropped in front of his own door. It was just getting light, and that was the very time appointed for receiving his bride. Everybody was frightened to see him appear so suddenly, but he told them everything that had happened and they were all filled with joy. The people all said: "This is your reward for being an honest man."

Then there was a woman who had likewise made a vow to Count Hu when she was afflicted with smallpox. Because of this she had recovered from the smallpox without a single scar. So now she wanted to make the pilgrimage to fulfill her vow. However, since her feet hurt her very much and she was hardly able to walk, she wondered how she would be able to get there. Finally, when the day for the pilgrimage arrived, she decided to pay no attention to the pain and go anyway. She walked along for a few dozen *li* (one *li* is about .2 miles), and soon she found that her feet no longer hurt her. She quickly completed the pilgrimage and thanked the gods. Everyone said that it was a miracle performed by Count Hu.

(I, 2-3 — from Tung-yang)

5.

We have customs associated with the procession to Fang-yen in our locality, but how these customs arose is not clear. Usually a family in which a son has been born will make offerings for three days (namely the three days after the birth).[10] The offerings are prepared ahead of time and placed in the main gate of the house or in some open place. One then makes the offering in the direction of the crags of Fang-yen. The women of the village quietly murmur various words during the offering, for the most part wishes such as: "X has had a son on such and such a day in a certain month. I hope that Count Hu will protect him, that he will be lucky, that he will grow fast, that he will not be sick and will have no pains..., and when he is sixteen years old (either sixteen, twenty, or twenty-four years old), then we shall let him bring incense in person to our Lord, Count Hu..." After this offering, another offering is made to the P'u-sa,[11] and to the ancestors. Whoever can afford it, goes in person to Mt. Fang-yen on behalf of the child. If this is financially impossible, then it is not done.

When the child reaches the age that was indicated in the vow, then he must take all the things necessary for the offering, such as sacrificial paper and candles, and set out on foot on the pilgrimage. Otherwise it will not be right and Count Hu will send a punishment.

For some three days before he is to leave, everyone in the boy's home eats nothing but vegetables. During this time his mother (and if his mother is not living, then his wife) must pray every morning in the direction of Mt. Fang-yen, just as is done during the "Three Mornings."[12]

If one is at an inn while visiting Fang-yen and is served something containing chicken, pork, or other meat, he must say nothing about it but rather eat quietly what has been given him. A person should not say something like: "These vegetables seem to contain some meat." If a person says that, then he is no longer considered to be living as a vegetarian, and this can anger Count Hu, for Count Hu will say: "This man is not sincere. How can he eat meat when he comes to me?" (Since whoever goes there to worship with a sincere heart will certainly not do this!)

There once was a man who went to Fang-yen with four or five others to worship. But his wedding day had been set for the third day after the start of the journey, and since his home was 350 *li* from Mt.Fang-yen, he could never make it there and back in three days. His parents and everyone else tried to tell him that he could not make it back in time for his wedding day, but he was determined to go and all their warnings did no good. After he had arrived in Fang-yen and made his offering, he went out to wash his hands, when suddenly there was a clap of thunder and he fell to the ground. Looking more carefully, he found that he was at home lying in his own bed.

Then the wedding was held and everyone praised Count Hu. The next year
this man had a son who later became a government minister.

                                        (III, 48-49 — from T'ang-ch'i)

The earliest references to the deified Count Hu of which I am aware are
found in two late works dating from the Sung period, *Wu-lin chiu-shih*
(chap. V, 7a) and *Meng-liang-lu* (chap. XIV, 3b). In the second work we read
the following: "The Hsien-ch'ing temple is near the Yen-ch'ing temple in the
Dragon Fountain Valley near Hang-chou. Its deity is named Hu, with the
surname Tsê. He comes from Yung-k'ang in the district of Wu. He governed
Hang-chou twice, and was always a very good governor. During his
administration, there was no damage from the rivers or from floods. The
emperor was informed of this, and Hu was appointed superintendent of the
War Ministry. He was buried on Mt. Dragon Fountain. In Hu's home village
on Mt. Fang-yen, a gang of bandits had formed. One night they saw a vision
of a heavenly figure in a purple robe and a golden sash who was holding a red
banner high in the air. After this the robbers were destroyed. In appreciation
of this, the emperor built him a temple and donated a temple plaque in his
name. He was given the rank of a 'Count Possessing Magic Powers,' and a
gravestone with the title 'Shining Power of the Visibly All-Hearing God' was
also set up for him. The country people worship him in Fang-yen." The same
account is given in the *Ch'un-tsai-t'ang pi-chi* of Yü Yüeh.[13] According to
him, Hu Tsê ruled Hang-chou in 1016 and 1033. The incident with the
bandits is given as occurring about 1030. Yü's principal source stems from
the later half of the thirteenth century (the *Hsien-shun Lin-an-chih*). Hu had,
during his career as an official, also been in the southernmost province of
Kuanghsi, and there, as well as in Fukien province, had helped people in
their needs.[14] Fan Chung-yen (989-1052 A.D.), who wrote his necrology,
mentioned that he helped sailors, and even non-Chinese natives during his
period of office on Hainan Island, which is a part of Kuanghsi province.[15]
He later fell victim to a traitor while defending a city in central China, and
was killed together with all the members of his family...[16]

There is no reason to doubt these early sources. There are many cults
which can be traced back to beginnings in the Sung period. The question,
however, is whether the cult on Mt. Fang-yen was always connected with
Count Hu or whether it was not much older, and that it was only later that
its deity became identified with Count Hu. There are numerous instances of
such shifts in identification. There are several places, for example, where the
cult of Huang-ti has been transferred to that of a later deity, Kuan-ti, the god
of war. It is easy to see why the personalities of these deities could be so
easily confused, since these personalities are so vague in nature. One of the

texts even calls the deity Count Wu, instead of Count Hu, a change of names outwardly ascribable to the influence of local dialect pronunciation.[17]

The form of the cult on Mt. Fang-yen is similar to that of folk cults, particularly that of all mountain cults. The procession to Miao-feng-shan near Peking, (*illustration 2*) in which I myself participated on May 12, 1935, was of a similar nature. There was fasting beforehand, the departure was at night, one was not permitted to ride any sort of conveyance, and one was required to eat nothing but vegetables. The pilgrims brought along incense and sacrificial paper, prostrated themselves before the main god and associate deities, made vows, and bought souvenirs and toys for their relatives.

2. Announcements and proclamations of pilgrimage organizations are made in front of the temple on the *Miao-feng-shan,* famous center of pilgrimages near Peking, 1935.

The stories told about the magic powers of Count Hu are also similar to those told elsewhere about other deities. This can be seen by a perusal of the types of these tales listed in my *Typen chinesischer Volksmärchen* (FFC No. 120), Type Nos. 127-129.

The time at which the pilgrimage is undertaken appears, however, to be an important difference. While the pilgrimage to the Miao-feng-shan is made in the spring during the beginning of work in the fields, we have noticed here in several texts (Text I, 4-5 and III, 74) that the pilgrimage is begun after the harvest. The various texts indicate various dates:

the entire 8th month	(Text I, 40; I, 33; I, 35a; III, 199c; III, 73; III, 83g; II, 29b II, 111c)
the 8th to the 9th month	(III, 74; III, 68a)
the 1st part of the 8th month	(II, 111a; I, 35c)
the 1st part of the 9th month	(III, 67)
departure on the 1st of the 8th month	(I, 1-2; I, 4-5; III, 83e)
departure on the 8th of the 8th month	(II, 111)
departure on the 10th of the 8th month	(I, 55)
departure of the 11th of the 8th month	(I, 102)
departure on the 12th of the 8th month	(II, 109)
departure on the 13th of the 8th month	(III, 6; II, 306)
departure on the 14th of the 8th month	(III, 82)
departure on the 15th of the 8th month	(II, 29d; II, 96)
departure on the 18th of the 8th month	(I, 65)
cult worship on the 11th of the 8th month	(II, 111)
cult worship on the 15th of the 8th month	(I, 64; II, 31; II, 30)
cult worship on the 16th of the 8th month	(I, 234a)
cult worship on the 17th to the 19th of the 8th month	(III, 12)
cult worship on the 24th of the 8th month	(III, 83c)
cult worship on the 9th of the 9th month	(III, 188)
return on the 17th of the 8th month	(III, 6)
return on the 18th of the 8th month	(I, 2-3)

Some of the writers of the texts say that they no longer know the exact days. Most of them write only the day of departure which must vary with the distance from Fang-yen. But it seems to be certain that the principal day of the cult is on the fifteenth of the eighth month and the immediately following days, in other words, just the time of the full moon. At present the festival of the full moon falls on the fifteenth day of the eighth month, but there is considerable evidence that formerly there was an ancient harvest festival on this date.[18] Such harvest festivals at the time of the full moon remind one of the full moon festival of the Yao culture, which was also connected with the harvest, as well as with spring planting. Since the Yao have played an important role in the development of Chinese culture,[19] it is not impossible that these festivals were influenced by them. It is an established fact that the high culture of China had no festival connected with the full moon. (The festival held on the fifteenth day of the seventh month is purely Buddhistic). On the other hand, the high culture has a "mountain climbing" festival celebrated on the ninth day of the ninth month. Being on the ninth day of the ninth month, this is a festival date typical of the high culture. Without going into greater detail on this festival, I would merely like to suggest that it is probably likewise a canonization of an older folk festival which came from a different region, and was originally observed at a different time. With this in mind, it is easy to understand why the writer of one of the texts mistakenly places the date of the festival of Count Hu on the ninth day of the ninth month.

The second important matter for us is the question of the age at which the pilgrimage is undertaken. The texts show unusual uniformity in this regard:

with the 16th year	(III, 12; III, 48)
with the 15th year	(III, 67)
with the 16th or 20th year	(II, 109)
with the 18th year	(I, 1)
with the 19th year	(I, 43)
with the 20th year	(I, 2; I, 45; I, 64; I, 65; III, 6)
about the 21st year or from then on	(I, 103; I, 35c; II, 306; II, 31; II, 96; III, 100)
over 50	(I, 35a)
50th-60th year	(II, 109; III, 199c)
60th year	(III, 188)

All references can be summarized as follows: the pilgrimage to Count Hu is made at the age of twenty or sixty. The sixtieth year signifies a turning point, since a cycle of sixty has been completed, this being the normal life span of a human being (cf. Type No. 71 of my *Typen chinesischer Volksmärchen*). One asks Count Hu to prolong life beyond the normal limit.

The other time period, however, appears to be more important. In the high culture, the ceremony of "capping," in which the boy is accepted into the community of adults, was performed at the age of twenty. But there are numerous examples in which this ceremony was performed at an earlier age,[20] and this is exactly like the state of affairs alluded to above where even younger people can make the pilgrimage to Count Hu. The ceremony of capping has usually been associated with an ancient initiation rite, and in the case of the cult of Count Hu, we must make a similar assumption. Like the full moon festivals of the Yao peoples, this mountain festival is also based on the notion of fertility and sexual freedom. The texts, to be sure, express this only in a negative manner by relating how the deity punished those who desired to take liberties. Nevertheless, the fact remains that the mountain visits and the temple festivals on mountains were considered objectionable, and that legal measures were often taken.[21] The main objection was that it was impossible to separate women completely from men during such pilgrimages, and, according to Sung-period Confucianism, women should not walk around and be seen by men other than their fathers, brothers and husbands. Furthermore, mountain temples were often a retreat where men could arrange secret meetings or could indulge in prostitution. In spite of these laws, pilgrimages continued to the present time.[22]

Genuine initiation rites are known among the Yao peoples. Only after initiation is the boy permitted to take part in the dances and festivals of the adults. Here, too, the boy must be a certain age before he is allowed to take part in this festival, which likewise puts emphasis on fertility. The protective rites which must be observed, as well as the stories about dangerous punishments meted out by the deities, are perhaps survivals of older initiation rites. It doesn't seem a mere coincidence to me that a particularly large number of texts deal with the young man who was just about to celebrate his wedding, but was absolutely intent upon making the pilgrimage first. These are the very tales in which the young man always encounters the most dangerous miracles.

Only in one single text is there any indication that Count Hu becomes the godparent of a newborn child, and that the pilgrimage is undertaken out of gratitude for this sponsorship. I am not certain whether this is an original motif or rather a later contamination. It is very customary, particularly in the area of the cult of the deity Hu, to choose camphor trees as sponsors for a child. In other areas, other deities are chosen as godfathers.[23]

Although the collection of texts on the cult of Count Hu is quite large, the various texts are deficient in many ways. It is therefore impossible to provide a really complete, detailed description of the cult. Moreover, we lack similar text collections for other mountains, particularly in the provinces of Fukien and Kuangtung.

In addition, there is to my knowledge no analysis of the organization of these pilgrimages. We know that the form of organization is often loose. Some interested people begin to propagandize the pilgrimage a few weeks or months before the start, and whoever is interested joins. But we also know from a few remarks in a study from Taiwan[24] that some sectors of the population of one area visit one mountain, while other sectors visit another mountain. This seems to be connected with the origin of the different sectors (clan origins, ethnic origins, origins of immigrants). None of the many texts on Count Hu clarifies these problems concerning the organization of the pilgrimages.

3. CHINESE BUILDING MAGIC*

Among the Chinese folktales collected by Ts'ao Sung-yeh in Chin-hua (Chêkiang province, central China) which I brought back with me from the field, we find a large and distinct group of tales dealing with building magic.[1] The underlying concept in these tales is that by including certain objects in a building under construction, one can bring about certain effects on the later inhabitants. There are other types of building magic practiced in China, such as the hanging of certain objects supposed to guarantee the security of the house from the gable, or attaching objects supposed to guarantee the safety of the inhabitants to the exterior of the house (e.g., the stone from T'ai-shan, etc.), but these will not be discussed here. First we will present the text of several of the tales:

1.

Once there was a mason who worked for a rich man. Now earlier, the mason had always received meat on the six-days (the sixth, sixteenth, and twenty-sixth of the month). When the time for a six-day came around again, the man naturally gave him his meat, but since the mason had eaten too little, there was still something left over, and he saved this for the following day. The lady of the house noticed the left-over meat, mixed it with a lot of dry vegetables, and made it into a dish of dry vegetables and meat which she served him the following day. She meant no harm by this, but the mason thought she had some evil intention in mind, and so, when he was at work on the gate, he put six dice with their numbers arranged in the order 1, 2, 3 into a bowl, and built this into the gate.

The master of the house liked to gamble and had always had good luck. But after the gate was finished, he lost every time, and declined day after day until he had finally lost all his possessions. Then the mason happened to come by once again. The lady of the house told him how they had lost everything since the time the gate had been built. They had been able to treat the masons well, she said, but now that was no longer possible. She gave him all the details of their story, and then the mason suddenly realized

*Revised and translated version of "Chinesischer Bauzauber," *Zeit-schrift für Ethnologie* LXXI (1940), 87-99.

that he had done the wrong thing, and he said to the woman: "Bring me a ladder." The woman brought the ladder, the man climbed up on the gate, removed a brick, and switched the dice to the numbers 4, 5, 6. From then on the family became prosperous again.

(I, 133 — from Lan-ch'i, Chêkiang)

2.

South of my home Lan-ch'i there is a village by the name of the "village of the Shih family." There was a rich man living there who liked a flower hall that he had seen in the city so much, that he hired some workers to build him one too. He gave the workers soya-meat and soya-chicken at every meal, and treated them well. But when the job was nearly finished, one of the apprentices thought to himself: "I work hard all day long from morning til evening, and the man doesn't treat me at all well. Every day all he gives us is this burned meat, and there isn't even any white-cut meat (this is boiled meat cut in large pieces, prepared without any soy sauce or other spices — it is customary among us). This is really terrible! " For this reason he took the chopsticks and the bowl used for eating and placed them over the still unfinished door of the flower-hall. Afterwards they completed the hall.

After a few years the head of the house gradually became poor. And his sons were poor wretches.

After several more years had passed, the apprentice heard about all this in a neighboring village, and also heard how well the man had treated his workers. He was very surprised and returned to the man for whom he had built the hall. Now the man had already passed away by then, and his sons told the mason that after building the hall the family had not had any more good fortune. Now they had no fields left, yes, they no longer even had any more food and clothing. Despite this they invited him in, since he had come from so far away, and they bought wine and meat for him with some of the money they had saved. At dinner they said to him: "When you were here before there was such good food. Now all we can give you is this white-cut meat! " Then the mason realized that he acted wrongly, and he removed the chopsticks and bowl from above the door. And gradually the family became wealthy again.

(I, 247-48 — from Lan-ch'i)

3.

There was a family living somewhere and they built a house, and every day they served white-cut meat. Now, who would have imagined that a craftsman would take a loathing to this food, buy the tail of a pig, and put this in the rafters? From this moment on the family slowly declined. But the house was still not yet finished.

Now the lady of the house came out one day with the food and said to the craftsman: "I'm sorry, but we don't have any more money, and the only thing we can give you is fried meat." Only then did the craftsman realize that these people considered white-cut meat to be a very special dish, and he quickly removed the pig's-tail. After that the family gradually became wealthy once again.

I can also tell you the following things about the superstitious traditions of carpenters or masons who secretly do evil things while on the job:

1. Masons: They wall up a bowl at the foot of the wall in front of the gate, and place a chopstick in the bowl. Then the family will surely decline and their grandchildren in later generations will be beggars. But if one puts the same thing under another gate, then the family is supposed to become very wealthy and respected. Or they hide a ship made of paper in the shade-wall.[2] If the front of the ship is pointing toward the outside, then the wealth of the family will diminish. If it is pointing toward the inside, the family will gradually increase in prosperity. Or they secretly hide a clay rat in the rafters of the roof. Then this rat will make a lot of noise at night. Or they fashion a human figure from clay holding a night-pot in his hand, and hide this figure in the rafters. Then the men and women always have to urinate in their beds at night.[3]

2. Carpenters: They drive a nail into a newly-built column. Then the master of the house will have no descendants. Or they hide a small wooden doll on the top of the column of a recently-built house. Then the people will always hear disturbing footsteps and other sounds at night when it's quiet. Or they make an impression of a hand on the bottom-side of a toilet seat. Then anybody who sits down there gets a slap in the behind.

(I, 235-36 — Chin-hua)

4.

Not far from our village is another village in which an old man once lived. He was certainly not rich, but there were eight or nine people in his family and the rooms were not enough for them. So the man decided to add a couple of rooms. And since he wanted to start building the same year, he bought wood and bricks, and in less than two months he had accumulated all the necessary building materials.

Then the old man went out one day and hired some carpenters and masons to build the house for him, and they started in to work almost right away. The old man treated them very well. At mealtime they always had meat, chicken and other things to eat. In this way, he hoped that he could induce the men to work faster and more carefully, and thus to finish the house in a few months.

One day the old man couldn't get any pork in the village, and it was too far to go to another village and buy it there. So instead of meat he gave his workers duck eggs. But although everybody else ate the eggs, the master carpenter refused to eat them and was very angry. He secretly took the eggshells, painted a human head on one of them complete with eyes, nose, ears, a mouth, eyebrows and hair, and put this shell in a hole he had made at the top of the stairs. He then covered up the outside of the hole with some wood. From that time on the master carpenter was in very good spirits. Time passed quickly, soon the house was finished, and things were comfortable again for the old man.

For the next two or three years or so the house was very good, and nothing happened. But one summer night during the third year, the egg that the master carpenter had concealed started to move, and rolled down the stairs with a loud noise. Everybody in the house heard this sound, and they all thought that something or other had rolled down the stairs, but they didn't check right away to see what it was. Pretty soon they heard this racket again. This time they began to get suspicious and were very afraid besides. The old man went to find out whether there was a man or a ghost on the stairs, but when he got there he couldn't see a thing. Then he started to get a bit scared too. He wanted to go back to his room, but soon he heard the loud noise again. Then he became so frightened that his hair stood on end and his face turned white. He ran as fast as he could to his bedroom, threw himself down on his bed, and didn't even dare to breathe. There was so much noise that night that people were falling unconscious from fright. The following day everyone was half dead with fear and acted as if they were in a stupor most of the time.

But then the old man said to his wife: "That noise last night was undoubtedly the work of the carpenter. But I've got a very good plan. Since the stuff the mason or carpenter used in his plot against us is surely made of wood or plaster, it ought to roll down on these things too. So tonight let's put down charcoal ashes on the stairs, and if the thing rolls down, then it has to leave a trail in the ashes. Then we can tell where it comes from and how far it goes. Once we know that, we can put a chamber-pot in its path, and it'll roll right into the pot. And when it smells the stink, then it won't be able to get up and leave.[4] Then we'll discover it and we can burn it." When the wife had heard this, she exclaimed joyfully: "Very good, very good! " So they spread a thick layer of charcoal ashes on the stairs and the floor.

That night the thing rolled down the stairs again, but didn't make any more noise. But they thought it had stopped rolling altogether, so they became very peaceful and were no longer afraid.

However, when they went to check the next morning, they found the tracks of an egg on the stairs, and they realized that it had come the previous night as well, but because of the ashes it hadn't been able to make any racket. The old man thought about the matter for a long time, and finally it occurred to him that once he had served a meal of eggs. So that was why the workers had done this to him.

The next night he took two chamber-pots and put them where the thing would roll down. The following morning he went to check, and sure enough, there was an egg. It had turned into a ghost. So he set fire to it, and from that time on everything in the house was peaceful and quiet.

(II, 200-202 — from Chin-hua district)

5.

Once upon a time there was a very wealthy family, but the head of this family was very miserly. Whenever he undertook something, he would dream up some devious little trick or other, and after giving the matter considerable thought, he used to try it out. These stratagems always involved money. He didn't want to pay a cent too much! And so the villagers who knew him called him by the nickname of *k'o-sih-kui* (this is a dialect term for a miser and for people who love money more than their very lives, and who always take without giving in return. Such people are called "be-dead-ghost" or "killer-ghost"). Once this man thought to himself: "I already have many sons, and pretty soon we won't be able to live in this house any more. It's not big enough." Besides, that house was too old and in bad condition. His son wanted to have a new house built, and he thought about this matter for a long time, because building a house is not so simple. You have to spend a big pile of money, buy bricks, roof tiles, and all that, and hire some workmen. So instinctively, he shook his head and said: "That won't work. It'll be better if we build a few units of straw houses." After he had decided on this, he returned. But his wife and children warned him that a straw house would have to be renovated every year, you would need rice-straw that would have to be bound together for that, as well as bamboo rods to keep it steady, and all that would mean a lot of work. A brick house would be much better. His oldest son continued to speak: "You know, we can certainly do the rough work involved (All the easy, non-professional work is called rough work, as long as it is not very difficult. Thus, a house is built by carpenters and masons, but carrying wood and bricks is considered rough work.), and the carpenters can call us 'cousins'." The miser could save some money in this way, so he thought it over and said: "O. K., fine. So go ahead and buy the cheapest wood you can! " And his sons had to carry the bricks, call the workmen cousins, and work together with them. He himself supervised the work, had his sons carry bricks and smooth down the foundations, and soon the carpenters were finished with the gable. But the masons had not gotten so far with the walls. So the carpenters left while the masons were still at work.

One day the foreman (that's the fellow among the craftsmen who bosses the work crew) thought to himself: "This family, this miser is having a house built here. The head of the carpenters is supposed to have been his relative. Now if he hadn't been related, I'm sure he would have played a dirty trick on him. But I'll do it instead! "

Soon somebody came over and called them to dinner, but all they found waiting for them were the same old rotten vegetables. At best there were a few pieces of bean-cheese mixed in. The man was even more furious with the owner after this, and decided to really put one over on him. The snack that day was very good. They had dumplings made of glutinous rice. The mason took the dumplings and put them in the wall above the gate. After a few days his work was finished too. The miser was very glad to see the house finished, and he was even more happy about the fact that he had spent so little money. So he quickly picked out an auspicious day and moved in.

After they had lived in the place three or four years, everything was still quiet and in good order. But unexpectedly one night, while everybody but the skinflint was asleep, a knock was heard at the main gate. He figured it might be robbers, and lit the lamp. He checked, but found nothing, so he went back to bed, but pretty soon he heard it again. So he got up and checked once more. But by then everything was quiet again. This happened again and again, and the miser didn't get a wink of sleep all night. After that it was the same story every night. And on top of all this, one day one of his cows would die, the next day a pig, many misfortunes befell him, and he was always having some kind of litigation with somebody. After a few years of this, all his possessions were gone. He and his family wandered about without a home.

One night the miser slept in an old temple. Upon entering he greeted the Buddha[5] there and said: "I've had no good fortune since the time I built my house. I had to sell all my fields. The only thing still left is that unfortunate house. I'd sell *it* too, but the people have heard that there are supposed to be ghosts in the place and don't want to buy it. Have pity, Buddha! Who is responsible for all this? "

Then the image of the Buddha spoke: "Skinflint, do you know what you are? Do you feel any remorse now? " The miser nodded his head: "Yes,

I feel sorry." The image then spoke again: "Since you regret what you have done, ask the mason who built the house to help you"" And he thanked the Buddha many times over. But it wasn't the Buddha to whom he had said all this, but rather the mason! He knew that the miser was filled with remorse, and so he had hidden behind the image of the Buddha!

The miser threw himself down at the feet of the mason and begged him for help. The mason promised to help, went into the house, and uttered a few words at the gate. Suddenly several gleaming dumplings fell out of the gate. They had already turned into ghosts. That's why they looked the way they did. He burned them immediately. But the miser kept the mason for dinner, and the mason explained everything to him. Then the miser realized what he had done, and said that he would never do it again. With this the mason left.

The man gathered together his family again, and gradually they regained their wealth, and nobody ever used the nickname again either.

(II, 216-218 — from T'ang-ch'i)

There is another group of tales closely related to this one which deal with the making of some object rather than the building of a house. It is always a bed or a toilet. Here is one text representative of this group:

6.

Once upon a time somewhere there was a wood shop. The owner had a daughter, and after a while she grew up. The business grew more prosperous from year to year, and the owner became richer every day. Then someone learned that he had a daughter and wanted to marry her, so he sent a go-between to request her hand in marriage. But the father refused the man and said: "Ask around first, and then come back." So the go-between went about asking neighbors and relatives whether the man who wanted to marry her was a clever and capable fellow, and he heard nothing but praise everywhere he went. So the wood-dealer gave his permission for the marriage. The wedding presents they received were numerous as well as beautiful, but it was still not enough for the girl, nor was it good enough. She wanted her father to make her a marriage bed himself. But since he owned a store, he was very busy day and night, and he complained: "As if I hadn't given her anything! Well that's really the limit! " And he began to get very angry with his daughter. On the other hand, however, he was afraid he might miss the proper time for the wedding, so he finally gave in and agreed to do it, despite the fact that he was still against it. So when he made the bed he finished everything and put it all together, but in one corner he stuck a small figure of a Buddha with wild hair.[6] On the day before the wedding, they brought the bed over to the house of the groom, and when the appointed time had come the next day, the bride went over too.

That night, after they had climbed into bed in the bridal room, they started in to hit each other.[7] As soon as they got out of bed, they made up and were very much in love. This went on for several days, but they refused to believe their senses. By this time, everyone in the house knew about the situation, and nobody could believe it. They all advised: "It must be due to the bed." But some of them still didn't believe it, so they called in a carpenter to check over the bed. Now, after he had carefully taken it apart piece by piece, he really found the small figure of a Buddha with wild hair concealed in a corner of the back side of the bed. They destroyed this figure and reassembled the bed. After that they always got along well with one another, even when they were in bed together, or next to it, and they didn't fight any more. This had only been a trick of her father.

(I, 242-243 – from Wu-i, Chêkiang)

The rather numerous additional texts in our collection from Chin-hua and vicinity are all more or less similar to each other. The only element that changes is the manner in which the magic is brought about. Here is a summary of the various types of magic:[8]

a)   Walling up of dumplings or noodles. These make noise at night.

b)   Walling up of a ship with the bow pointing toward the outside, or of two ships, the smaller one pointing toward the inside, the larger one toward the outside. This causes the family to become poor.

c)   Putting dice with the lower numbers on top. The family grows poor by gambling.

d)   Painting a hand on something. It strikes the person who uses the object.

e)   Walling up a bowl with chopsticks. The family grows poor.

f)   Walling up a doll or a figure of a deity. It appears as a ghost.

g)   Placement of a paper figure. It appears as a ghost.

h)   Walling up of a cart containing money and traveling in a direction away from the house. The family becomes poor.

i)   Painting eyes on something. The family turns blind.

j)   Placement of a knife. It brings death.

k)   Placement of a nail. It makes noise at night or brings death.

l)   Walling up of a straw figure. It appears as a ghost.

m)   Placement of a piece of wood. It makes noise.

n)   Placement of the tail of a pig. It causes poverty.

o)   Inclusion of wood chips. They cause harm.

p)   Placement of a small watering device. It causes poverty.

q)   Placement of a shoe. It is supposed to cause harm.

r)   Placement of the figure of a tiger. It is supposed to devour the family.

s)   Placement of a thread with ink. It is supposed to cause harm.[9]

t)   Placement of a broom. It is supposed to cause harm.

u)   Placement of a coin or the figure of a cat. Noise at night.

v)   Placement of the figure of a cow. Harmful.

w)   Placement of a chopstick. Harmful.

x)   Writing down the sign of Leo. Supposed to kill.

y)   Placement of a bowl of water. This makes it impossible to light a fire.

z)   Dripping some blood in. Harmful.

aa)   False placement of a brick. Brings poverty.

ab)   Rotation of the main pillar of a house. Causes misfortune.

ac)   Putting of lice in bed. Brings ghosts or lice-plague.

ad)   Burning of a model of the house made of incense wood. A fire is supposed to break out.

ae) Placement of a man made of straw carrying a match in his hand. Fire is supposed to break out.

af) Walling up of a colorful cloth. The house is struck by lightning and burns down.

ag) Placement of oil-cake. This leads to suicide.[10]

In other cases, there is no exact indication as to which type of magic was employed. There are also a large number of cases in which the apprentice imitates his master's trick and achieves an opposite, favorable effect.

Now, I was informed that the masons and carpenters (the clay workers who pound the clay walls are also often included here) perform this magic based on a secret art, the secret art of Lu Pan. Numerous texts also mention this fact. Lu Pan is the patron of carpenters and artisans. It is no longer possible to establish whether there was ever any real historical personage behind this figure. In any event, we find that Lu Pan is conceived of as a supernatural divine being as early as the Han period (e.g., *Han-shu* LXV, 7a). A gate was named after him (*Hou-Han-Shu*, LIX, 5a). In the literature of the pre-Han period he is considered to be the inventor of several tools, such as the grappling hook, the cloud ladder and the ram. It is also reported that he carved a bird which was able to fly for several days.[11] Occasionally he also appears as a painter.[12] In this story, by painting while holding the brush in his toes, he succeeded in painting a spirit that was so ugly he did not want to be painted. The spirit got so angry that he disappeared in the water. The picture is now painted on doors in order to protect houses from spirits. He is associated with the building of houses (in the drama *Ch'ün hsing hui*), and with the construction of bridges (in the drama *Hsiao fang niu*). While the story of his efforts at painting, known already prior to 300 A. D., is the first one to connect Lu Pan with building magic, a story from the ninth century already has elements which are also contained in the modern versions. His father, the story reports,[13] had been killed by the ruler of Wu, while Lu was living in northwestern China. He made a sculpture of a man whose hand was pointing toward Wu. From then on, there was drought in the kingdom of Wu until the hand of the figure was cut off. From all this data it appears likely that Lu Pan, originally perhaps an historical figure sometime several centuries B. C., became the patron of carpenters in the Han period, or a short time later.[14] The *Book of Lu Pan (Lu Pan ching)* is supposed to be in the possession of the masters. Cheng Shih-hsü reports as follows:[15] "In this book, which is the holy book of the three master craftsmen (carpenter, mason, clay-worker), there are many paintings, both good and bad. Here one finds ghosts with dishevelled hair, ghosts with their tongues hanging out, as well as pictures which attract wealth. On the day when the ridge-piece is put into place, the master first prays very fervently to the heavens, and then blows open a page of the book and uses the picture he has found in this way. Their behavior is in complete accordance with the instructions of their protective patron, regardless of whether the head of the house has treated them well or badly." I also heard this view expressed. Nevertheless, all the texts explicitly state that the craftsmen perform some unfavorable magic only when they are treated badly, and that we are therefore dealing here with an act of revenge.

I have attempted to obtain a copy of this *Book of Lu Pan,* and although I have not come across any manuscript copies, I am convinced that some still exist. The only copy I was able to obtain was a small modern printing *Hui-t'u Lu Pan ching (Illustrated Book of Lu Pan).*[16] In the main, this pamphlet contains astrological and geomantic advice on building a house, including drawing and some practical information on measurements. An imperial chief inspector of public works in Peking by the name of Wu Jung is listed as the author. It is impossible to find either the author or the book mentioned in any of the large biographies or bibliographies. In view of the nature of the book, it would be impossible to date it earlier than the Ming dynasty. Whether or not portions of the book derive from considerably older materials is another question. We are not going to deal with the contents of the book here, since this would have to be done in the broader context of an explanation of all the geomantic rules. The important fact for us is that several pages entitled the *Secret Book of Lu Pan* have been added at the end of this book. Symbols which should be affixed to the outside of the house, such as the T'ai-shan stone, etc., are mentioned first, followed then by the section in which we are particularly interested (chap. IV, 18a-19a). The translation is as follows:

"All craftsmen, if they are alone and nobody else sees them, make use of the first picture they find after opening up the book with their eyes closed."

Thus, the notion we find expressed here is the same as the popular tradition reported above. This is followed then by a series of twenty-seven pictures, accompanied by rhymed and unrhymed captions. These rhymes are folk rhymes similar to other types of folk poetry, and very different from formal high literature. I will now translate the captions, giving in parentheses an explanation of the picture as well as of the magic involved:

1.   If one conceals a cinnamon leaf in the brace, the master of the house will pass his exams." (Picture of a cinnamon leaf. The basic idea is probably that a cinnamon leaf *'kui'* is associated with an honored position *'kui'*.)

2. "They also hide a ship in the brace. Then the bow of the ship can be pointed toward the inside, which leads to wealth for the owner. The ship should not be pointed toward the outside, since this brings about a loss of wealth." (Picture of a sailboat. The basic idea is that the ship can bring wealth in or carry it away.)

3. "If one hides something which is not bent somewhere, the master of the house will have long life." (Picture of a pine branch. The pine is considered in folk belief everywhere to be a symbol of long life, since it doesn't die during the winter.)

4. "If you hide these five ghosts with their tightly-bound hair in the pillar, then there will be sadness and death." (Picture of a man, with the magic symbols for the four elements, metal, wood, water and fire, in the four corners of the picture. The fifth element, earth, is thus the man himself. This is probably similar to the Taoistic magic of conjuring up the evil spirits of the elements.)

5. "A coffin, a corpse. If there are two, it means double punishment. If it's large, the the house will mourn an adult. If it is small, the house will lose someone small. It is concealed in the crossbeam in the hall." (Picture of a coffin. Symbolism clear. This saying is in the form of a four-line, seven-character poem, with the last line in prose.)

6. "A black sun hidden in the house, such a house has no happiness, time passes sadly, darkly. If you undertake something, it is as if clouds hid the sun. One is always sick and never leaves bed. – Hidden in the crossbeam over the door." (Picture of a circle surrounded by cloud symbols, with the character for the sun in the center. Symbolism clear. Poem similar in form to the preceding.)

7. "An iron lock containing the wooden figure of a man. Something like a human being painted brightly on the surface. In such a house five people die in one year. In three or five years everyone is dead. This is concealed in the well or in the wall." (Picture of a Chinese castle. Written on the castle are the words: "in the center a man carved of wood." – This probably alludes to the notion that the life of a man is contained inside. Poem in the same form as the preceding.)

8. "Bamboo leaves, entirely green, three leaves tied together. The words 'great peace and quiet' are written on top. Concealed well on the highest ridge-piece, it brings man peace, quiet, and eternal happiness. It

is nailed in place underneath the ridge-piece and is forbidden on top of the piece." (Picture of a three-lobed leaf. The words "great quiet" or "peace and quiet" or "great happiness" are written on every leaf. Bamboo symbolizes permanence. The form of the poem like the others.)

9. "If one paints the gauze hat on the beam, the boots on the pillar, and the belt on the crossbeam, it's just right. If one has sons, they pass their exams with the highest grades, become Han-lin officials and write books! " (Picture of the hat, belt and shoes of an official. This expresses the wish that the children should become officials. Poem in four lines like the above, but lacking the final line in prose.)

10. "If one hides a spot of China ink in the chink of the door, generation after generation of clever men and high officials will come forth. If they don't become literary officials, then they become painters; and a house in which good has accumulated, has faithful and loyal members." (A line-drawing, similar to a kind of fork. The ink is supposed to represent involvement with literature or painting. Poem in four lines like the above.)

11. "A fragment of an eating bowl, a chopstick, those who come later will be beggars. They will always have to go cold and hungry, they will have to sell the house and live in a mountain temple. It is hidden in the crossbeams of the entrance gate." (Picture of a small piece of earthenware and a chopstick. The broken bowl and the single chopstick are supposed to symbolize the beggar. Poem like No. 5 and similar ones.)

12. "If one hides a turned-over boat north of the house, whoever embarks on a business journey will drown in the river. His children and daughters drown themselves, his wives will die in childbirth. It is buried in the earth directly to the north." (Picture of a simple boat turned over. Symbolism clear. Verse like No. 11 above.)

13. "A sword and a ribbon, buried somewhere in the ground. Married couples, fathers and sons will quarrel, many will hang themselves with a rope. Can be buried anywhere." (Picture of a sword with a thread tied to the hilt. Symbolism obvious. Verse form as preceding poem.)

14. "Two swords painted on white paper is a reckless hero, a murderous firebrand. But whoever kills others is sent to jail and does not escape punishment in the autumn. It is concealed in the white-tiger headboard

in front of the gate." (Picture shows two short knives. Symbolism clear. In ancient China death penalties were always carried out in the fall. Poem like the preceding.)

15. "A man, a horse, a lance, fame in military service, and great happiness. The name becomes famous in the world, the barbarians surrender; however, death as a general in the field." (Picture of a man on a horse with a lance, but not a warrior. Symbolism clear. Poem in four lines like No. 9 above. Apparently the final line in prose, which tells where the picture should be mounted, is missing. The fourth line is a contemporary proverb!

16. "The white tiger must sit in the main hall. Because of this the head of the house will always be involved in quarrels, and the women in the house will have many diseases. It doesn't do anything to the children, only to the wife. It is concealed in the beam with the head facing toward the inside. This is unlucky." (Picture of a sitting tiger. The white tiger is a symbol of the west. It is therefore associated with feminine qualities. Poem like no. 5 and others.)

17. "Hide rice in the supporting beam, then the household will surely become wealthy and prosper a thousand riches, ten thousand cords of money. Security in the house. The rice spoils in the granaries, the chests are full of clothes. It is hidden in the supporting beam." (Picture of a pile of rice grains which are supposed to represent wealth. The spoiling of the rice should be understood as a consequence of the large surplus of which no use is made. Poem as above.)

18. "A piece of tile, a broken saw hidden at the point where the beams join. Then the husband dies, the wife marries again, the sons wander off, the slaves run away, and nothing is left. It is hidden where the beams meet." (Picture of a roof tile, on which the words "eternal passing" are written. The tile symbolizes the broken house. Poem as the preceding.)

19. "Two coins placed on the left and right sides of a beam, bring long life, wealth, happiness, and a good job in great abundance. The father becomes famous, the son is honored, the wife is enfeoffed and receives other gifts, and children and grandchildren wear the clothes of officials for generations. It is attached to both ends of the main crossbeam, one coin at each end, upside down." (Picture shows two old cash coins, one bearing the inscription *yüan* /'original'/, the other *chiu* /'nine'/. Symbolism clear. Poem as the preceding.)

20. "Seven nails make a pack, seven persons will never get lost, but if another person is added, and if someone takes a daughter-in-law, then one will always have to leave when another comes. It is concealed in a hole in the pillar." (Picture shows nine /! / nail-like dots. *Ting*, meaning a 'nail,' can also be used to denote 'person' /*ting*/, so seven nails are equivalent to seven people. Poem as the preceding.)

21. "A piece of good China ink and a brush bring wealth, honor, fame, and a high position. One will help the court and become a minister. If the brush tip spoils, one loses the office. It is hidden in the beam." (Picture shows a block of dry ink bearing the inscription 'ink'; a brush next to it. Both symbolize the scholar. Poem like the preceding.)

22. "If one writes this magic sign in the water and wood (i.e., in the wall), one will see spirits and ghosts in the house, stones knock about, sand flies, and the place is always haunted. Many women and children die of disease. This is inscribed in the crack of a tree trunk." (Picture shows a Taoistic magic symbol, apparently formed from the components 'door' and 'ghost.' Such magic signs have been common from at least the fourth century A. D. The usual poem.)

23. "If the red bird is written in front, there will be much strife. If he is an official and has no misfortune, then he will constantly quarrel with others. The family possessions are lost, people die, and it doesn't cease until the house is sold. This is written on the beam above the main gate." (Picture of a square. The red bird is a symbol of the south, therefore one should actually expect fire. Symbolism not clear. Usual poem.)

24. "Inscribe the 'bushel-prisoner' in the gate entrance, then misfortune will befall the house when it is finished. Great accusation and prison, where one remains until death. It is hidden in a crevice in the gate entrance." (Picture shows a black square similar to a bushel-measure inscribed with the character for 'human being.' Probably is supposed to express the idea of being a prisoner. Usual poem.)

25. "Hide a cow's bone in the house. This brings sorrow and distress. There is no coffin to be buried in when one dies in old age. Grandchildren in later generations will be poor. It is buried in a room."(Picture shows a bone with the inscription 'cow's bone.' Next to it a black ring of unknown significance. The bone probably symbolizes decline and death. Usual poem.)

26. "A sword wrapped in the hair of the head, then sons and grandchildren will be bald and run from the house. One has sons, but no man, one is never happy, but remains widowed and alone. This is concealed in the ground underneath the gate entrance."(Picture shows a sword cutting through a bundle of hair. Symbolism alludes to the cutting off of the hair, signifying the entrance into a holy order of monks. Usual poem.)

27. "Paint a flask-gourd on the wall and on the beam. Then one understands the philosophical and religious teachings. All who live there possess special arts. There are many doctors, fortune-tellers and astrologists. It is painted on the wall and at the place where the beams are joined together." (Picture shows a black flask-gourd. This is an attribute of magicians and holy men, which explains the meaning of the symbolism. Poem as usual.)

The number *27* is undoubtedly symbolic. It may be related to the number *9* which, as a number signifying completion, plays a particularly important role in all magical speculation. Perhaps there are also connections with the stations of the moon, although the Chinese number of moon stations is actually twenty-eight, and was only occasionally shortened to twenty-seven as a result of Indian influence. The entire text appears either to have been handed down in incomplete form (this is why the first four pictures lack verses), or to derive from various different sources. It is more likely that the text is incomplete, since irregularities occur in other verses as well. Incomplete transmission is, of course, especially common when it comes to folk traditions.

If we compare this 'canonical' enumeration of building magic with the folktales from Chin-hua, we find that the folktales indicate completely different magical practices. Only the ship (No. 2) also appears with the same meaning in the folktales. Therefore, we may definitely assume that our text of the *Book of Lu Pan* was not the basis for these tales. Probably these tales had no underlying text, and the masons and carpenters simply made use of various kinds of magic according to the particular circumstances involved. The *Book of Lu Pan* offers proof of this custom only for an earlier period. Unfortunately, however, we cannot determine the exact age of the book.[17]

The question arises as to how old this custom really is. From what could it have developed? The first mention of a similar custom is in the Han annals.[18] It seems there was a large affair involving magic in which many thousands of people were implicated. Human figures made of T'ung-wood were found buried in a palace, and also along the roads which the emperor was supposed to travel. This was supposed to kill the emperor magically. Hun magicians were involved with this magic. This is entirely comparable with the later building magic, even if there are certain differences. The magic is not planted by craftsmen, and is not intended to have a lasting effect on every dweller in the house, or every traveller on the road, but is explicitly designed for use against the emperor. In general, we can say that these and similar cases belong more to the field of image and analogy magic, a type which is well attested both for ancient China and the Huns.

I believe the actual origin of building magic should be sought in the building sacrifice. Whenever a new building was constructed, human beings who were supposed to protect the house were walled up in the foundation. We can see here the same basic idea as in building magic, namely that some entity walled up in the construction can have favorable or unfavorable later effects. We have many attestations for the presence of such a building sacrifice in China. Excavations in Yin-hsü, the capital of the Shang dynasty (before 1050 B.C.), have shown that sacrifices were placed under the foundations of pillars of palaces. Later texts taboo the custom of human sacrifices, and speak of immolation of dogs under pillars. This may have been a custom which co-existed with human sacrifices. The dog protected the house magically, just as a human sacrifice could. The custom of immolation and sacrifice is known in many forms. Very similar folktales concerning the construction of a dam at which human beings are sacrificed, and like customs connected with the casting of a bell, the dedication of a new brick oven or a new porcelain oven, will not be discussed here.[19] A recent modern example reported by Chen Shih-hsü[20] relates that in Nanking, when they were digging the grave of Sun Yat-sen, a rumor was circulating that the souls of small children were being purchased for the grave. In the tale about Meng Chiang (Kiangsu province) there is a remark to the effect that people bearing the family name "Wan" (=10,000) were buried in the city wall in order to render the wall particularly strong and solid (10,000 years of durability).[21] Apparently, even in recent times, such practices were common in Shantung province.[22] The practice of building in figures could thus be regarded as a substitute for the walling-up of human beings, although this type of burial of figures for magic purposes is an ancient custom that can be traced back to a very early period. It is difficult to establish a definite area of distribution for this custom, but it appears to be concentrated particularly in southern and eastern China. This impression, however, may only be due to the fact that adequate information is not available for other areas.

4. THE SUPERNATURAL IN CHINESE FOLKTALES FROM CHÊKIANG*

The "Great Tradition" of Chinese religion – to use a term coined by Robert Redfield – is by now fairly well known; at least, we know the content of the main religious texts and the forms of worship. Parts of the "Little Tradition" are also known. The forms of popular worship, the names of popular deities of different areas have been studied. A number of "secret societies" and their cults have also been analyzed. Yet, the question remains: what are the religious ideas and beliefs which are in the minds of the ordinary farmers – not in the minds of local priests or more or less educated persons. Folktales can be used as *one* source to find out what the common man believed, especially if such folktales do not consist only of the more or less "standardized" tales, but also include local legends or happenings which are supposedly true, but which are told without the official names of the actors and without the name of the place. If personal name and place name are given, a Chinese would regard a story as a historical text of some kind and not as a tale. Of course, a study of tales cannot give us the whole picture; it should be supplemented by other information, especially from the life histories.

As the source of the following discussion, I am using a collection of some five hundred texts, collected for me by Mr. Ts'ao Sung-yeh in Chin-hua (Chêkiang) in 1934.[1] The stories were collected from school children with an average age of twelve years. The children came from the surrounding area, from villages and towns and may represent a cross-section of the general population. The stories do not contain examples of all Chinese tale types: some tales occur very often, others do not occur at all in this collection. Therefore, to a degree, the collection reflects motifs which occupied the minds of the children most strongly. The material does not render itself to statistical analysis; yet, in my opinion, some conclusions can be drawn from it.

1. Gods:
    (a) *The Persons:* Most common is "the Buddha" (2,44; 5,35; 6,86; 7,7), an unspecified deity of Buddhism. Never is any further detail given as to

*Reprinted from *Humaniora,* eds. Wayland Hand and Gustave Arlt (Locust Valley, New York, 1960), 335-341.

which of the many Buddhas is meant. Next to Buddha, the Earth-God is important (5,8; 6,2c; 6,69). His temple is in every village and town and every child has seen him often. All other deities occur more rarely. There is the highest Taoist God, Yü-huang (6,16; 6,23); the Thunder God (6,64; 6,65); the daughter of the Dragon King (7,27; 7,28), a female Star God (7,39), the God of Pestilence (6,29), a Treasure God (6,57), and a God of Fate (6,58). The Sun occurs once (6,54), but not really as a deity: she has a house and much gold.

(b) *Activities of the Gods:* The Gods live on sacrifices (5,8), have families (7,27), marry (7,28), have the same social values as men (7,27). Some live in caves in luxury and with many concubines (6,87), others play chess (6,58). They get angry when persons kick their statues in the temples (6,2a); they speak out of figures or out of the person which they want to punish (7,7; 2,44), and in general punish the bad or kill them and help the good (6,64; 6,65; 6,69; 6,86; 7,1; 7,7; 6,58).

(c) *Service to Mankind:* Gods also have definite functions and, on occasion, have to serve man. If a man is destined to become an emperor, the Gods show their devotion to him (6,2b; 7,48; 7,49), and if they fail to do so, the future emperor can punish them (6,2f). They protect treasures for the right owner (6,57). If necessary, they marry humans (7,28). Scholars who recite texts can change the intentions and plans of Gods (7,39) and the statues can be used to impress moral teachings upon people, even if a trick has to be used (2,44; 5,35). Gods might even participate in tricks and cheating in order to help a future emperor (6,2c), and they can be cheated by man (5,8). They may make use of an invention made by man, for their own purposes. The thunder was invented by man and used by the Gods (6,23).

Gods, thus, are not much different from human beings. They have more, but not unlimited power. An emperor is more powerful than most of the Gods. Most of these deities are usually regarded as belonging to the Taoist pantheon, but our tales are not much interested in their official character. Often a God could easily be replaced by another one.

2. Deified Persons:

(a) *Origin:* Usually persons who sacrificed themselves for their community became deities or the community built a temple and began to worship them (7,37; 6,21; 7,8; 7,10; 7,11; 7,14; 7,34; 7,35). Sometimes a person who exhibited unusual feats became deified (7,12, a quick captain).

(b) *Activities:* Their most important activity is to help the good (1,2; 1,7; 1,12; 1,14; 1,23; 1,33; 1,41; 2,4). They give children (1,10), but expect that the children later give them sacrifices as a reward (3,27). They continue to help the community by giving rain (7,37; 7,35) chasing away demons

(6,21) or by general protection (7,8; 7,10; 7,11; 7,34). They are easily offended and get angry (1,6) and punish persons who are not sincere when they come to worship (1,1; 1,3; 1,6; 1,8; 1,10; 1,31; 1,40; 1,42).

These deified persons, then, are much closer to the people. It is with them that people have most often contacts, not with the Gods. Their names and often traits of their life are well known, much better than the Gods are known.

3. Saints:

(a) *Origin*: A person may learn the art of becoming a saint from a Taoist (7,23) or his fate may be changed but the change was incomplete so that he did not become a God (7,48; 7,49). Saints can be recognized as they remain young (7,23).

(b) *Activities:* Saints know the future (6,8; 6,51; 6,55), perform miracles (6,79; 6,7c; 7,16) which sometime are socially valuable, but in most cases have no importance for man. Sometimes they sell good things, but people do not recognize it (6,6). They help good persons who often do not recognize with whom they are dealing (7,49). But normally, they help people (7,16), assist the good and punish the bad (6,5; 6,55; 6,59; 6,62; 6,72; 7,50; 5,66). They are, in general, similar to the deified persons, but they cannot be asked to do something, mainly because they do not have temples where they can be reached. Their use to mankind is limited to their own fancy and cannot be directed.

4. Ghosts and Demons:

(a) *Origins:* Most often persons in coffins which have not yet been buried, or not been correctly buried, become demons (6,27; 6,31; 6,32; 6,33; 6,34; 6,38; 6,41; 6,104; 7,9), but also pieces of the coffin itself can become demons (1,4; 3,50; 6,30; 6,35). The hanged often become ghosts (6,28; 6,37; 7,30; 7,31; 7,32; 7,33). Such persons are usually young women who have been forced to commit suicide and who have not lived out their lives. Murdered persons, too, can become ghosts for the same reason (6,63). Finally, all objects which are very old, can come to life (7,2; 7,4; 7,45).

Ghosts are often of female sex (3,50; 6,28; 6,30; 6,36; 6,37; 6,38; 6,44; 7,9; 7,13; 7,29; 7,30; 7,31; 7,32; 7,33), but male ghosts also exist (6,39; 6,42; 6,63). Some ghosts are in animal shape (6,40; 6,84; 6,83). Ghosts are very ugly (1,4), hairy (6,35; 7,47), with short hair (6,36), and have big, black teeth (6,52). Often, they at first look beautiful, but then become really ugly with long tongue and with claws (6,28). They like to transform themselves into frightful shapes with long hair, long tongue, and blood all over (6,30; 6,37; 7,32; 7,33). They emanate a red glow (6,34; 6,35; 6,44) and dress in white, the color of mourning (6,53). When they jump into the water, they make no sound (5,60). In general, their character is bad (1,4; 6,26; 6,83; 6,84), and the more time goes on, the more powerful they become (6,104).

(b) *Their Social Life:* Ghosts, too, have families and like to stay together (6,41); they have sex life among themselves (6,44) or with humans (6,38; 6,83). They even have a king (6,52). They visit the theatre (6,38), talk in groups at night (6,53) and discuss human affairs (6,42). They make tricks just in order to have some fun (6,43). They go to human judges to claim their rights (6,63).

Ghosts collect riches (6,52) and food. Their food may be ordinary food like melons (6,52), but normally it is human flesh (1,4; 3,50; 6,32; 6,33). For this purpose, they go out at night-time (1,4; 3,50; 5,60; 6,27 et al.). Ghosts try to induce people to commit suicide in order to serve as their replacement (6,28; 7,30; 7,31), or to drown themselves for the same purpose (5,60; 4,61) — both interesting ways to explain suicide as actions for which the victim is not really responsible. Ghosts, on the other side, fear spirits of the hanged, because these are powerful (7,31).

(c) *Actions Against Man:* Ghosts and demons are normally harmful and attack people for no reason (6,27; 6,34; 6,40; 7,29), try to frighten people by assuming frightful shapes (6,28; 6,30), or really to kill them by frightening (7,4). They trick people into graves and kill them there (6,30), rob princesses for no reason (6,84), capture girls (7,29) or cut off the pigtail of a man for no reason (6,26). They may catch souls (6,39) and steal (6,83). They try to seduce a man (7,13) or have sexual relations with him (6,38). Usually, they then try to draw his life essence out of him in order to strengthen themselves; the man finally dies of exhaustion. They also can have sexual relations with women (6,83). It is rare that they just play with a man without harming him (7,45).

They revenge themselves if they are cheated (5,60), kill people in order to keep a treasure for the right person (6,56). But very rarely they also do good things, such as protecting a man against another ghost (7,31) or giving food to a man (7,30). People are, therefore, interested in getting rid of ghosts. This can be done by several methods. Ghosts can be tricked by ink (1,4; 3,50; 6,38; 7,47) or by the classical texts (6,27; 6,32). Both methods are favorites among scholars. They also can be eliminated by burning (1,4) or burning of the coffin (7,32), filling of the coffin with dirt (6,33; 6,35; 6,44) or by removing the cover of the coffin (6,27). They die when the sun rises, if they cannot take refuge in their coffins (6,33). Fire-crackers frighten them away (6,36; 7,32; 7,33) or statues of Gods protect against them (6,34). Even dogs may prevent their attacks (6,40). It is also helpful not to talk to them (6,36). If a courageous man can force them to eat rice, they will have to change into human beings (6,38), and some men even have forced ghosts to serve them (7,47). Persons who are drunk meet ghosts more often (7,31; 7,33).

Ghosts and demons seem to play a very important role, though almost always a negative one. They seem to be ordinarily *Wiedergänger,* walking dead, and exhibit a bad, aggressive character. Chinese religious theory would explain that such walking dead are in possession of the "animal soul" but not of the "personal soul." The animal soul does not recognize friends and is by nature bad. But our tales do not go into such speculations. Ghost stories are very common in the short-story literature. Here, too, ghosts have similar traits, but the sexual element is much more underlined than in our tales. It seems to me that this is not only the case because the stories were written by children, but that, on the other side, the writers of short-stories used the concept of a ghost to describe sexual and other emotional events which they could not ordinarily describe because of social taboos.

5. Animals:

Animals formerly lived in heaven (4,73; 6,17) and sometimes were punished by being made to live on earth for a while or forever (5,73). Some human beings became animals as a result of a bad treatment given to them (6,15), or as a punishment (6,14). Animals can be good or bad: they help man (5,73; 6,60) because man has helped them (6,76; 6,77; 6,78), they punish the bad (2,26) and those who do not believe in them (6,45). They revenge themselves if they are killed by man (7,36). Sometimes, they like to play tricks on man (6,45), but sometimes, they are outright bad (6,76; 6,77; 7,6; 7,45; 7,46). Some may become bad in time (7,5). Their role is quite limited in our tales, and those animals which have a bad character are really demons in animal form, often snakes or dragons.

6. Magic Things:

Magic objects are also quite similar to the ghosts and demons: blood (2,17; 3,28; 3,65) or a painting (2,20) can produce magic actions. But in most cases reported in our stories, some craftsmen made small models of objects and enlivened them by magic formulae (1,5; 1,17; 1,20; 1,30; 1,36; 1,37; 1,44; 1,47b). The magic which is produced in this way may work immediately, but often it begins to work after several days or as long as after three years (2,9; 2,44). The magic just plainly terrifies people (1,5; 1,17; 1,20; 1,30; 1,36; 1,37; 1,44; 1,47; 1,47b; 3,42; 2,17; 2,20; 3,28; 3,65), but it may also cause harm to them (1,16; 1,21; 1,22; 1,24; 1,25; 1,27; 2,2; 3,5) or may change the whole fate of the family (1,15; 1,19; 1,18; 1,22; 1,28; 1,29; 1,35; 1,43; 1,44; 1,45; 1,46; 1,48; 2,1), or may change the luck in gambling (2,8; 2,13; 2,32). Magic may spoil the bridal night completely (1,30; 1,25; 1,24; 2,30; 3,5), or may only spoil food (2,31). If the magic is discovered in time, its effects turn against the person who made it (1,23; 1,27; 1,22). A bed-pan can avert magic (2,9; 2,31). Magic rarely serves a moral purpose, such as punishing greedy persons (2,13). But it might be said that magic which is started by craftsmen served a social function: the employers were afraid and did, therefore, not dare to mistreat the craftsmen too badly. Magic which is not caused by man often does not cause any effects.

7. Geomancy:

Finally, one typically Chinese belief has to be mentioned: geomancy, or the belief that the place where a house or a tomb is built influences the future life of the owner or his family. It may also be an unusual feature in the landscape which influences the life of the people living nearby. Any action against a future gravesite influences the fate of the future generations (6,98). The right site may make the family rich after generations (6,100). Such a site may provoke fires (8,101) but may still be good (6,102). Bad places should be destroyed (6,103), but the killing of stone animals or figures (6,97) may lead to a loss of good luck. Such figures may have indicated a place where a future emperor was supposed to be born (7,18; 7,20; 7,21), and when they are destroyed, no emperor will be born (*ibid.*, and 7,19). Even a camphor tree may influence the fate of people: when a tree was trimmed, people began to die (4,1).

Conclusion

In popular belief, as expressed in folktales from Chêkiang, deified persons are the main source of good, and ghosts or demons the main source of bad. Deities seem to be aloof and are not as potent and actively interested in human affairs as the deified persons are. Saints are too unreliable to be a real source of good. Animals are not important at all – and in general, Chinese folklore is quite poor in animal tales. Nature has some powers in itself which can be socially useful, if not destroyed, and magic objects have power which can be used for social purposes if they are not detected.

The "Little Tradition" which these folktales exhibit does not deviate much from what we can also find in collections of short stories written by educated persons. But there seems some difference in weight: less interest in sex, greater fear of the dead, and much more belief in the effectiveness of magic objects. The stories exhibit little real, emotional, religious feelings; the supernatural is regarded as a part of the social world, only with some more powers than the ordinary society has. Man is not helpless against these powers. He can defeat them. The supernatural beings are not ideal pictures of the good, but have character traits pretty much like ordinary beings, if they are not basically bad in character. It is clear from all stories that human society is the real, legal society: the other worldly powers, although also organized in form of a society, have basically no autocratic rights over human society and have not given laws to nor created human society.

5. BULLFIGHTING IN CHIN-HUA (CHÊKIANG PROVINCE)*
by Ts'ao Sung-yeh

The following essay is a slightly abridged but close translation of a previously unpublished manuscript given to me by Mr. Ts'ao Sung-yeh. Ts'ao belongs to the young generation of Chinese folklorists who have formed the Chinese Folklore Society (*Chung-kuo min-su hsüeh-hui*), and is probably the greatest authority on the folklore of his native Chin-hua. He has already distinguished himself by the publication of several essays on special characteristics of this area.

This paper on bullfighting introduces us to a custom about which little has been written, and also attempts to answer questions concerning its origin and history. Although Ts'ao's theories deserve a detailed examination, I would only like to touch briefly on two points here. I have dealt with these more thoroughly elsewhere.[1] (1) The question as to when the Chinese began to use cattle or water-buffaloes for plowing is still very much under discussion. It seems to be certain that by the fourth century B.C. plowing with animals was fairly common in the developed parts of China, but whether animal power was already used in the Shang period (before 1050 B.C.) has not yet been definitely established. (2) Ts'ao Sung-yeh is not the only writer who regards bullfighting as a custom typical of Chin-hua. Another nineteenth century source makes the same statement and adds that the age of this custom is unknown.[2] However, we know of a number of Chinese reliefs and paintings which depict such fights. The Berlin Anthropological Museum had a copy of a painting from the Sung period showing a bullfight (inventory number I.D. 34069). The famous poet and statesman Su Tung-p'o (1036-1101) mentions that one of his acquaintances in Szuch'uan province had an old scroll depicting a fight, which was criticized by a shepherd boy who said the painting was incorrect.[3] Another source of the Sung period mentions another painting.[4] But reliefs from the Han period (probably first or second century A.D.) already show scenes which might refer to bullfights.[5] Bullfights, therefore, would seem to be old in China. The question remains whether those of the Han period refer to another custom which has no connection with the Chin-hua bullfights, and whether the

*Revised and translated version of "Der Stierkampf in Chin-hua," *China-Dienst* III (Shanghai, 1934), 941-945.

paintings depicted the Chin-hua type or not. The Berlin painting, as far as I can recall, did depict this type. Unfortunately, however, we don't know where the painter got his inspiration. On the other hand, I agree with Ts'ao that bullfights of the Chin-hua type are typical of the Miao and related tribes,[6] and Yüeh tribes are still living in the area of Chin-hua today. It might be mentioned that bullfights were put on in connection with the festival of the fifth day of the fifth month in southern Korea,[7] an area which, as I hypothesized in my *Lokalkulturen,* II, was influenced by Yüeh culture.[8]

But now to the text of Mr. Ts'ao's essay.

Although there has been bullfighting in Chin-hua for a long time, the custom has remained almost unknown to outsiders. Recently, however, guests from Shanghai, Hang-chou, and other cities, had an opportunity to see bullfighting in Chin-hua while attending the festivities held in conjunction with the opening of the Hang-chou-Kiangsi railroad, and the associated exhibit of products of the areas served by the railroad. This celebration, usually not witnessed by outsiders, made a great impression on the guests, and all the Shanghai newspapers carried stories about it. But since these outsiders had only a short time for observations, and since everything was unfamiliar to them, they were only able to give superficial and false accounts. I was born in Chin-hua district in an area where bullfighting is quite widespread, and used to see these fights even as a child, including the place where the fights are held and its surroundings, and thus am better qualified to report on the subject. I would first like to give the reader an accurate description of the fight itself, followed by a scientific explanation.

1. *When do the bullfights take place?*

In all the districts belonging to Chin-hua, the temples are the clan centers, or, in other words, every clan meets under a temple. The sphere of influence of such temples is sometimes limited to one or a small number of villages, but may extend to more than ten villages. According to the prevailing custom, the temple is renovated once every ten years, and the image of the god is repainted or restored. If the villages or market-towns belonging to a temple are wealthy, or if they have a rich harvest, then they ask the god for an oracle one year prior to renovation. A piece of bamboo four to five inches long and split in two is used as an oracle. If, after the oracle has been cast, one side is facing down and the other up, this means that the god approves of the bullfight, but if both are facing in the same direction (either up or down), then he does not approve. For this reason approval comes only in years with a good harvest. In years with a poor harvest there is no oracle, in order to avoid having to arrange a bullfight..

2. *The animals*

The animals used in bullfighting are all brown bulls. No water-buffaloes are employed. Large bulls with a short neck, a solid compact body and a short tail, like a lion, generally make good fighting bulls. If it is thought that a certain bull has potential as a fighter, bulls of approximately equal value are selected, paired off and taught to fight. Once the bulls stand face to face, some sniff each other first and then attack, others attack immediately. If they are not powerful chargers, they thrust only at the hind legs. But they are expected to be powerful thrusters. If bull *A* is superior, they pull down vigorously on his nose so that bull *B* hits him in the neck. At the same time the people taking care of bull *B* strike its hind legs, so that it tries harder. Then again, sometimes they raise his snout so that he takes the blows in the chest. Only after the bull is well trained in fighting is it permitted to enter the actual arena of battle. During training the animal is usually kept on the rope, since many bulls want to run away after the first blow.

3. *Feeding the bull*

The feeding of the fighting bulls is considered very important. Their stalls are particularly clean. When there are no greens, they get dry rice-straw, and if greens are available they are given chaff. When Ch'en Ch'i-yüan writes during the Manchu period[9] that "They lie on a mat made of green silk," he is referring to this. Recently, someone claimed that they were given real mosquito nets for protection against mosquitos and flies. This practice may occur, but is not common. The best bulls get two meals a day, and are fed wheat between meals. In addition to these two meals, they are fed supplementary rice-straw in the winter, and they are given fresh fodder at other times. It is sometimes necessary to go back deep into the mountains to locate this fodder. The animals are let out once every day to promote digestion. One day before the fight the best bulls get rice brandy, sugar, or ginseng. Some even give them opium. The average bulls don't get rice brandy or weak wine until right before the fight.

4. *Decoration and value of the bulls*

When a bull is sent from one place to another, a sign bearing his name is affixed to his head. Two short pheasant feathers are attached on top of the sign, and it is encircled by all kinds of brightly-colored patterns. A red blanket made of satin or plain red cloth is placed on his back. On top of this is a flagstand in which triangular pennants pointing in all directions have been placed, just like with a general on the stage. If the bull has the reputation of being invincible, a pennant with the inscription "Commander-in-Chief" is added to those on his back, or is carried by someone walking on ahead. The lead-reins are made of hemp, and sometimes, in the case of some of the first-class bulls, are partially of silk. If the bull is led to another place, horn-players, drummers and gong-players lead the procession, and up to ten ropes are used to guide the animal. Upon arrival, a sacrifice is made to the deity. The statement sometimes heard to the effect that the same festivities are put on when the animal is led to the arena, is not true.

During a bull sale the prospective buyer first takes the animal to the arena so he can see his abilities. If he is satisfied, he engages a middle-man, discusses the price, and pays the deposit. — The price of a bull is higher than that of a common head of cattle. First-class specimens cost about 3000-4000 Chinese dollars, average ones bring about 100-200 dollars, and fair to mediocre animals run about 20-30 dollars or more. If the price of an animal is 80 dollars, an additional 20 *mao* in small change is added, and then it is said that the animal is worth 100. Thus, if one hears that a first-class bull is worth 1000 dollars, it means they have added several hundred *mao (mao is approximately equal to* 8¢) so as to arrive at a nice, round high figure. Even the good bulls have to assist when there is work to be done in the fields, and only the very best animals are exempted. It is not true that a bull who has not won a fight is not used again for working the land.

5. *The arena*

The arena is generally selected in an area adjoining a small hill so that one has a place for the audience to sit. In Chin-hua there is a saying: "The *Tung-ts'ih-yen* is a place for noise, the opposite mountain is a place for meeting." A place for noise is an area for bullfighting, and the meeting place is the spot where up to ten theater groups meet and hold a competition. This often occurs at the time of the temple festivals. The *Tung-ts'ih-yen* is the most famous temple in the northern part of the district of Chin-hua.[10] More than 100 pairs of bulls are used each time they have fights there. There are mud walls on which spectators can stand at both sides of the arena. The opposite mountain is today the railroad station T'ang-ya of the Hang-chou-Kiangsi line. It used to be a small plain on which numerous theater groups could put on performances. Such an arena consists of an irrigated field several *mou* in size.[11] Before the fights, the mud is plowed up, and two gates are erected on both sides of the arena. These are made of bamboo and are covered on top with red cloth. They are known as arena gates. The arena is then roped off and surrounded by wooden barriers to keep the spectators off the field.

6. *The fight itself*

The bullfights generally begin in the 8th month according to the old calendar,[12] but may also take place in the second and third month. Sometimes there is fighting all year long, sometimes only for eight months, with a contest scheduled every eight or ten days. In extremely hot or cold weather, and during work in the fields, the fights are suspended. The contests usually start about one o'clock in the afternoon. First there is a fireworks display at the arena gate, and then the fight begins. The seconds are already waiting in the arena with covered heads and bare legs. During the fight they wind leather bands around their forehead for protection. The two opponents are lead into the center of the arena, and their lead-ropes are removed during the fight.

Now the owners of the bulls and their seconds are standing next to them. The eyes of the two bulls facing each other turn red. They prick up their ears in anger and work themselves into a fury. While some are still busy making preparations in the arena, and others are removing the rope from their bulls at the arena entrance, they all suddenly let loose together with a loud cry, and the bulls attack each other. They meet in the center of the arena, and each animal tries to do his best. If they separate during the fight, this is known as "pulling out the head." If one bull can succeed in bringing down the other, then his opponent is held down by pulling on the nose-ring, and the bull then charges the neck or leg area. When the nose-ring is pulled, the seconds, if they have been bribed, may use the opportunity to stick their fingers into the nose of the opposing bull, making it difficult for him to breathe and causing him to bolt. If a bull is a fast fighter, this is called "*Hsiang*," and if he splits the nose of his opponent in two, this is known as "rupture." If they continue to fight after the rupture, this is known as "removing the nose-ring." Only very specially trained bulls can go on fighting after this. The permission of the opposite party must be obtained and this leads often to differences of opinion. During the fight there is a young man stationed behind every bull who strikes its hind legs to make the animal fight harder. After a fight of one-two hours, the end is signaled by firing off a rocket, and the seconds bring cake, wine and meat for the so-called "meal in the arena" (there is another large meal after the fights). If there are few bulls present, only one pair of bulls goes into the arena at a time. Otherwise, several pairs do battle simultaneously. First the mediocre bulls fight, and the first-class animals come last. After a certain period of time has elapsed, fights involving first-class and average bulls are stopped in order to protect the animals. But this is only true of regular contests. In final fights they must battle to the finish, because it is a question of victory or defeat, and the owners want to get as high a price as possible. To be sure, some animals also fight to the death. They always let the mediocre animals fight to their maximum ability, and only if they have already been sold are precautions taken to protect them. Poor-fighting animals sometimes run all around the arena, or slash with their tails, but veteran fighters walk with composure. Bolting bulls sometimes will break through the barriers into the audience and cause great disturbances. Some even start attacking human beings as soon as they enter the arena. When a bull bolts, then they don't say that the bull has bolted, but rather that Mr. X (the owner) has bolted. Naturally, you can see better the closer you are, so that the spectators often break through the barriers and get themselves dirty. This is supposed to prove they are really interested in bulls. During the pauses between fights, bulls are constantly paraded through the arena to show the audience the animals of the various breeders. Then, in jest, the seconds on both sides start throwing mud at the bulls, and their guides and the spectators join in on the fun with loud laughter. The owners of the victorious bulls leave filled with joy, but it is probably exaggerated to say that they light fireworks as an expression of their joy. The owners of the defeated animals hang their heads in sadness.

The seconds look very funny, since they are covered with mud from head to toe. Sometimes they are even struck rather hard, and are sent flying into the mud. During the fight everything is quiet, but as soon as a bull has won there is a loud commotion. Naturally, you get the most out of a bullfight if you sit together with old experienced spectators, and hear from them what the qualities of the respective animal are.

7. *How long has there been plowing with cattle in China?*

After our description of the bullfight, we would now like to examine the question of when the custom probably arose. To do this, we must first answer the question of when the cattle were introduced as plowing animals in China, because bullfighting also probably dates from this period. Hsü Chung-shu has examined the problem of plowing with cattle in detail in an essay on ploughshares.[13] Hsü enumerates the various points of view, criticizes them, and then advances his own, still somewhat questionable view, namely that the domestication of cattle and horses appears to have come about as a result of their use in fighting.

As Hsü states, "We can determine the beginning of plowing with cattle only on the basis of the archaeological finds. Now a named ploughshare has been preserved pre-dating the Ch'in dynasty (middle of the third century

B.C.). This was so large that it was impossible for humans to move. We conclude on the basis of this instrument that people were plowing with cattle before the Ch'in period. But it is unlikely that there was plowing with cattle before the time of the Contending States, because the *Shih-chi* reports about a certain Li K'ui[14] who advanced agricultural theories, and only talks about greater or less care in cultivation, but makes no mention of a difference between hand-plowing and cattle-plowing. According to this then, the agricultural implements had not yet undergone any changes up to this time (fourth century B.C.)." I believe, however, that this report contained in the *Shih-chi* has been too liberally interpreted, because the amount of yield from cattle-plowing is, after all, also dependent on the degree of care exercised.

I believe that the origin of plowing with cattle can be ascertained from the implements used by the Yin.[15] These Yin were constantly on the move, so that hand-plowing still played a great role in their life. But when, at a later date, the king of the Yin, P'an-keng, wanted to move again, he encountered violent opposition. It appears that at that time they were already using cattle to plow, and were, for that reason, more bound to the soil. Therefore I would not like to support the hypothesis that plowing with cattle did not begin until after the Ch'un-ch'iu period (eighth to fifth centuries B.C.). Thus, bullfighting can have started somewhere already prior to the period of P'an-keng.

8. *Origin of the bullfight in Chin-hua*

After having examined the question of when bullfighting originated in China, we would now like to consider the question of its time of origin in Chin-hua. According to a widespread tradition, it is said to have appeared sometime between the Sung and Ming periods (960-1640). Hu Tsê[16] from Yung-k'ang (Chêkiang) is supposed to have petitioned the throne to abolish the high poll-tax in his districts. For this the grateful inhabitants erected temples in his honor, and offered bullfights for his amusement. The aforementioned poll-tax is supposed to have been introduced subsequent to a census, but afterwards the system remained the same as it was before. There are grave doubts concerning the validity of the story about the petition of Hu Tsê. In addition, not only is the bullfight put on in honor of Count Hu in front of his temples, but north of Chin-hua Count Ching is usually the patron of bullfighting. Wang Ch'ung-ping, in his work on Chin-hua, writes as follows: "Count Ching's first name was Chih, he was the ninth child and came from the village of Ch'ih-sung in the district of Chin-hua. His mother dreamt that a spirit entered her body and gave birth to him." He lived during the Sung period. This report makes Count Ching into a local deity. Both stories take place about the same time, but since they are both mythological, and the story about the poll-tax does not appear to be historical either, this offers no proof that bullfighting began between the Sung and Ming periods.

The settlement of the Chin-hua area by Chinese took place, according to family genealogical chronicles, predominantly in the Chin (fourth century) and Wu-tai (tenth century) periods, and particularly during the latter period. If, then, the custom of bullfighting was imported by the Chinese from another area, then this custom must have already been present during the Wu-tai period.

If, however, bullfighting was a custom of the pre-Chinese population of Chin-hua, then it must be considerably older. The entire Chin-hua area appears to have been inhabited by the mountain Yüeh previous to the arrival of the Chinese. The notion that the Yüeh (according to the *Shih-chi*) are the descendants of the emperor Shao-k'ang of the Hsia dynasty, is certainly a later construction. But Han Fei-tse[17] writes: "The Yüeh run around barefoot and cut their hair short." And in the *Shih-chi*[18] it states that the Yüeh have long necks and the language of a raven. The names of their rulers cannot all be explained by means of the Chinese language. All of this considered together is proof that the Yüeh are a branch of the original first inhabitants of southern China.

After the Yüeh state was destroyed by Ch'u, the mountain Yüeh developed in the course of the Ch'in, Han and following dynasties from the descendants of the Yüeh who had settled in southeastern China. This became the most vigorous segment of the Yüeh people. Yang-chou province was divided in the Ch'in and Han periods into five counties with some seventy-eight districts. In the Hou-han period it had six counties with a total of ninety-seven districts. Under the Wu dynasty (at the time of the Three Kingdoms) there were already fourteen counties, and under the Wei two more were added for a total of sixteen counties and 147 districts. Thus, the extent of Yang-chou remained more or less unchanged during the Ch'in and Han periods, and increased considerably under the Wu. Of the ten new counties, seven were inhabited by the mountain Yüeh. The present-day district of Chin-hua is located in the county of Tung-yang, which came into being at the time of the Three Kingdoms. It can, however, no longer be determined where the county capital was located at that time. But at a later time, during the separation of North and South, it was located in what is now Chin-hua. One of the greatest advantages that the land had to offer were the large fields of the mountain Yüeh. If these Yüeh were not yet familiar with cattle-plowing, the Chinese certainly must have taught it to them when they conquered the area at the time of the Wu empire. If, then, the custom of bullfighting is derived from the mountain Yüeh, it must date back at least as far as the period of the Three Kingdoms.

9. *The meaning of the bullfight*

After having discussed the origin of the bullfight, we will now examine its meaning. There are some who believe that the population of Chin-hua is made up of farmers, and that they take particular pleasure in physical combat. This supposedly gives rise to constant feuding. Now, since people disliked the killing of human beings, the bullfight was selected as a substitute. There are others who say that the people of Chin-hua are cruel and enjoy fighting. Later they decided to let the bulls fight with one another in place of human beings. Both views amount to the same thing, and probably arose as a result of the fist-fights which break out at bullfights when one bull loses. Others are of the opinion that bullfighting is a kind of contest between breeding animals. This view reflects modern ideas. Such may well be the case on breeding farms in Shanghai, and contests like this are extremely useful, but are out of the question as far as Chin-hua is concerned. The most satisfactory explanation was furnished by my friend Chung Chin-wen. In an essay on the bullfight he states:[19] "If one wants to magically increase the powers and strength of the domestic animals, festivals are organized during the fall harvest or before the spring work in the fertile fields begins. In these festivals one requests or gives thanks for a good harvest, and the bullfights take place at this time. Aside from its practicality, it gives pleasure to both the individual and his deity." He goes on to say: "The conception that the present-day population of Chin-hua has of the bullfight has changed considerably from the time when cattle-plowing was first introduced. Today nothing more has remained than a popular amusement." By and large, Chung's views are probably correct, but I would still like to express my opinion that bullfighting developed from a kind of magical ceremony.

Among primitive peoples we find fertility dances, in which, among other things, sexual intercourse between men and women takes place. These dances are meant to promote the growth of vegetation. Thus, this is a magical ceremony for the field spirits, although it is not certain whether these spirits are conceived as being human or non-human. By magic we mean verbal or non-verbal exorcism. Now, the fruits of the field belong to the spirits under the earth, and the magic is supposed to bring them to life. Magic is employed against the spirits in order to gain their approval. In primitive agriculture, magical thinking is extremely prevalent, and among such peoples prayer has not yet been separated from magic. Later agricultural procedures still preserve traces of magical practices.

When the cult of spirits was later transformed into the worship of gods, magic became prayer. The difference between the two is that in prayer, whether or not a wish is granted depends on the deity, while in magic great pressure is brought to bear on the spirit. Prayers are always accompanied by expressions of gratitude. In fact, the god is always thanked before new requests are made. In an ode of the *Shih-ching* it says: "We loudly sound the drums for our field ancestor. We ask him for sweet rain so that we may have a good harvest, and food for our men and women." And in the *Chou-li*, in the chapter entitled "Official of Spring," we read: "During all harvest requests to the field ancestor, the clay drums are beaten for his pleasure." These things have a truly magic character. It is not certain whether this field ancestor was once a god.

He probably was somewhere between a god and a spirit, since one cannot effectively use magical ceremonies against a god. By the way, the custom of sacrificing to a field cousin still exists today in I-wu (Chêkiang). A human figure is fashioned out of straw and is burned. After the sacrifice children then eat the remaining sacrificial offerings. Here too the concepts of god and spirit are confused. Even our grain gods and other local deities developed, to a great extent, from field spirits.

For this reason, the origin of the bullfight must be sought in a magical ceremony contra the spirits. The use of cattle in this ceremony can probably be attributed to the psychological fact that cattle were considered particularly valuable at the time plowing with cattle was first introduced. By this time the earth spirits had undoubtedly already been transformed into celestial deities, but, as has already been stated, the period of transition between spirits and gods lasted an especially long time in China. This can still clearly be seen from the historical records and the present state of affairs. Thus, the present-day bullfight in Chin-hua developed into a kind of expression of thanks. For this reason, I find it impossible to agree completely with Chung Ching-wen, who sees in the bullfight basically nothing more than an amusement and a means to increase the power and strength of the domestic animals. I consider both of these to be later developments.

10. *Conclusion*

Many observers consider the bullfight of Chin-hua to be a barbarian custom. But if we view it in the manner as indicated above, we come to realize that the custom has a long history and is a survival from an ancient period. Bullfights are held only in Chin-hua. The assertion that bullfighting is also found in numerous neighboring districts is untrue. The custom in Chin-hua is now already on the decline as a result of the poor economic situation of the peasants, and if their distressed condition does not improve, bullfighting will probably disappear here as well.

6. CHINESE SCHOOLBOYS TELL TALES*

The following tales were written by students in Li-shui (Chêkiang) in September, 1934. Mr. Fang Szu-hai stimulated the writing, but did not influence the students as to the topic they should select. Thus, some of these stories are folktales, others are simply tales. Their main interest, perhaps, lies in the simplicity of expression and the manner in which actions and events are reflected in the mind of a Chinese child living in a middle-size town. The name of the writer, his place of birth and age at the time of writing are given in parentheses. The original Chinese manuscripts were deposited in the Berlin Anthropological Museum and perished during World War II.

1. *A Strange Present* (Kuan Li-hua, 13 years., Li-shui)

The house of Hsiao-chin was very far from the school, and one also had to cross a small river — otherwise you couldn't get to school. One day he was on his way back from school, and the river had risen because it was raining so hard. So he rolled up his trousers and went very carefully across the river. Just as he reached the other side, a sick and very old man suddenly appeared behind him, and called to the boy to lend him a hand and help him over. The child thought it over a while: he certainly coudn't carry such an old man in his arms or on his back. And after considering the matter, he took some stones, and with a great effort, placed them one next to the other across the river. Then he took the old man by the hand, led him and asked him to jump from one stone to the other. Then the old man said: "Thank you, my child. I don't have anything with me I could give except a fine hammer, so I'll give you that! " The child didn't want to accept it, but the old man put the hammer in front of him and went away. So the child took the hammer and went home and told the story to his mother. His mother said: "That probably was a saint who wanted to test you. Now, you helped him get across the brook and so he knows that you're a good child. Maybe this hammer will be of very great use to you later on some time."

*Revised and translated version of "Chinesische Schulkinder erzählen Geschichten," *China-Dienst* IV (Shanghai, 1935), 279-281, 363-364, which is included in my *Erzählungsgut aus Südost-China* (Berlin 1966, W. de Gruyter & Co., pp. 275-287).

2. *Killing the Brother* (Liang Hsien-ts'ui, 12 years, Li-shui)

In 1930 in the village of Hsia-ch'en there was a coffin shop in which three brothers worked. The oldest one was called Ping-yao, the second Ping-sung and the third Ping-lien. Every day they made coffins to sell. One day Ping-lien went to buy some wood. He still hadn't come back and there was only one piece of wood left in the house. Then the two brothers each took an ax and chopped up this piece of wood. Ping-sung raised his ax and was the first one to strike, and because he was a little careless he chopped off his brother's head. Just then his other brother came back, and they both cried a long time. Later they didn't make coffins anymore, but rather became farmers.

3. *The Husband Hangs Himself* (Cheng Ch'en-ch'ang. 10½ years, Li-shui)

Once there was a man who used to fight with his wife, and since he couldn't overpower her, he hated his wife. But she was taken by some other people out of the house. But after a while the man grew so ashamed that he took a rope, hung himself from a beam, and died. Now when the wife returned, she saw her husband hanging from the beam, and she quickly cut him down, but he was already dead. Then she cried very much. After that she bought a coffin through some other people, and had him quickly removed and buried in the ground.

4. *Catching a Tiger* (Chou Chih-ch'u, 11¾ years, Li-shui)

Once there was a very clever person living in Chin-yün. One day he climbed up a mountain to see the view, and when he reached the top he saw a tiger. Then he went back into the city, bought a piece of meat and put a bullet inside. Then he went up to the top of the mountain again and placed it down there. And he hid himself under a big stone. When it was almost time for dinner, the tiger saw the piece of meat and ate it. But as soon as he had it between his teeth, the bullet exploded and the tiger was killed. The next day the man called many people to bring the tiger down in order to sell it. There was a pharmacy that wanted to buy the tiger in order to cook medicine from it, and so he sold the tiger to the pharmacy for 100 dollars.[1]

5. *A Wicked Man* (Lü Tê-ming, 10 years, Li-shui)

There was a man by the name of Lü Tê-kui living last year in Ch'u-chou (=Li-shui) at the Huo-shao gate. He had taken a wife and had a comfortable life. Later, after his wife's death, he married again and opened up a salt shop in his house. But year after year he had great losses, and after a while his capital was gone. Then he stole money from his wife,[2] and first there was an argument with her about this, but in the evening she hung herself from a beam and died. The next day his parents-in-law found out about this and bought a coffin for 52 dollars. But secretly Tê-kui went to the coffin shop and bought another coffin for six dollars, and pocketed the rest of the money for himself. Later on the parents-in-law found out about this too, and they demanded back the coffin for 52 dollars, but he had already put the corpse into the coffin, and besides this he had taken off all the clothes she was wearing. His wife's parents were angry about this too, and unconditionally demanded ten new dresses from him. They made eight dresses themselves too, and then they put all twenty dresses on the corpse and buried her once more.

6. *A Mother Who Didn't Instruct Her Son* (Chou Wen-hui, 10¾ years, Li-shui)

Once there were two people in my village. One was a young man, and the other was his mother. She was always at home, but her son roamed around all day long in the streets. One day when he was out on the street again he saw a fish-seller. And very secretly he stole a fish. He did this without making a sound while the fish-dealer was busy with some other people. So he took the fish and ran back home. He said to his mother: "Mother, fry this fish for me! " His mother said: "You are really very clever and I'm very pleased with you! " From then on his courage to steal grew from day to day and later on he really became a robber. He was caught several times by the authorities, and was finally sentenced to death. When the day of his execution arrived, he said to the executioner: "Please call my mother! " And then he told his mother: "The reason I'm being killed now is just because not only didn't you scold me when I stole fish that time, but you even praised me. That's why I became a robber! " After that he struck his mother with his fish and then was killed himself.[3]

7. *Don't Buy Any Foreign Products!* (Li Ch'ang-shou, 12¾ years, Li-shui)

Once there was a pupil who went out with his grandmother and came to a store. Then his grandmother bought a foreign-made doll and gave it to him as a present. The pupil said: "That's a foreign product, I don't want it. I'm Chinese and don't want to play with foreign products! " His grandmother asked him deliberately: "But why don't Chinese take any foreign products? " The small pupil said: "Just because I'm Chinese — That's why I don't want any foreign products. If all the Chinese buy Chinese products, then all the money will stay in the country and circulate, but if everybody buys foreign products, then all our money will go into the hands of foreigners! "[4]

8. *Cutting Off the Pigtail* (Ch'en Ken'liu, 11¾ years, Li-shui)

There was an old man who was carrying firewood with a carrying-pole, and he had just arrived at the river when two policemen came along with a knife to cut off his pigtail.[5] The old man said: "Wait until I've put down the carrying-pole, and then cut! " He put down his firewood, took the bamboo carrying-pole and pushed the two policemen into the river.

9. *Collecting Money for the Police* (Li Ts'un-hsin, 11¾ years, Li-shui)

About half a year ago I was studying in Hsiao-ching, and when I went home for spring vacation I heard that a man had come to our village to collect money for the police. After a while there was a policeman by the name of Hsia Hsi-yü who collected together with him in our village. Hsia Hsi-yü told this to a man by the name of Li Pao-erh, went to Wan-ling and killed the policeman. The next day Hsia-yü and Li Pao-erh were caught by the police of Ch'ing-t'ien, and after three months in jail they were both shot.

10. *The Quarrel about the Wedding Money* (Wang Ai-chu, 14¾years, Li-shui)

There was once a man who lived near Ch'u-chou-fu. His mother was dead already, and his father had married another woman who already had a daughter. But this daughter was already engaged and the bride-price had already been set at 100 dollars. Her father thought he would take the whole 100 dollars away from her, but the child's mother had already taken 50 dollars for herself. Now her brother and father demanded the money from her, but her mother didn't want to give it up, and so the three of them started to quarrel. During the night, the son and his father killed the mother. The daughter wanted to start screaming, but the father and son said: "If you scream any more, we'll kill you too! " The girl didn't dare to scream again. The next morning the district officer heard about the matter and sent soldiers, bought some white sugar and put the corpse in the sugar for three days in order to test whether she had really been murdered.[6] Then he took the son and the father to the *yamen* and punished them.

11. *Stolen Money* (Lo Shih-fen, 11 years, Li-shui)

The wife of Huang Shih-wang was very clever and wise, but a neighboring family hated her and was always devising plans to bring her to ruin. Her workers brought a load of sugar into the house from outside. Then the neighbor took more than thirty red pills,[7] put them secretly into the sugar, and at the same time made a secret accusation at the police station that the woman was selling red pills. She saw the workers bringing the sugar in, and since the sugar seemed too coarse to her, she took away a little of the rice-straw on top, discovered the many red pills, was very astonished and burned them immediately.

The police arrived to search the house to check whether there was anyone dealing in the forbidden red pills. She said: "What kind of proof do you have that you can come into my house like this and search for red pills? Who on earth made the charge? Please give me an explanation! " The police pointed to the neighbor and they also had his place searched and finally they found the pills. Then they dragged him off to the station and he had to confess.

12. *Ten Good Friends* (Chou Wei-chieh, 12 years, Li-shui)

The farmer A-ch'un got up early, went to the fields and worked terribly hard all day long. And so he worked day after day, and when the time for the harvest came, his harvest was more abundant than that of the others. The other farmers in the village were very surprised about this and asked him: "Why do you have such a good harvest year after year? " He said: "I have ten good friends who help me every day! " The farmers didn't understand him. Then A-ch'un took his two hands and showed them to them. Then they finally understood.[8]

13. *Something about Misery during a Drought* (Hsü Lien-yü, 13 years, Li-shui)

When there is a long dry spell then everything in the fields dries up, and how are the farmers supposed to go on living? — In the country there lived a large family of eleven, eight of them children, along with an old mother, a man and his wife. They had a little more than ten *mou* of land and usually were able to live on this. But what about this year? The rice they needed in order to live had completely dried out under the sun. The children cried all day long from hunger, but what were the man and his wife supposed to do? Now the neighbor's wife had harvested a few loads of grain. And although they had suffered just as much on account of the drought, one day, because their crying made her so sorry, she gave them five pecks of rice. They could grind this rice and make enough food for two days from it. But the hard-hearted husband of the woman thought: In such a year of drought they could hardly survive themselves, so how could she give rice to others? And without asking any more questions, he struck his wife with great force. But his wife became very agitated and hung herself. The pitiable couple heard about this and they felt that they had been the cause of the woman's death. How would they face the woman now? So they took the rest of the rice and put poison in it so that everybody died. And really, of the eleven members of the family ten died at the same time, and only an 8-year-old child was spared since it had not yet returned from tending the cattle. That's really a sad story! "[9]

14. *"A Foot of Jewel-Jade Is Nothing, an Inch of Time Is Better."*   (Ch'en Hung-ch'i, 12 years, Li-shui)

Wang-erh lived in a very poor house and the money for his studies came completely from the handiwork of his parents, but he worked and studied very well and all his fellow pupils and teachers thought highly of him. One night he was lying in bed thinking of how he might study even better, and he fell asleep with these thoughts. Then he dreamed that an old man came up to his bed and said: "Child, let me tell you, in a place very near here under a tree on a mountain there is a lot of gold. Take it for yourself and you'll immediately become a rich man!" Wang-erh made note of this when he woke up after that, and in a short while it was light outside.

When he got up in the morning he told his mother what had happened. The mother said: "Go ahead and go there if you want to! " Wang-erh said: "No, I'm not going! Dreams are false, and if I go up on the mountain, won't I be wasting half-a-day's time? I noticed that it is written in *Ch'ien-tse-wen:* 'A foot of jewel-jade is nothing, an inch of time is better! ' Isn't time even more valuable than gold?"[10]   And after that he went right to school. And really, this man later became a very famous scholar.

15. *In the End You'll Always Fall In Yourself!* (Wang Ta-Chia, 13 years, Li-shui)

In the village there lived an unmarried man who was probably more than 50 years old. He was always helping people light incense and candles in the temple. He had a very bad character and liked to hurt others. One year there was a man by the name of Pao-fu, who had somehow been so wronged by him that he lost his house and property, had to sell all his possessions and was forced to move to another place, bringing only his wife and mother along with him. But he kept his hate in his heart, and still definitely wanted to take revenge. One night while everyone was asleep, Pao-fu took a knife, forced his way into the temple and wanted to stab the man. The man was sleeping, and so he tried to stab him but missed. And so he thought a moment and decided then that it would be better to put out the man's eyes, since then not only would he not be able to do his job, but he would also have a rough life all the way around. So he quickly took his knife and put out the man's eyes. Then he ran away. The next morning the man knew that the culprit had already gotten away, so without any proof, he accused another man in the village with whom he was on bad terms and who was very poor. When the poor man heard about this, he cried a lot and asked the people in the village to be witnesses for him, but since he had no money they couldn't come. The day of the trial he borrowed a few dollars from his father-in-law as traveling money for the witnesses. Fortunately the judge decided after the hearing that he was innocent. But the other man wasn't satisfied and made another accusation at the next court, but there too the poor man was declared innocent, and the other man had to pay a fine for his false accusation.

16. *Playing* (Wei Hung-piao, 13 years, Li-shui)

Several years ago in our village Hsia-ho there was a pharmacy. The son of the owner was called Chu-ko Pao, and was an excellent player. One day he wanted to go outside and play, and his wife found out about this. Then she took away his playing stones. He demanded them back, but she refused, so he grabbed hold of his wife and hit her. During the night his wife took a rope and hung herself.

17. *The Good Fortune of a Village Depends on a Mu-lien Vine* (Wu Hsing-chung, 12 years, Li-shui.

It is said that in former times we had a good dragon-vein, because outside the east gate, at the place called Shui-k'ou, there was a *Mu-lien* vine which had formed a sort of tent, like a bridge, and that's why the people in the village were usually very rich. Now a family in the village had a son who went off and became an official, but in more than ten years he didn't send a single letter or come back, and nobody had any news about him. The old mother in the house thought about her son, and cried every day under a big tree alongside the road. After she had cried for three days and three nights she met a geomancer. This geomancer noticed that she was crying very much and asked her why. Then the woman told him her reason and the geomancer said: "There is a means by which he can be brought home within three days. Do you have a white dog in the house?" "Yes," the woman answered. "Then take this white dog and put his blood on the bridge made of the *Mu-lien* vine, chop it down, and then your son will return within three days." The woman really did as he had said. In less than three days her son was killed by enemies and the corpse was brought home. At the same time the rich people in the village gradually became poorer, because the *Mu-lien* vine was the very thing which had made the entire village wealthy!

18. *The Drought* (Hsü Shih-liang, 12 years, Li-shui)

The year 1930 was a very bad year because there wasn't a drop of rain. At that time there was a farmer whose field had been completely dried up by the sun. He went to a pond and drew out water with a treadmill. While he was drawing water, another farmer suddenly came along, and when he saw the farmer drawing water at that pond, he came over and said to him: "I made this pond at great expense. How is it that you're drawing water out of it? " The other farmer said: "You claim to have made this pond? I'll keep on drawing water in any case! " Then the other farmer moved even closer and said: "That farmer over there will tell you, just ask him! " "When I have time I'll ask him." Then the second farmer took his hooked stick and plunged it into the other one's stomach, so that his intestines poured out and he soon was dead. When the other farmer saw this he ran away very fast. But finally he was caught by some other farmers and spent more than ten years in jail. Don't you also think that behavior like that is very coarse?

19. *The Beggar Who Became Governor* (Lü Te-ch'ang, 12 years, Li-shui)

Several hundred years ago there lived a man by the name of Wang Wei-yü. His house stood at the side of a small river. He had completed his studies (in a school somewhat similar to the secondary school today).

One year the harvest was bad (first there was very strong sun and drought, then suddenly rain for more than two days). A flood began and everyone in his family drowned. Only he alone climbed onto the roof and had nothing to eat for three whole days and nights. He couldn't sleep either. After the water had subsided, he climbed down and found that everyone in the house had drowned, and that all the utensils in the house and all the money and valuables had been completely washed away by the water. Nothing was left. So then he could do nothing more than put his sack on his back and go begging.

Day in, day out, probably for about two to three years, he went along begging in this way. One year during the eighth month he noticed that some people had taken chicken and wine and a few straw mats, and since he didn't know what they wanted to do, he followed them, because he was hoping to get something to eat. So he followed them to the Li-yang Hall. Then the people took the food and the other things, put them on the table and started muttering prayers. After this they laid out the mats and went to sleep. When

Wang Wei-yü saw this he did the same, muttered prayers and lied down to sleep. But unfortunately there were so many people who wanted to have a dream in the temple that they didn't let Wang Wei-yü sleep there, but forced him to go outside.[11] For that reason Wang Wei-yü had to sleep outside on the bridge in front of the Li-yang Temple.

Shortly before the rooster's cry, a cold wind came and awoke the beggar (Wang Wei-yü). Then he said, as if talking to himself: "The lord Li-yang told me I should go to such and such a water-mill and sleep there! That was his word." In this way he startled the people who were in the temple looking for a dream, and after that they chased him away. But Wang Wei-yü wasn't troubled at all by this, but rather continued on very cheerfully to the water-mill. When he arrived at the door of the mill, he saw a ghost's head there covered with wild hair. It was wearing the cap of a minister and had on a dragon-coat in red. After he had seen this, he ran quickly back to the bridge where he had been sleeping before, and went back to sleep again.

The next morning the dream-seekers gave him cup after cup of food, and he ate it, but since he wasn't able to eat it all by himself, he put the rest in his sack and sold it to another beggar. With the money he received, he went to a fortune-teller and had his fortune told. Then the fortune-teller said: "Soon you will become an official! " But he didn't believe it. Then the fortune-teller gave him some more details about this, but he still had his doubts. After that he gradually went on his way begging into other parts of the country.

One day there was an exhibition of essays in the emperor's palace, and many people came to look at them. There was a pond near the imperial palace. Now, unfortunately the emperor's child was careless and fell into the pond. When this happened everybody was busy looking at the essays, and nobody noticed it. But the beggar went to the lake, saw what had occurred, rescued the child, and brought it to the emperor's palace.[12] The emperor appointed him governor of the three great districts of Ch'u-chou, Wen-chou and Chin-hua.

Later the emperor died and an assembly to determine the succession to the throne was convened at the court. The chancellor commanded him to attend the assembly too, and when he heard this he became very sad, packed his bags and wanted to go to the capital. But after he had been traveling for five days, he suddenly became very ill, and it appeared very serious, so that the sedan-bearers brought him back, and when they had reached the city he died. Later an honorary commemorative arch was erected on the spot where he had died.

Just think: such a beggar can become a high official! And so I ask all of you not to look down on other people. The local proverb says it well: "A stone slab can turn a man around." That has this meaning too.

After you have read this story, you'll all say that it's a lie. But it's really true, since my grandfather told it to my father, and my father told it to me, so that it's not at all untrue!

20. *The Murdered Cattle-Boy* (Chi Fang-hsün, 14 years, Li-shui)

In the spring of 1919 the east wind was blowing so beautifully, and the sun was shining down on the earth so brilliantly, and beautiful birds were chirping everywhere, and out in the fields there were beautiful blossoms in the shade of the pastures and clear water in the radiant mountains. Everything was sparkling with life. It was a wonderful sight.

Gentlemen, every spring people like to get out sometime and enjoy the beauties of nature. There was an old pine-tree then outside of the village out on a flat meadow. The story about this tree was that it had been planted a long time ago by the village ancestors. Now the people protected this tree very much, and no-one was allowed to dig it up. From time to time they sacrificed incense under this tree and worshipped it.

One warm day the sky was cloudy, a young cattle-boy came riding along on a cow. He had a short flute in his hand which he played now and then, and by and by he rode up to the tree. Since there was a flat meadow there covered with a lot of beautiful grass, it was a good place for him to pasture his cattle. After a while the sky suddenly turned black, great masses of clouds formed, a heavy rain fell, the thunder rumbled and the lightning flashed. Now the cowherd was very poor and this time he hadn't brought along any raincoat. So he went under the tree to protect himself from the rain. Suddenly there was a flash of lightning, and the old pine and the boy were struck both at the same time, and the poor boy found his death under this tree. The villagers saw the boy, and when they saw him hit by the lightning they felt extremely sorry for him. So now there is a temple on the spot in which the villagers pay him their special respects. People still sometimes tell this story even today.[13]

21. *Wang Ching-yüan Insults the Mayor* (Hsü Hao-nien, 14 years, Li-shui)

In Shui-ko in Li-shui district there was a man more than thirty years old by the name of Wang Ching-yüan. He had a village pharmacy. One day the village mayor came to his house to collect some money. Wang Ching-yüan wasn't at home, but his wife was in the shop. Then he asked: "Your husband? " Then the woman said: "He went out, but will probably be back soon. Come back again tomorrow." He said: "Fine! " When Wang Ching-yüan returned home, his wife said to him: "The mayor was here to collect money." When Wang Ching-yüan heard this he became furious. In the evening he took a lump of excrement and waited for the mayor to come so he could shove the lump into the mayor's mouth. Now the mayor really did come to the house, and Wang Ching-yüan took the lump of excrement and smeared it all over his mouth. The mayor spit it all out right away, and saw that it was shit. Then he pounded on the table and became terribly angry. But Wang Ching-yüan had already run away. The next day the mayor went into town and filed a complaint against him. The judge questioned him about the episode and the two of them accused Wang. So Wang Ching-yüan was kept in jail for half a month, and then everything was all right again.

22. *The False Son* (Miss Chang Ts'ui-yün, 14 years, Li-shui)

Our neighbor's son used to be a dealer in silver. And he had already been away for more than a year, and no letter had come. His old mother and wife hoped very much that he would return.

One day a man who had the same name as the son telephoned from Sung-yang. The old mother was very happy about this and went to the telephone office right away. When she returned, she had tears in her eyes, and the neighbors asked her how her son was.

The mother said: "My son has fallen ill and wants his father to come to him! " She said this and cried. The neighbors said: "But he doesn't have a father! How can he make such a crazy call? There must be a mistake." Another person said: "That's hardly a mistake, but he's probably so sick that he had somebody else phone for him, and this other person didn't know whether he still had a father. That's probably what happened." The old mother said: "If he's that sick, it's best that his wife go to him."

The next day when it got light, his wife packed her bag and went to the bus station. She wanted to ride with the bus, but since it wasn't time to leave yet she waited at the station. After a while, a mailman came over from the post office and said: "Here's somebody who has the same name as your husband! " His mother went straight to the house of this man, and asked whether the person in Sung-yang was really her son or not, and called his wife back from the bus station. The next day her son sent a letter from Lung-ch'üan, and everybody was terribly happy.

23. *The Magic Turtle* (Miss Li Yü-chih, 12 years, Li-shui)

In Li-shui, in the town of Tsao-shu-yin ("shade of jujubes"), there used to be a large jujube tree, and underneath this tree there was a large turtle. As soon as it started to get dark, it began to climb out. The turtle climbed out very often, but then the people cut down the red jujube tree. But even now there was something uncanny about the place. After this they put up a theater stage, and after that an image of Buddha, but there was still something mysterious about the place. Then the people thought up something else: they erected a *Wu-lu-pao* ("raven-oven-jewel")[14] and put up a saying inside. After that things were quiet on this spot.

24. *Attack of Robbers* (Hu Shou-chin, 12 years, Li-shui)

At 5:00 A.M. on the morning of February 19, 1932, my grandfather and I were sound asleep when we suddenly heard several shots which awoke us. When I heard the shots I thought they were fireworks, and so I said to my grandfather: "It's getting light, I hear people shooting off rockets! " Then he listened carefully and noticed that they were gunshots, and after it became light we knew it for certain.

Somebody said to me: "The bandit Hu Ch'ao-fu has come along with more than two hundred robbers, and wants to surround the city. There was only one detachment of troops stationed in the militia barracks. The section leader Ch'en said: "If we're surrounded, we'll be killed. Maybe it would be better to rush out together and try to defeat them! " Then they burst forth from all four sides and the robbers thought that a large detachment of the army had come and they took flight, since they were just a very irregular bunch. But the section leader Ch'en continued to pursue them and was killed by a bandit's bullet. When the troops saw this, they returned to camp and reported: "Our leader has gone to heaven! "

Later the bandits were completely wiped out, and they kept the head of the chief bandit as a memento. The section leader Ch'en, who had given his life for his country, was subsequently made a commander in honor of his memory.

25. *The Bear Woman* (Chang Mei-ying, 12 years, Li-shui)

In the city of Li-shui, outside the Li-yang gate, there lived a farmer whose name I've forgotten. He was a very honest and hard-working farmer, and was a bachelor besides. One day he went into the mountains to cut wood. Along the way he met a female bear. The bear grabbed hold of him, but she didn't eat him. She dragged him off carefully to her cave, and there they became man and wife.

After two years the bear had already given birth to a boy and a girl. The farmer, who had to sit in the cave day after day for more than a year, was very depressed and said to her: "Bear woman, I'm very distressed that I have to sit here in the cave. I'd like to go out with the children for a walk! " When the bear heard this, she allowed him to do it. The farmer took the children and was very happy. He said to the children: "Children, wait in the temple for me next to the north-wall bridge. Don't go out! " The farmer told them this and the children went there. The farmer gathered together many fruits, laid them in the path, and called to the bear woman: "Hurry up over here. There are a lot of fruits here. Pick them up fast! " When the bear heard this she came running quickly. And when she saw the farmer going someplace, she followed right behind him. She followed him for a long time, and saw that he was fleeing to the temple, and she followed him there. When he had called to her, he was walking slowly, but now he was going very fast. The bear soon caught up with him. But in the temple wall there was a hole. Then he took his son and ran away. But the bear saw the girl still waiting outside, and she took her along and followed after the farmer. The farmer came to the Li-yang gate. But they were just about to close the gate, so he started to call out for them to close the gate more slowly and to let him in. The gatekeeper heard this, and opened the gate again and let him in. When the farmer came inside, the bear woman was also just about at the entrance. But when the bear woman saw what he had done, she was at her wits' end and she smashed herself against the gate. When the farmer heard sounds, he opened the gate and saw that his daughter was standing there and that the bear was already dead. Then he buried the bear under a single camphor tree[15] and took the girl home. That was my story!

7. POPULAR POETRY ON TEMPLE WALLS*

In China, the entire walls of famous temples, pagodas, or inns along the road are often covered with drawings and inscriptions (*illustration 3*). For almost every poet, there are poems he is supposed to have written on temple walls.[1] Every novel,[2] collection of short novels,[3] or literary collection[4] contains such poems, and these are often really quite beautiful. In fact, in large works, as for example in the one about the Holy Mountain of the West, the Hua-shan, a special chapter is devoted to the inscriptions of famous men.[5] Inscriptions of names are naturally still very common today, and are often extremely interesting, particularly when they date from the creation of grottos to Yung-chêng (1723-1735) period, as in the caves of Tun-huang,[6] or into the Ming period, as in the case of the Wild Duck Pagoda near Hsi-an. But otherwise we find that even today the walls are still decorated predominantly with poems, and among these poems there are many which evince both taste and sentiment. Sometimes these are famous old poems, more or less altered, sometimes the poems have been improvised and praise the beauty of the locality, sometimes they are jocular in mood, and sometimes contemplative and philosophical. On occasion we even come across pieces from folksongs or folk sayings. The form of the short poem *(chüeh-chü)* – four lines, each with five or seven characters – is the preferred form. This is a form of the classical poem, but one in which the laws of rhyme and tone are not so strictly followed, and it comes close to being a transition to folk poetry, which makes use of other rhymes (the *shih-san-chê*). There are, however, other forms as well: quatrains with four characters per line, and also short couplets, both forms especially common in poems derived from folk poetry, theater, or folk sayings.

The poems presented here, which I collected in central and north China in 1934-35, have undoubtedly all been written only in the last few years. It is difficult to confirm their age by means of the inscription alone. Usually the manner in which it has been preserved is the telling and crucial factor. They are hastily dashed off with a brush or in pencil, and don't last for very long. But it is all the more unusual then, that among the almost eighty poems I collected there is not a single "modern" poem (i.e., one composed

*Revised and translated version of "Volkspoesie an Tempelwänden," *Sinica* XI (1936), 127-136.

3. Wall paintings on the walls of a pagoda in Su-chou, Kiangsu, 1934.

Both paintings were found together with poems.

in the new colloquial poetic form (*pai-hua*). This shows how little this new form has penetrated into the folk, and how much people still adhere to the old forms, especially if these forms have been made more flexible as a result of assimilation to folk poetry.

Only one, or perhaps two, of the seventy-seven poems have obvious sexual meanings. A few more have sexual connotations. This is not a consequence of my bashfulness. I recorded all poems which were still legible, making no selection. Over the years, I have seen some obscene inscriptions in mainland China and in Taiwan. Usually these were of a very famous curse. Occasionally I have also come across obscene drawings. Yet I would guess that other types of drawings are more common. Although there is probably no statistical material available, I would conjecture that a collection of inscriptions (graffiti) on the walls of buildings in the United States comparable to the Chinese buildings from which I took inscriptions, would yield almost only names and dates, occasionally a longer prose inscription of the type "Kilroy was here," and some obscene inscriptions and drawings. Hardly ever would we expect to find a poem on walls in the United States or in continental Europe. I am unable to give any explanation for this difference, especially since the Chinese have a very rich obscene folklore. However, whenever I have attempted to get Chinese friends to collect erotic and obscene folklore, I have encountered considerable resistance to putting such things down on paper. These friends were of the opinion that an obscene text in a temple or pagoda would offend the deity, and the deity would try to punish the writer.

There are certain provincial differences between wall poems in China. Although in central China the walls are covered almost exclusively with poems, in east and south Shensi the poem-like riddle predominates. They go so far there as to write such riddles as advertisements on small restaurants or inns. Famous places, however, which are visited by travellers from all over the country, such as the Hua-shan, only have poems composed in praise of the beauty of the spot. These poems are often of particular loveliness.

WALL POEMS

1. From the Chiao-shan-kung in Li-shui. Written with charcoal on the wall. September 19, 1934.

> I have a poem,
> nobody in the world knows it.
> If someone comes and asks me,
> then I don't know it either.

2. From an inn below the Nan-ming-shan, Li-shui. September 20, 1934.

> Unfortunately my wife does not have a kind heart
> the married couple has no harmony, until today.
> I went away for a full two years,
> Today I returned, and everything is the same again.
>
>   —Sigh of Chou I-fang.

3. From the same inn. September, 20, 1934.

> The whole way was really fine
> the land of Buddha is truly beautiful everywhere.
> Unfortunately the wife Huang accompanied me,
> during the day we walked in the mountains, at night we slept.

4. See No. 3.

> If one crosses the river and strolls in Nan-ming,
> then the sweat drips from your body when you walk.
> The ancients all praised the area of Nan-ming,
> its beauties surpass those of San-yen and Tung-ch'i.

5. See No. 3.

> The soldier knows hardship,
> daily in mountain exercises the sweat flows,
> I can never see the woman in the house.
> And, besides, the officials are still quarreling.

6. See No. 3.

> Three inches of small golden lilies,[7]
> as flowers they float on the water.

7. See No. 3.

> Three people walk together in Nan-ming,
> Nan-ming's beauties really please.

8. From an inn below Nan-ming-shan, Li-shui. September 20, 1934.

> You wanted me to die, but I won't do it.
> If I wash my eyes clear, I can see you dying.

Heaven wants someone to die: that's not hard.
You want me to die: that can never be!

9. See No. 8.

One day goes by and then another
and in one's heart it's as if one were being boiled in oil.

10. See No. 8.

Someone with money married a daughter Huang
The Huang is using me and isn't serious.

—Sigh of Chou

11. From a hall wall of the Nan-ming-sih. September 20, 1934.

I have lived in the dust of the earth more than 60 years already,
everyone praises my great age.
Sons and grandsons fill the house: riches, honor and joy:
But on the final day I'll cast it all aside anyhow.

12. From the wall of the destroyed temple below the lower pagoda near Li-shui. Written with chalk on both sides of the God of Wealth. September 22, 1934.

The riches which you bring,
you can't bring to yourself.
You have wealth but go hungry,
of guests almost none come to you,
To summon wealth for people
around here you can do this
only for your golden body!

13. From the wall of an inn near Yün-ho. September 24, 1934.

When somebody knows a poem,
why smear it right away on the wall?
When the yellow dog walks across the land,
he leaves his footprints everywhere.

14. From the same inn; present in two versions. September 24, 1934.

Last night in the bridal chamber we blew out the vermilion lamp
The beautiful maiden thought distantly of the river water.

In an instant on the pillow I was in a dream of spring.
In the morning I was many thousands of miles away in Kiang-nan.

15. From the wall of an inn near Yün-ho. September 24, 1934.

When I see my cousin
I have been in love for years.
How don't you know that I love you?
heaven and earth forgive me, lover.

16. From the wall of a temple on the Ma-an-shan near Yün-ho. Written in pencil. September 27, 1934.

In the district of Yün-ho there is good hiking,
And to see the setting sun on the Horse Saddle Mountain.
With my friend Wu-shu,
we people from P'eng-ch'eng[8] made this poem.

17. From the wall of an inn below the Pao-shu Pagoda, Hang-chou. This poem was also found in the Pe-sih Pagoda, Su-chou. October 6, 1934.

The heavens have peace, the earth has peace,
but the human heart has none.
But if the heart is at peace,
then the whole world has peace.

18. From the wall of the Pai-sih Pagoda, Su-chou. November 3, 1934.

The dancing of the phoenix,
pearls and trifles —
the women pay attention to these,
but it causes true men to meditate.

19. From the wall of the Pai-sih Pagoda, Su-chou. This poem was found twice in the pagoda. November 3, 1934

Good, good, good
really, really good.
a thing even more beautiful
doesn't exist.

20. From the wall of the Pai-sih Pagoda, Su-chou. November 3, 1934.

Life and death are predetermined
Happiness and honor lie in the hand of heaven.[9]

21. See No 20.

When a person doesn't seek riches and honor, and doesn't care about poverty
one can be completely independent.
Buddha also has many worries, and how many more have I.
If heaven be compassionate, how can it forget man?

22. See No. 20.

Satiated I gazed upon the world for 40 years
five grandsons I had, but not love in my heart.
When my household declined, for some unknown reason,
I lost my wife and sons and my tears became a spring.

23. See No. 20.

Beautiful is the green pine, and bad the flower,
because today you see the flower before you,
but if hoar-frost and snow come one day,
then one sees only the green pine, and the flower no longer.

24. From the wall of the Pai-sih Pagoda, Su-chou. November 3, 1934.

Suddenly a clap of thunder
the body climbs into the ninth earth[10]
Man can cheat the others well, but heaven can't be cheated.
Man wants to intimidate the others, heaven can't intimidated.

25. See No. 24.

When I climbed the pagoda for the first time,
I had no money to buy gold and silver.
Then I left a poem,
and the whole province gave me gold and silver

26. Pai-sih Pagoda, Su-chou. November 3, 1934. The poem is dated March 15, 1931.

> Good friends came to meet one another,
> the opportunity had arrived.
> It was just rather fortunate
> We went to Shanghai to take care of some business and came through
>   Su-chou, and asked to walk in the Pai-sih Pagoda.

27. See No. 26.

> In the pagoda I climbed one storey, and then eight more,
> There were three of us, all with the same ideas.
> Everywhere we asked about each famous mountain,
> But nowhere yet have we met a real other-worldly monk.

28. From the wall of the first inner gate of the Imperial Palace, Peking. Written in chalk. November 30, 1934.

> The unfolding of the emperor's power can still be seen,
> and it makes the onlooker sigh and shed tears.

29. See No. 28. Written in pencil.

> Mighty are the rooms just readied,
> the old goes, the new comes, the things grow clearer then.
> Before this was a doubly forbidden area,
> Today it is a ....[11]

30. From a watch tower of the Great Wall near Ch'ing-lung-chiao. Written in ink. December 7, 1934.

> Commerce penetrates the four oceans,
> the source of wealth reaches the three rivers.[12]

31. See No. 30.

> The great Tao brings forth wealth,
> here it is really beautiful.

32. See No. 30.

> Try hard in your duties, as if
> you wanted to climb the eight chains of hills.[13]

33. From the west pavilion of the Coal Mountain, Peking. Written in pencil. December 11, 1934.

> With goals one governs the people.
> I am also one of this people
> but all my knowledge is in vain,
> because our mountains and rivers have been sacrificed to the Japanese.
> If the goal is not good, then the empire is difficult to preserve.
> Who can save us if China falls?
> We don't want to be angry with the past.
> it is still possible to do one's utmost and save the empire!

34. From Hua-ch'ing-ch'ih, Lin-t'ung district, Shensi. August, 1935.

> The Hua-ch'ing spring is a survival from an ancient time,
> its beauties are already in the annals,
> But unfortunately times change
> and almost nothing remains left for us.

35. See No. 34.

> Now or when
> do we march against Japan?
> first remove the disgrace of the country?
> then get rid of the dirt.

36. See No. 34. Next to it the erotic picture of a girl.

> The modern girl smiles at me,
> how beautiful, how seductive, she tempts me.
> If she can sleep with me on a common pillow,
> then I'd like to stay here for the rest of my life.

37. On the Li-shan, in the Li-shan Lao-mu-tien. August, 1935.

> If one wants to visit the mountain, one has to go up the ridge,
> Once you're on top of the ridge, there's an old temple there.
> In the old temple is the old mother.
> and I come to the old mother and burn incense.

38. See No. 37.

> If the right time has not come, one has no happiness,
> it's like when moving clouds cover the moon,

If a person has Tao, then the time of happiness will come some day,
The driving clouds will be pushed aside, one sees the clear moon.

39. See No. 37.

I think of the years when we were not yet poor,
and we had wine and guests the whole day long.
All were intimate friends
Why is no-one here any longer?

40. On the wall of the Shih-fo Temple on the Li-shan. August, 1935.

All teachings boil down to one good thing,
the great Tao does not have two doors.
If you ask about the teaching of the earlier Tao,
then you will find it in one word: character.

41. In the grotto of Ch'en Hsi-i in Yü-ch'üan Temple at the foot of the Hua-shan.

T'ai-tsu came here in his early years,
and desired to play a game of chess with the lord.
But when the game was over,
he had lost a mountain for the Sung dynasty.[14]

42. In the Yü-ch'üan-yüan at the foot of the Hua-shan.

Three times I came here on a trip,
it is an unusually beautiful spot.
And if later I should return home sometime,
then I always will remember and never forget Yü-ch'üan-yüan.

43. See No. 42.

If there are many clouds in the sky, the moon isn't clear.
If there are many stones on the mountains, the path isn't smooth.
If there are many fish in the water, the water isn't pure.
If there are many people in the world, then the heart isn't so pure.[15]

44. See No. 42.

With friends I journeyed to the Hua-shan,
the Yü-ch'üan is really beautiful.

The woods thick, the mountains deep; one forgets months and years.
And doesn't know how far it is to come here.

45. See No. 42.

I only wish to eat three times a day
don't long for wealth and position.
I only don't want to become a traitor to my country
too bad I live alone on the North Sea!

46. See No. 42.

How will this life of mine probably turn out?
If what lies before me is mighty, I will break down mountains,
When my shoes have grown thin from trembling and fear,
only then will I find rest for my life.

47. See No. 42.

Three went from the south peak to the heavenly palace,
and underway came to a cave; there they lifted up the brush,
for truly it is a country of saints.

. . . . 16

48. See No. 42.

Five went together to visit the Hua-shan
outwardly common, but pure within.
We look for no riches and fame,
we only desire to wander about in the world.

49. See No. 42.

Smashing stars, carrying the moon, we made this trip.
the world was shaken, the creatures trembled,
After I have seen the beauties, it strengthens my heart,
Read the Buddhist scriptures well, then there is peace!

50. See No. 42.

In 1931 I traveled to Hua-shan,
how beautiful are turquoise mountains and green forests.
Everyone honors secluded rest and quiet.
Therefore I left a poem in Yü-ch'üan-yüan.

51. See No. 42

My heart was restless when I came to Yü-ch'üan
But as soon as I entered the courtyard I was at peace.
And when the cold clouds move on tomorrow,
earth, mountains and rivers are like a hand—

52. In the first inn encountered after the first five Li along the road.

Amid the five holy mountains the Hua-shan has
the most beautiful temples and the most gods.
To read holy scriptures and books — any one can do that.
but who knows about travail when in repose?

53. In the hall of the Sha-lo Temple, after ten Li along the road.

Across ridges and through brooks I came to Sha-lo
the night was calm, the people peaceful — beautiful.
Then I heard armor — and the sound of halberds,
are 10,000 horses and 1,000 soldiers passing?

54. In the cave of Mao-nü, 15 Li further on.

She left Shih-huang-ti and his palace
she came to the Hua-shan, to become a saint.[17]
Day by day she perfected herself in the cave
Thus Mao-nü lived for thousands of years.

55. See No. 54.

A palace lady of Shih-huang by the name of Yü-ch'iang
fled and came here.
From hunger she ate pine-nuts and let her hair grow,
she reached the Tao, became a fairy and lives forever.

56. See No. 54.

The old cave of Mao-nü lies in the West Mountain.
and a monster in front blocks the way.
But if one has a pure heart and a believing spirit,
then the monster[18] clears the way and lets you pass.

57. See No. 54.

> The Hua-shan is the most beautiful mountain in the world,
> its five peaks and steep cliffs make one shudder
> We came, four of us, with the same desire, and looked at everything.
> and next year we wish to return and to fulfill our vow.

58. On the wall of the last inn which the sedan-bearers reached.

> That I might escape the dust of the world, I came to the Hua-shan.
> I came first to the Ch'ing-a Wall.
> I'm not looking for riches and fame,
> I simply wish to become a pupil of Tao in the hall of the Holy Mother.

59. See No. 58.

> Thick clouds obscure the old temple
> the temple is old, the clouds thick.
> The peak is high, the moon hangs small
> the small moon hangs over a lofty peak.

60. See No. 58.

> I want to go up to the Hua-shan and came here,
> in Ch'ing-a and the eight-fold view there is beautiful repose.
> A place of thick white clouds and seclusion,
> The Holy Mother, how old can she be?

61. On the north peak of the Hua-shan, in front at the entrance.

> Two visited the peak of Hua-shan
> and came first to the Cloud Terrace Peak.
> Silently they stood and gazed around:
> This mountain truly has magic power.

62. See No. 61.

> From afar one sees the beauty of the mountain
> from near one no longer hears the water.
> Spring is gone — the flowers still here.
> Come — the birds are not afraid.

63. See No. 61

> The cloud-dragon flies far,
> the heavenly horse itself rises into the air.

64. See No. 61.

> I always heard them talk about Hua-shan
> only today did I come here.
> The five peaks of the Hua-shan are really beautiful,
> and all the gods are here.

65. See No. 61

> When one climbs the Hua-shan, one comes to the north peak.
> There I was received by saints.
> At night I hear recitation, morning shines from afar.
> and the disciple greets me the worldly one.

66. See No. 61

> Two of us came to the Hua-shan
> went to the north peak and visited the temple
> and when we have visited all five peaks,
> we will have protection for the entire year.

67. See No. 61

> Shadows on the north peak
> body and soul free of the worldly,
> It is like a dream
> only afterwards you understand that it's truth.

68. On P'u-chiu-sih in Yung-chi, Shanhsi.

> This is really a beautiful area
> I don't know who built the temple.
> I searched (?)
> and only now come here to look at it.

69. In Yen-ch'ing-sih near T'ai-yüan

> Human upon human: heaven covers the earth.
> Flesh in flesh: Yin encloses Yang.

Out of nothing, a true pearl comes forth
How could I stop this battle?[19]

70. Station-house No. 7 of the busline in the district of Wen-hsi.

A bride is pregnant
The mother-in-law calls her a dog
You tell her husband
Where does the pregnancy come from?

71. Riddle verse in a restaurant on the bus route in Tung-chen.

The character 'word' unseparated from green
Two human beings walk on the earth
To the character 'beg' add a mouth
Man lives in the grass.
    (Solution: please sit down and drink some tea)[20]

72. Riddle verse in the Hou-t'u temple in Wen-hsi, Shanhsi.

The man goes to the family of his mother-in-law
and carries two flowers on his head
He stays there two months
and rides back home again.
    (Solution: to fall in?)

73. Riddle verse at the same place.

A mountain — isn't high
A snow — which doesn't melt
A path — isn't far
One runs far — and doesn't arrive.
    (Solution: ?)

74. See No. 73.

It can walk and has no feet
It can eat and has no mouth
It has a river and no water
It dies and has no ghost
    (Solution: an animal?)

75. See No. 73.

    A girl without shame
    pulls a young gentleman with her hand and walks in the street.
    Upstairs in the house she kisses,
    downstairs again she lets her little feet be kissed.
      (Solution?)

76. See No. 73.

    In the mouth of the character '10,'
    Tree and eye tied, the heart hangs underneath
    Under three waters and one leather a girl
    A girl in the house of her husband.
      (Solution: I think of my wife?)

77. See No. 73.

    "Autumn night in the quiet cell'
    The insects buzz, the flowers rustle,
    In the shadows I walk around the temple, the moon is full
    Alone in the passage-way, I do not sleep
    And see (?) pines amongst banana leaves.

8. THE PAST AND PRESENT STATE OF THE FOLKLORE MOVEMENT IN CHINA*

Introductory Note: The following essay was written by our colleague Lou Tse-k'uang in Hang-chou specifically for his German and Japanese friends. In the course of our correspondence, we had occasionally made the observation that modern Chinese folklore studies are much too much neglected. There has been relatively little and often poor work in this field on the part of Western scholars, but the work of our Chinese colleagues has remained unknown, or has not received sufficient recognition in the broadest scholarly circles.

Lou belongs to the group of leading folklorists active in China during the 1930's, and we have repeatedly had the opportunity to refer to important studies he has written. At the time this essay was being written, he was again at work preparing a large comprehensive study on Chinese folklore. To an certain extent, his previous works such as his collections on *Chinese New Year's Customs*[1] and on *Stories about the Clever and Stupid Girl,* as well as his study *Chinese Marriage Customs,* can be regarded as a part of this long-term project.

In the following essay, he describes the beginnings and organization of folklore studies in China. One can see the kind of economic and psychological difficulties which this pioneer generation of folklorists had to contend with. In the second section we are afforded a glimpse of the results and achievements of the discipline. This second section should prove particularly important for our work, principally because of the short bibliography given in the appendix. This bibliography, together with the brief annotations on content which we have occasionally amplified, covers, of course, only a portion of the total number of books published. Moreover, the numerous folklore journals issued by the various folklore societies are at least equally as important. The Hang-chou society, presided over by Lou Tse-k'uang and Chung Ching-wen, is now in the process of publishing the second year of its monthly journal.[2] Special issues of other periodicals[3] and supplements to daily newspapers are also appearing. In any event, it is

*Revised and translated version of "Früherer und jetziger Stand der Volkskundebewegung Chinas," *Zeitschrift für Ethnologie* LXV (1934), 316-325.

evident that in the eleven years during which folklore studies have been in existence in China, once the initial difficulties were surmounted, there has been a series of achievements which no scholar can afford to overlook any longer.

Up until now, specialists in the comparative folktale have had very few Chinese folktales at their disposal. And even many of those available were not genuine folktales, but rather literary tales, as is the case with such a large number of the tales contained in the well-known collection by Richard Wilhelm entitled *Chinesiche Volksmärchen.*[4] A look at the materials collected by our Chinese colleagues reveals that a large number of our most familiar folktale motifs can also be found in China. This will probably require us to approach many problems in comparative research from a new perspective. The question of whether folktales change or are preserved intact for centuries, and according to what laws this occurs, cannot, in our opinion, be studied anywhere better than in China. A work such as *Studies on the Tale of the Meng Chiang,* by Ku Chieh-kang, in which he traces a folktale motif through some two and one-half millennia, and demonstrates how practically nothing survives of the old half-historical report in later versions, is much more illuminating for this question than any mere speculation. The monograph *Stories about the Clever and Stupid Girl,* by Lou Tse-k'uang, who traces this motif over a period of some two thousand years, is another enlightening case in point. It is of course unnecessary for us to underscore the importance of folklore studies for the comparative history of religions, sociology and other disciplines.

We sincerely hope that these studies will continue to be pursued to the same extent as before, despite the still considerable difficulties, principally economical, which they must face. It is also our hope that this short essay, for which we are extremely grateful to the author, will help to fill the gap that still exists in our knowledge of Chinese culture.[5]

After the interruption of his work by the Sino-Japanese war, and later by the civil war, Mr. Lou continued to publish in Taiwan, partially reprinting and re-editing some of his earlier works, but in part also continuing to collect tales in Taiwan from Taiwanese Chinese and from aboriginal tribes of Taiwan. His former colleague Chung Ching-wen remained back on the mainland, and is now an important figure in the Communist movement to utilize folklore for propagandistic purposes.[6]

I.

View about the folklore movement in China. — Folklore studies in China have been widespread for only approximately eleven years. — The Folk-Song Research Society and the Folklore Research Society of Peking

University of 1922 – Publications and achievements of the Folk-Song Research Society. – Influence of the Folklore Research Society. – The Folklore Society of the Sun Yat-sen University which was newly formed in the South after the collapse of the northern society. – Accomplishments of the southern Folklore Society over a period of three years. – The preservation of folklore studies by the various local societies after the death of the southern society. – The founding of the Chinese Folklore Society on the shores of the lotus-covered West Lake in Hang-chou.

1. Friends and colleagues who are engaged in studies in Chinese folklore have recently expressed themselves about their work. By no means does each and every one of the scholars who has turned to working on behalf of this movement approach the problems from the standpoint of folklore. No, many stated that they used folklore solely as supporting material for other types of studies. Others again were of the opinion that all three branches of folklore studies could not develop at an equal pace. They sensed that to a certain degree the various branches of our discipline were developing independently of and in opposition to each other.

I believe that both these views are somewhat deficient It is hardly an accident that both these opinions can be encountered within the broad field encompassed by the Chinese folklore movement. It undoubtedly corresponds to a stage in our development, and reflects the self-confession of a weakness of which the representatives of the movement are themselves well aware. Nevertheless, one can recognize in all this a first step toward progress in the Chines folklore movement.

I consider the first opinion mentioned, namely that one should not proceed from folklore studies proper as a point of departure for one's involvement in the movement, definitely to be a developmental disease. If a scholar makes use of folklore only as supporting material for other kinds of studies, then it is hard to avoid the formation of regrettable divisions within our camp, because one scholar will specialize while the other dissipates his energies by taking an interest in too many things. If one starts out from a base of bonafide folklore research, however, it won't be long before he goes off in a bookish, library-oriented direction. Now, compared to the first possibility, this is even more unfortunate, at least as far as folklore studies are concerned.

In my opinion, the fear that the various branches of folklore studies could develop in opposition to one another is unfounded. In every type of growth process, we find that there are some parts which develop more rapidly, and some at a slower rate, and as long as scholars don't get too far away from each other, this does no particular harm.

2. It is a period of some 121 years from the publication of Henry Bourne's *Antiquitates Vulgares* (1725), through Brand's *Observations on Popular Antiquities* (1820) [1777], to the first appearance of the word 'folklore' coined by W.J. Thoms in *The Athenaeum* (August 22, 1846). From the first coining of this word until the present time we can count a mere eighty-six years. The spread of this term as far as China, however, has only taken place in about the last 11 years.

We can confidently consider the beginning of folklore studies in China to be the founding of the Folk-Song Research Society at the National University of Peking in 1922. Although this organization was not formed specifically for the purpose of folklore research, it is nevertheless impossible to assert that the society had no connection whatsoever with folklore studies. This becomes evident once we look at the introductory editorial statement published that year in its official organ, the *Folk-song Weekly*:

> Our society pursues two aims in the collection of folksongs: a scientific aim and an artistic one. We believe that the study of folklore in present-day China is a very important matter. Nevertheless, no scholar has given it sufficient attention to date. And only a few interested parties have occupied themselves to a degree with the material. But earnest efforts should be devoted to this study. At least, one should offer some materials for the investigators, or attempt to awaken the interest of others. Folksongs are an extremely important type of folkloric material. We intend to collect and print such materials in order to make serious specialized studies possible. This is our first aim...
>
> (*Ko-yao chou-k'an*, No. 1, p. 1)

It is possible from these words to gain some insight into the intentions expressed and the difficulties encountered at the time of the formation of the society. The leaders of this society were Chou Tso-jen,[7] Ku Chieh-kang[8] and Ch'ang Huei.

The Folklore Research Society was the sister of the society for the study of folksongs. It was founded in response to the fear that the Folk-Song Research Society would not be able to assume responsibility for all the work in the field of folklore. Chao Ching-shen and others took over the direction of the society. Its achievements are as slight as its short life, but its surveys of research on folklore studies, and the clear and energetic manner in which the work was pursued, managed to win the respect of many scholars.

The life of the Folk-Song Research Society was by no means long, only somewhere between two and three years. Nevertheless, in this short time it published ninety-six numbers of the *Weekly* and several monographs, and amassed a collection of more than twenty thousand folk and riddle songs.

The first major study in its series was the universally acclaimed *Studies on the Tale of the Meng-Chiang-nü,* by Ku Chieh-kang, along with such important studies as the folksong monograph *He saw them,*[9] *Marriage Customs,* and *Reports on the End-of-the-Year Festival.* Publications such as these helped to elevate the folksong, which was, so to speak, lying in the village streets, from its lowly position. But in the vicissitudes of the time, the Folk-Song Research Society went the way of the Folklore Research Society, and it also perished.

3. But after the collapse of the society, the great slumbering powers lived on, like a body which had died in the north, but whose soul has fled south to be reborn there. What I am alluding to now is the Folklore Society of the Sun Yat-sen University in Canton, which was formed out of the earlier research section for archaeology, history and philology. It too developed out of studies in folk literature, and received certain direct and indirect stimuli and guidance from the two Peking societies. The leaders of the Canton society, such as Ku Chieh-kang, Chung Ching-wen and others were, for the most part, already close friends back in the north.

The fate of the Canton society was very similar to that of the Peking society: it lasted only three years. But if one compares the work of the two organizations, then it becomes evident that the Canton society made some substantial contributions in respect to related academic disciplines when compared with the latter society. As far as the scope of the movement is concerned, the Canton organization initiated folkloristic seminars, folklore exhibits, and also sent out investigators to Shao-kuan, Yünnan and elsewhere to conduct field research on the spot. The publication of their weekly journal amounted to some 110 numbers between March 1928 and April 1930.[10] In these three years, thirty-four collections were also published, the most important of which I will mention in the appendix. The last number of the *Folklore Weekly,* No. 109, again contained many valuable essays and original materials.[11] Special issues on such topics as Chinese deities, riddles, folksongs, folktales, the betel-nut, the Tan (a tribe in Kuantung province), the mid-autumn festival, the story of Chu Ying-t'ai (a woman from the east Chin period), sacrificial ceremonies on the Miao-feng-shan, etc. all have their particular value. Unfortunately, however, issues of the periodical were not widely distributed, and the number of readers was small.

4. When the Canton Folklore Society was breathing its last, the local societies which it had inspired inherited its job. Everywhere in Hang-chou, Ning-po, Amoy, Fu-chou, Chang-chou, Swatow and elsewhere, both in the interior and on the coast, the small lights of the local folklore societies now appeared. This was a period of transition which helped to keep folklore

studies alive in China, and for that reason it is worthy of our consideration. I will therefore briefly sketch the situation of each of the societies:

Hang-chou: Although this society published only nine issues of its *Weekly,* it is nevertheless of importance for the tenor of the folklore movement in Chêkiang. Ch'ien Nan-yang and Chung Ching-wen were its directors at that time.

Ning-po: Five issues of a *Folklore Ten-Day Journal* and ten issues of a weekly devoted to folksongs, riddles and folktales were published. Among collections there was a volume of folksongs from Ning-po. The society was very well received in eastern Chêkiang, and didn't collapse until its president left Ning-po. Later it merged with the Chinese Folklore Society mentioned later in this article.

Amoy: The society was founded relatively early in south Fukien. Its directors were Hsieh Yün-shêng and Su Ching-yü. Publications include stories from Fukien, two collections of folk traditions from Ch'üan-chou, and a folklore weekly of some forty to fifty issues. Nowadays, however, the society is no longer as active as before.

Fu-chou: The weekly journal is still published, and numbers about 130 issues to date. The publication has a wide circulation in Fu-chou. The directors of the society are Wei Ying-ch'i and Chiang Ting-i.

Chang-chou: More than thirty numbers of the weekly journal have appeared here, as well as two small volumes of folk traditions from Chang-chou. The director is Wêng Kuo-liang.

Swatow: The society arose in connection with those of Ch'ao-chou, Hong Kong and Lu-fêng. It probably also exerted some influence in Canton. Its weekly journal appeared up to No. 33, and recently it has also merged with the Chinese Folklore Society. It is now known as the Ling-tung Branch Society, and its director is Lin Pe-lu.

5. In the summer of 1930, the Chinese Folklore Society (*Chung-kuo Min-su-hsüeh huei*) was born on the shore of the lotus-covered West Lake in Hang-chou. It came into being as a result of the co-operation of Chiang Shao-yüan and Chung Ching-wen, and is now in its third year of existence. In its work it is not so subject to external influences, as were the societies in Peking and Canton. Although its directors had energetically gone about the essential preparations, and although members had sketched extensive

programs and had great hopes, in practice numerous obstacles arose. For this reason, their first publications, as they readily admit, do not yet contain any very significant contributions. They have already published two large volumes entitled *Collected Folklore Studies*.[12] These are collections of papers on the theory of folklore, and are publications of our co-workers which should win the praise of our colleagues in Europe, American and Asia. Our monthly journal[13] and our weekly (70 numbers to date) appear regularly, and give equal coverage to both theory and original source materials. Collections already published or in press are as follows:

Lou Tse-k'uang: *Chung-kuo hsin-nien fêng-su chih. (Chinese New Year's Customs).*[14]

Chung Ching-wen: *Lao-hu wai-p'o ku-shih chi. (Collection of Folktales about the Tiger-Grandmother).*

Liu Ta-po: *Ku-shih-ti t'an-tse. (Types of the Folktale).*

Lou Tse-k'uang: *Ch'iao-nü ho kai-niang-ti ku-shih. (Stories about the Clever and the Stupid Girl).*

Chung Ching-wen: *Chung-kuo min-t'an hsing-shih-piao. (Survey of the Types of Chinese Folk Narratives).*

Ch'ien Nan-yang: *Min-su chiu-wen. (Folklore from Ancient Sources).*

Lin Pe-lu: *Min-su-hsüeh lun-wen-chi. (Collection of Essays on Folklore).* Issued by the Ling-tung Branch of the Society.

Lou Tse-k'uang (trans.): *Hsi-tsang lien-ko. (Tibetan Love Songs).*

Chang Chih-chin *et al.: Hu-chou ko-yao. (Songs from Hu-chou).* Issued by the Su-chou Branch of the Society.

Miss Ch'iu-tse: *Jen-hsiung-p'o. (The Bear Woman).*

Lou Tse-k'uang: *Yüeh-kuang kuang-ko-chi. (Collections of Moonlight Songs).*

Miss Hsüan-pao: *T'ien-lo-nü. (The Snail Woman).*

Lou Tse-lun: *Chu Ying-t'ai. (Stories about Chu Ying-t'ai).*

Shih Fang: *Tou niu. (Bullfighting).*

We have found helpful colleagues in almost all the provinces, in all probably more than two hundred individuals. There are branch societies in Ling-tung, Su-chou, Shao-hsing and elsewhere. We have plans to send a research expedition next spring to the Hsia living along the coasts of Chêkiang, Fukien and Kuangtung.

All those persons interested in folklore have by now gradually come together within the framework of the Chinese Folklore Society. By co-operative efforts, they hope to encourage and promote the study of Chinese folklore throughout the entire world.

II.

The difficulties of folkloristic research. — Chou Tso-jen and Ku Chieh-kang as forerunners. — Chao Ching-shên, Chung Ching-wen, and Lin Lan collect and study folk narratives. — Ku Chieh-kang's *Studies on the Tale of the Meng-Chiang-nü.* — The collection and arrangement of the *Moonlight Songs* and the *Stories about the Clever and the Stupid Girl* by the present author. — Chiang Shao-yüan's *Studies on the Beard, Nails and Related Concepts.* The shorter studies of Huang Shih. Ku Chieh-kang and Liu Wen-chang: *Wedding and Mourning Customs in Su-chou and Canton.* — The first sections of the *Folklore of China* by the present author. — The translation of van Gennep's *Folklore* — A. Robertson Wright's *English Folklore.* — Charlotte Burne's *Handbook of Folklore.* — New areas of Chinese folklore.

1. Now we will discuss the works on the various scholars engaged in the study of Chinese folklore. Folklore studies came to China, as was mentioned above, only some eleven short years ago. Within this period it has become evident that, given the scope of the discipline and the size of the country, not only is the material collected growing at an inexhaustible rate, but the classification and working up of these materials is particularly difficult.

Thus, our colleagues have partially devoted their energies to assembling broad and intensive collections, and in part to initiating the first systematic scholarly studies of these materials amassed. Although admittedly no world-shaking publications have yet made their appearance, I strongly believe that the studies of each of these scholars, if they pursue them with perseverance and vigor, will mark the first folkloristic awakening of East Asia.

2. Folkloristics is like a large garden without any borders, and is criss-crossed by numerous paths running through this garden in every

direction. But in China, the broad domain of literature adjoins this garden as a close neighbor, and there is a very active exchange of traffic between the two areas. For this reason, the third great field in the three major subdivisions of folklore (according to Burne's classification), namely that of folktales, songs and sayings, has enjoyed a particularly vigorous development in China. We need only think in this connection of the accomplishments of Chou Tso-jen and Ku Chieh-kang. All of us know that Chou was the first person to seriously collect and edit folktales, and Ku's compilation of songs from Su-chou, as well as his study of the Meng-Chiang tale, reach even beyond the limits of folklore into the field of history. They were followed by the important works of Chao Ching-shên, Lin Lan, and many others. But most of these scholars go into folklore studies from their activities in literature or from teaching. This can also be said regarding Chung Ching-wen's investigation of folktales and his classification of them into specific types. I myself have been collecting so-called "moonlight songs" and folktales dealing with the clever and the stupid girl for about some seven years now, and already have amassed an extensive collection. I hope soon to be able to present this material to the scholarly world, after having carefully examined and worked through the data.[15]

If we now want to discuss the state of research in the second major area of folkloristics, that of religion and cult, then the first scholar we have to mention is Chiang Shao-yüan, who got into folklore from the study of religion, and who emphasized that the history of religions and folklore are closely related disciplines, especially since religion is an integral part of folk belief. Typical of Chiang's folkloristic writings is his *Studies on the Beard, Nails and related Concepts,* in which he describes in great detail the folk beliefs and folk behavior associated with the hair, beard and nails in ancient and recent times in China. In this monograph he presents many additional examples in support of Frazer's analogies, and proposes two great laws involved in the beliefs. This is indeed a very impressive piece of scholarship. Writings of equal importance are those by Ku Chieh-kang on the Miao-fêng-shan and the Tung-yüeh-miao (their temples and cults). In addition to these figures, one scholar, Huang Shih, has come to folklore from the study of mythology. Along with several mythological studies, he has also addressed himself to a number of similar folkloristic questions, and has already published several smaller studies.[16]

In the third major area, namely that of folkways and customs, there have been few recent publications. Ku Chieh-kang and Liu Wan-chang's *Marriage and Mourning Customs in Su-chou and Canton,* Chou Chen-ho's *Customs of Su-chou,* Yang Jui-ts'ung's *Customs of Ch'ao-chou,* are all recent works. In an earlier period, reports about various geographical areas, and on various social classes, and monographs proceeding in a so-called 'horizontal' fashion, were far more common. Studies which treated the folk itself and proceeded in a vertical direction, however, used to be extremely uncommon due to the gap between the educated classes and the folk. In the near future, I have plans to write a *Folklore of China*, in which I intend to describe the annual folk festivals and customs of the genuine "folk," the forms of life of each individual, contests, games, etc. The first part of this work has now been published as *Chinese New Year's Customs.*

3. In regard to foreign studies, probably the most important books for development of folklore in China have been the work by the French anthropologist Arnold van Gennep entitled *Folklore* (1924), translated by Yang Yeh, that of the president of the English Folk-Lore Society, Arthur Robinson Wright, *English Folklore* (1927), translated by Chiang Shao-yüan, and finally the *Handbook of Folklore* (1914) by the English folklorist Charlotte Burne, translated by Cheng Chen-to, Ch'en Hsi-hsiang, and Lo Sih-ping. Further relevant works, which also include other academic fields, will not be mentioned here.

The other specialists who have contact with folklore studies and who likewise, albeit for different purposes, draw on folkloric materials, such as historians, literary scholars, educators, archaeologists, sociologists, and others, have all made extensive progress in their respective disciplines. Thus, we find there are cultural historians now who plan to write a history of "uncultivated China," leaving to one side the materials relating to Chinese high culture.[17]

It would appear as if each of these scholars were hurling his lance on a separate path, so to speak, but in actuality they are all working hand in hand with folklore studies, and are advancing together along a common route.

4. The study of Chinese folklore is still very young. Together with our colleagues throughout the world, we hope to make rapid progress in the future.

Appendix 1.

Ku Chieh-kang: *Mêng-chiang-nü ku-shih yen-chiu chi.* Three parts. The first part treats the changes in the tale of Meng Chiang, studies on the tale, and explanations. Part two contains discussions by Ku Chieh-kang and his critics on the legend, presented in ten sections. The third part brings thirty-eight letters by Ku Chieh-kang and scholars from all regions of the Meng Chiang tale.

Chung Ching-wen: *Min-chien i-wen ts'ung-hua.* (*On Folk Literature*). Contains some seventeen sections treating such subjects as the literature of the Tan tribes, love songs of the K'o-jen, and children's game songs.

Ts'ui Tai-yang: *Ch'u-min hsin-li yü ko-chung shê-huei chih-tu-ti ch'i-yüan.* (*Primitive Psychology and the Origin of Social Institutions*). This work is divided into two parts: (a) *Primitive Psychology.* (b) *Origin of Social Institutions.* The first part is in turn divided into nine chapters treating such topics as the relations between the individual and the group, etc.; the second part has eight chapters dealing with topics such as primitive psychology, religion, morals, politics, social life, art, and education.

Jung Chao-tsu: *Mi-hsin yü chuan-shuo.* (*Superstition and Tradition*). Contains thirteen sections, treating such problems as the origin of oracles,[18] the Pao-p'o-tse, the god Erh-lang, and others.

Wei Ying-ch'i: *Fu-chien san-shen k'ao.* (*On the Three Deities in Fukien*). Reports in ten sections on the Lin-shui fu-jen, the Kuo-sheng-wang, and the T'ien-hou in Fukien province.[19]

Chung Ching-wen: *Ch'u-ts'ih-chung-ti shen-hua ho chuan-shuo.* (*On Mythology and Tradition in the Elegies of Ch'u*). Contains seven sections on gods, saints, demons and hero legends from the Ch'u elegies.

Ku Chieh-kang: *Miao-fêng-shan.* (*Mt. Miao-fêng*).[20] The cult on Mt. Miao-fêng, notes on the cult, investigation of the temple of the Pi-hsia-yüan-chün, and so on. Twenty-six sections.

Ch'ien Nan-yang: *Mi shih.* (*History of the Riddle*). Describes the origin of the riddle, as well as the place of the riddle in the course of history, its development and decline.

Yao I-chih: *Hu-nan ch'ang-pên t'i-yao.* (*Summaries of ballads from Hunan*). A short selection of several dozen songs widespread in Hunan; their style, type and character.

Yang Ch'êng-chih (Translator): *Min-su-hsüeh wen-t'i ko.* (*Folklore Questions*). The translation of Appendix B to Burne's *Handbook of Folklore*.

Chung Ching-wen, *et al.* (Translators): *Yin-Ou min-chien ku-shih hsing-piao* (*Some Types of Indo-European Folktales*). A translation of Appendix C to Burne's *Handbook of Folklore*.

Liu Wan-chang: *Kuang-chou erh-ko chia-chi. (First Collection of Children's Songs from Canton).* Contains one hundred songs.

Wang I-chih: *Wu-ko i-chi. (Second Collection of Songs from Su-chou).* Contains fifty children's songs and sixty-two folksongs.

Lou Tse-k'uang: *Shao-hsing ko-yao. (Songs from Shao-hsing).* Contains one hundred of the best known folksongs from Shao-hsing (Chêkiang).

Hsieh Yün-shêng: *Min-ko chia chi. (First Collection of Songs from Fukien).* Contains two hundred fifty songs from all over Fukien.

Chung Ching-wen *et al.* (Translators): *Lang-T'ung ch'ing-ko. (Love Songs of the Lang and T'ung).* Presents a new translation of thirty-seven love songs of the Lang and T'ung (south China), collected by the Manchu period scholar Li T'iao-yüan.

Yeh Tê-chün: *Huai-an ko-yao. (Songs from Huai-an).* Presents twenty-six folksongs from Huai-an (Kiangsu) and thirty-six children's songs.

Huang Chao-nien: *Hai-tse-men-ti ko-sheng. (Children's Songs).* Contains more than two hundred children's songs from central and southern China.

Ch'iu Chün: *Ch'ing-ko ch'ang-ta (Love Songs in Antiphony).* Three hundred love songs of the Hakka in Canton.

Wei Ying-ch'i: *Fu-chou ko-yao chia-chi. (First Collection of Songs from Fu-chou.* 224 songs from Fu-chou.

Chang Ch'ien-ch'ang: *Mei-hsien t'ung-yao. (Boys' Songs from the Mei District).* Eighty-four children's songs from Mei-hsien in Kuangtung.

Hsieh Yün-shêng: *T'ai-wan ch'ing-ko chi. (Collection of Love Songs from Formosa).* Two hundred love songs from Formosa.

Po Shou-i: *K'ai-fêng ko-yao chi. (Collection of Songs from K'ai-fêng).* Seventy songs from K'ai-fêng in Honan.

Ch'en Yüan: *T'ai-shan ko-yao chi. (Collection of Songs from T'ai-shan.)* More than two hundred songs from the district of T'ai-shan in Kuangtung.

Ch'ing Shui: *Hai-lung-wang-ti nü-erh. (The Daughter of the Sea Dragon King)*. Ten folktales from Wêng-yüan in Kuangtung: *The Daughter of the Sea Dragon King, The Marriage of the Snakes, The Tale of the Three-legged Moon-Toad, and others.*

Lou Tse-k'uang: *Shao-hsing ku-shih. (Folktales from Shao-hsing)*. Seventeen tales from Shao-hsing in Chêkiang province: *Gold-Thread Cat, The Old Woman, The Cattle Louse, The Tiger Ghost, The Snake Man,* and others.

Liu Wan-chang: *Kuang-chou min-chien ku-shih. (Folktales from Canton)*. Contains fifty folktales from Canton.

Wu Tsao-t'ing: *Ch'üan-chou min-chien chuan-shuo. (Folktales from Ch'üan-chou)*. Twenty-three tales.

Hsiao Han: *Yang-chou-ti chuan-shuo. (Folktales from Yang-chou)*. Contains approximately twenty tales from Yang-chou in Kiangsu province.

Liu Wan-chang: *Kuang-chou mi-yü. (Riddle Sayings from Canton)*. Composed of 130 riddle verses from Canton.

Po Ch'i-ming: *Ho-nan mi-yü. (Riddle Sayings from Honan)*. Contains six hundred riddle verses from Honan.

Wang Chü-hou: *Ning-po mi-yü. (Riddle Sayings from Ning-po)*. Presents 324 riddle verses from Ning-po.

Ku Chieh-kang *et al.: Su-Yüeh-ti hun-sang. (Marriage and Mourning Customs from Su-chou and Canton)*. A description of the customs.

Chou Chên-ho: *Su-chou fêng-su. (Customs in Su-chou)*. Divided into chapters covering such topics as temples and cult halls, wedding and mourning customs, and the customs of the various months. A description of customary behavior in Su-chou.

Appendix 2.

A Discussion with Dr. Eberhard on Chinese Mythology
by Chung Ching-wen (Hang-chou)

Introductory note: I had emphasized in a letter to the author just how important I felt his works and those of his colleagues on folklore and mythology were for an understanding of Chinese culture. These works put an end once and for all to the false notion still prevalent in our ranks that in China there is no ancient mythology. The answer of Chung Ching-wen — whose achievements were mentioned by Lou in the previous article — provides us with some valuable insight into the author's own works and projects, and is a welcome supplement to the essay by Lou Tse-k'uang. We would like to thank the author for his kindness in this matter, and will present parts of his reply in translation, and parts in abstract only.[21]

In his answer, Chung first rightly points out the great difficulties encountered by Europeans undertaking folklore research in China, and goes on to say that "the scientific value of these studies is extremely limited; in fact, in most cases it is quite impossible to even talk about any such value" (p. 36). In regard to this we are in complete agreement with Chung. This is precisely the situation as far as most of the Western studies are concerned. In part, this may be due simply to the fact that, up until now, there have not been many scholars who have been able to devote themselves seriously to Chinese folklore. If such research is to be successful, a long stay in the country itself is of particular necessity. The Japanese work, on the other hand, is more valuable in Chung's eyes. Chinese scholarship, Chung feels, is already assuming leadership in the field, despite its relatively recent appearance on the scene.

Chung then goes on to enumerate the sources on which we can draw for myths and legends: not only in literature, but from oral tradition as well. But this kind of collecting, Chung adds, happens to be fraught with a great many difficulties. Scholars are now busy collecting, and new materials, such as creation myths, legends of the origins of various beings and things, local legends, and the like, are constantly appearing. When this work has been completed to a certain extent, Chung states, it will prove of greatest importance, not only for Chinese studies, but for mythological research throughout the world. And now to the portions of the translated text:

For the most diverse reasons, only a few short disconnected fragments of myths and legends have been preserved in early Chinese literature. On the basis of this, all European and East Asian scholars have formed a unanimous opinion that classical Chinese culture did not produce such consummate and beautiful works as ancient Greece, Rome or northern Europe. I consider the correctness of this view to be quite doubtful. That the myths and legends found in ancient Chinese literature are often extremely fragmentary is a fact which must be admitted. But, logically speaking, it would be incomprehensible to think that some such consummate and beautiful works of myth and legend did not also appear in the course of the development of Chinese culture, particularly since we certainly have material contained in documentary facts of another kind which could undermine this hypothesis.

Chinese literature is unusually rich, so rich that it is easy to lose one's perspective. Apart from the older literature (*Shan-hai-ching, Li-sao, T'ien-wen, Huai-nan-tse*), beginning with the Han and Wei periods, works which contain various myths and legends, sometimes more, sometimes less, are really not so few in number.

To be sure, this literature contains a considerable quantity of ancient myth and legend, but the mouth of the farmers and fisherman's wives in the folk is the most abundant and valuable treasure-house of such myths and legends.

I, for one, am quite involved in these questions, and am devoting all my energies to their study. Already as early as ten years ago I noted down certain materials I had collected orally from the south Chinese folk. In recent years, I have been collecting and compiling material on the one hand, and writing preliminary exploratory general studies on the other. In the area of collection and collation, I have already compiled the following works, or intend to do so shortly:

1. Collection of local legends from Kuangtung and Kuanghsi.
2. Collection of myths from Lu-an.
3. Proofs for ancient Chinese myths.
4. Proofs for ancient Chinese legends.
5. Collection of Chinese nature myths.
6. Selection of ancient Chinese folktales.
7. Selection of contemporary Chinese folktales.

In the second area of general systematic studies, I intend to write the following two works in addition to the already published articles on Chinese local legends, Chinese flood legends, myths on the origin of tribes and races, myths on the origin of Chinese plants. Chinese swan-maiden myths, and a volume entitled *Myths and Legends in the Elegies of Ch'u:*

1. A book on Chinese mythology.
2. History of studies on Chinese mythology.

These projects are, of course, quite ambitious and difficult, but I sincerely hope to be able to finish my plan in about ten years. In addition, I have been quite busy recently with comparative studies of Chinese, Japanese, Indian and Korean mythology and folktales.

9. THE STRUCTURE OF A CENTRAL CHINESE LOCAL CULTURE*

This article, a brief summary of some of the results of my studies in central China in 1934-1935, is the first formulation of my ideas about local cultures in China, written at about the same time (1936) as the "new working hypothesis" in which I tried to combine the folkloristic-ethnographic approach with the historical approach. In my *Lokalkulturen im alten China* (Leiden, 1943), many of the ideas mentioned here are presented in more elaborate form.

Ethnology has generally shown considerable inhibitions when confronted with the task of analyzing the cultural structure of peoples with a so-called high culture. Thus, the high cultures of Asia have still scarcely been subjected to ethnological scrutiny. Nevertheless, it is clear that although such analysis presents more difficulties, its results are very significant both for methodology and for the evaluation of the history, science and art of the respective people. For it is precisely here among the high-culture peoples that we have the advantage of being able not only to inventory present-day culture, but also to become familiar with the culture of earlier periods by means of literary documents and other monuments as well. We thus find before us a broad span of culture – in the case of China, for example, a period of more than 3500 years – and we can deduce possible laws of change with far greater ease and certainty from cultural changes which have actually taken place, than from the almost history-less picture which generally emerges from the analysis of primitive cultures. In this way, it becomes possible to counter baseless hypothetical constructions with exact knowledge.

My 1934-35 field trip to China, undertaken on behalf of the Berlin Anthropological Museum, had, as one of its aims, the analysis of the cultural structure of one area in central China and one in northern China. We are still almost completely lacking in the requisite single detailed studies which, in view of the scope and complexity of Chinese culture, would have to provide an initial point of departure. This paper will cover only the results of the investigation in central China.

*Revised and translated version of "Die Struktur einer mittel-chinesischen Lokalkultur," *Artibus Asiae* VII (1937), 87-91.

I visited the eastern part of Chêkiang province for an extended period of time. This region, due to its mountainous character, remains a kind of backward area and is still partially underpopulated even today.

Upon initial examination, we seem to see nothing more than the same over-all picture of general Chinese culture whose basic characteristics are found in uniform distribution throughout almost the entire area of the empire. Subsequently, one notices the traits that assign this region to one of the four great regional subcultures of the North, Center, South and West. But closer scrutiny soon points up certain peculiarities in the area studied by the author (the vicinity of the city of Chin-hua and south of this) which cannot be found anywhere else in the neighboring districts.

The principal example is the bullfight in the form of a contest between two bulls. Bullfighting is unknown elsewhere among present-day Chinese. Nevertheless, the bullfight does occur among non-Chinese natives in Yünnan and Kueichou, and its presence in Sihch'uan province is also attested in the older literature. It is thus attested for an area which was of decidedly non-Chinese ethnic composition in the earlier period. The tree cult, usually associated with camphor trees which are designated as 'mother' or 'father,' has the same area of distribution. Here and there, special temples have also been built for the trees. In these temples we no longer find the trees themselves, but rather figures of gods which are worshiped as their representatives. This cult can also be compared with related customs found among south Chinese native populations. In addition, a considerable number of folktales, in particular a world-conflagration tale containing the motif of sibling marriage which is identical with narratives of the Yao tribes in southern China, represent a further local peculiarity. A number of other factors show that there appears to be a close connection between the cultural structure of this part of Chêkiang and that of areas in south China.

Now, there are still a number of non-Chinese, namely the Hsia-min tribe in four large clans, living right in this district. They are, as H. Stübel first demonstrated, the most northerly branch of a non-Chinese ethnic group which is most closely related to the Yao. Given these facts, one would have to assume that the peculiarities observed have been imported into the area by this segment of the population, even if these non-Chinese appear to have lost these same culture traits in the meantime. But here, in the case of China, we can go on to pursue the problem historically, and our end result reveals that this was a false initial conclusion.

Family chronicles of the Hsia-min, which were examined by Stübel and the author, show that the present-day Hsia-min did not start to migrate into this area of Chêkiang from Kuangtung and Fukien provinces until the beginning of the seventeenth century. But local chronicles and annals also reveal that this movement must have been a re-migration, since the Hsia-min appear to have already been situated in these areas by the beginning of the thirteenth century at the very latest. Later, in battles which took place at the beginning of the seventeenth century, a large segment of the population was destroyed, and many Chinese as well as Hsia-min migrated anew into the area.

Now, a picture located in the Berlin Anthropological Museum (#34069), a late copy of a Ming picture, portrays a bullfight apparently taking place in the same region, even before this new migration. The cult cannot be demonstrated in Chêkiang for an earlier period, but we can show the earlier presence of the cult of a number of female deities. This is also one of the special local traits. These deities likewise point to an origin in south China. We must therefore conclude that, in any case, the special local customs were not first introduced into the area by the present-day Hsia-min.

Somewhat to the north of the present location of the Hsia-min, near the city of Shao-hsing, we find another ethnic fragment, the To-min. Today they form a beggars' caste in which the men do the begging and the women act as marriage brokers and singers. The To-min appear to have lost their original culture. Sources attest their existence back to the early Ming period, and always as a caste of beggars. The earliest report about them,[1] however, discusses their own ancient forms of dress which they were still wearing at that time, and their customs. The women wore a so-called 'dog's-head' coiffure, and the men fashioned statues of cattle as well as lamps made of cattle-horn. This information is sufficiently clear: the To-min accordingly also emerge as the remnant of a non-Chinese ethnic group closely related to the Hsia-min and the Yao. They have also preserved elements of the cattle cult which is typical of so many south Chinese ethnic groups. In its most pronounced form, this cattle cult consists of the ceremonial sacrifice of cattle, bullfighting in the form of a contest between two bulls, and the preservation of the horns of the sacrificed cattle. Furthermore, the dog-cap or dog coiffure which is also shared by the Hsia-min and their relatives, the Yao, and which is always associated with the dog cult and the tribal dog legend, makes it appear even more certain that the To-min should be considered part of the Yao. It is thus possible to demonstrate the presence of the Hsia-min as well as the To-min in this area of Chêkiang well before the immigration of the present-day Hsia-min in the seventeenth century. These peoples were located there at least from the early Ming period, and apparently even earlier, and they are both related to the Yao tribes now living in south China.

Sources from the T'ang period and even earlier, however, do not mention any Hsia-min or To-min living here. They report that this area was inhabited by Yüeh peoples. Now, what is the relationship between the

Hsia-min, the To-min and these Yüeh groups? Closer examination reveals a number of connections between these peoples, some of which Stübel has already partially pointed out. Of particular importance is the very definite tradition of all Hsia-min which states that their original homeland was located around Mt. K'ui-chi, which is situated to the north of their present-day limit of distribution in Chêkiang. It is impossible to find any proper connection in the genealogical chronicles between this original homeland and the historically proven settlements in Kuangtung province. But the Yüeh likewise had the tradition that Mt. K'ui-chi was their original homeland. The Yüeh also possessed the dog myth. Likewise, the cattle cult is also typical of the Yüeh, and traces of it can be found wherever the Yüeh were formerly settled. Studies of ancient Chinese culture[2] were able to establish the oldest area of Yüeh settlement and expansion with great accuracy. This included approximately the areas of the present-day provinces Chêkiang, Kiangsi, Kiangsu, Anhui, and south Shantung. In the most northern part of their area of settlement, they clashed with other ethnic groups, partially merged with these groups and formed a component of what was later to become the so-called "Chinese" culture. But later on a contrast developed between this newly arisen "Chinese" culture and its various original components. The "Chinese," as a newly formed unit, pushed out in all directions, even toward the south into the actual ancient heartland of the Yüeh. Now, genealogical and local chronicles prove that extensive Chinese settlement in this area does not begin in earnest until the ninth century, although there was an initial wave in the fourth to fifth centuries. During this period, the Chinese settled mainly in the valleys among the old Yüeh population. By this action the Yüeh were split up, divided into numerous "tribes," and were forced into the mountains. To an extent, the Yüeh also began to migrate south. The Chinese adopted a number of their customs, and also assimilated the Yüeh racially. The Hsia-min, as part of the Yüeh peoples, remained living side by side with the Chinese settlers, or even mingled with them, while some of their number headed south with the general southern migration of the Yüeh and settled in Kuangtung. After lengthy stop-overs in Fukien, a group of the Hsia-min re-migrated to Chêkiang in the seventeenth century. In the meantime, the old Hsia-min in Chêkiang had been almost completely wiped out. But the To-min, by isolating themselves and forming a kind of caste, have preserved their independence down to the present day without any re-migration, although they have lost their original culture in the process.

This, then, is a general sketch of the cultural structure of this one region. It is evident just how complex the pattern of events is which led to the formation of the present-day form of culture. Without the use of historical materials, and thus without the use of the historical method, these events cannot be completely disclosed. If corresponding material should become available for a larger number of areas, it will be possible to state something conclusive regarding the general structure of Chinese culture during the historical period. We would like to emphasize here that investigations in northwestern China have yielded a similar result. There, too, we have been able to show that beneath the surface of a general Chinese culture, it is possible to discover the remains of local cultures. And there, too, we can trace these survivals back to earlier cultures, which, at the end of the second millennium, in combination with other early cultures, led to the formation of what we can call actual "Chinese" culture.

10. A TRADITION ABOUT A FLYING HEAD IN CHINA*

A note on the study by H. Nevermann, "Der fliegende Kopf. Ein Kapitel aus dem Geisterglaube der Indonesier," Weltkreis, II (1931), 133-139.*

"In the Ch'in period (220-200 B.C.) there was the Lo-t'ou ("falling-head people") in the south. Their head can fly. This race of people has a sacrificial ceremony called *Ch'ung-lo* ("falling of insects"), and from this the people got their name.[3]

At the time of the Wu dynasty (220-280 A.D.) general Chu Huan[4] received a female slave whose head suddenly flew away every night after she had gone to sleep. The head went in and out either through the dog's hole or through the window. The ears served as wings in flight. When it got light out, the head returned. This took place several times. The people were astonished about this and saw that during the night only her body was lying there without any head. The body was cool and was breathing quietly. Then they covered the body with a blanket. Toward morning, when the head returned, it was hampered by the blanket and couldn't get back to its proper place. After two or three attempts, it fell to the ground, moaned and was very sad. But the body was greatly agitated and looked as if it were near to die. When they removed the cover, the head rose again, attached itself to the neck, and immediately became quiet. Huan thought that was a great miracle. He was afraid, no longer dared to keep her in his custody, and let her go free. But when the matter was examined more carefully, the people learned that this was her nature. In those days the generals operating in the south found such beings everywhere. Once, when somebody tipped over a bronze dish on one of them, its head couldn't be attached again and it died."

This passage is taken from the *Sou-shen-chi*, a source which was supposedly written at the beginning of the fourth century, but the present text is undoubtedly a later falsification. A similar note on the "flying-head barbarians" is given by *Hsü-Po-wu-chih* in the twelfth century. Many other sources, especially the *Yu-yang tsa-tsu* (chap. IV, 4a-b) mentions cases of this type. All of them refer either to tribes in Southeast Asia, such as people in Champa or Laos (*Chien-hu chi, kuang-chi*, II, 2b) or to primitive tribes within

*Revised and translated version of "Eine Überlieferung von einem fliegenden Kopf in China," *Der Weltkreis* III (1932), 55.

the area of present-day China. In most cases, the art is known to women, but not to men. In my *Lokalkulturen im alten China* (II, 478), I have associated this belief with the culture of the Liao group.

11. A GENEALOGICAL CHRONICLE OF THE HSIA-MIN*

I.

The Hsia-min of southern Chêkiang province have been repeatedly studied in recent years, the most detailed study being that by H. Stübel and Li Hua-min.[1] During my stay in Li-shui (=Ch'u-chou) and Yün-ho, I also frequently came across Hsia-min and visited their settlements *(illustrations 4 and 5)*. In the process I had the opportunity to examine a genealogy of the Chung clan dating from the year 1804. The genealogy was very hastily written on bad paper, contained numerous mistakes, and had been repeatedly damaged. I had a copy of it made and will now present a translation of its most important sections. Because of the scribal errors and missing passages, the translation is often questionable and uncertain, and it is also partially based on supplementary oral explanations given to me. The translation is of especial interest in that the descent from a dog is more clearly expressed here than in the genealogies given by Stübel. It also demonstrates that apparently every family has its own genealogy, and that all of these are different. The time of composition for all these genealogies is about the year 1800. This is interesting in light of the fact that according to the gazetteer of Yün-ho, given below, admission to the imperial examinations was first granted to the Hsia-min in 1803. They were thus not recognized as full citizens until this date, after which they provided themselves with genealogical chronicles just like the Chinese families. The text is as follows:

The ascent of our original ancestor P'an-hu is...[2]

At the command of heaven in the fifth year *ta-sui,* in the fifth month on Mt. K'ui-chi in the "Cave of the Seven Wise Men," the king of Ch'u issued a decree[3] to the king P'an-hu, which sons and grandsons should pass on from generation to generation, and against which there must be no transgression. And if there are transgressions against this edict, then the imperial edict should be passed on to the proper district or county authority, and matters should be dealt with according to him. But in other cases agents should be appointed.

*Revised and translated version of "Zur Volkskunde von Chêkiang. Ein Stammbuch der Hsia-min," *Zeitschrift für Ethnologie,* LXVII (1936), 254-258.

It came from heaven, from the palace of the twenty-eight moon stations of the moon-heart-fox[4] down into the land of Yen and there it brought together all the brave men. The army of Wu[5] was harassed by them. They invaded the country, there was war, and the people suffered death and destruction. None of the vassals could help, several times they were unable to repulse the enemy;...received a command from the hall of heaven that Lou Chin-kou (Lou, the Golden Dog) should descend to earth and tame the moon-heart-tiger.... In addition, Yü-huang (Jade Emperor) commanded K'ang Chin-lung (K'ang, the Golden Dragon), and Niu Chin-nü (Niu, the Golden Girl), these stars,[6] to descend as helpers, but not to cross the threshold of humans. Now the Golden Dog descended into the palace of the emperor Kao-hsin, the liberator of the great empire....[7] And the doctors brought forth a golden insect. All the ministers of the court covered P'an-hu with lotus leaves and nourished him for several days. Soon he was transformed into a dragon-dog. He had 120 spots on his body. "I will remove the sorrow of the state and meet the king of Yen...." Then the emperor grew afraid and said: "We must make a proclamation: if there exists a brave warrior who can restore peace to the country, then I will give him the third princess and appoint him as imperial son-in-law." All the ministers.... Only the dragon-dog took the proclamation, went to the presence chamber, and said he could catch the enemies. All the ministers were pleased, and three times they shouted "10,000 years." "If you can protect the empire and bring it peace, your reward will not be small." The dog barked loudly three times, and then said good-bye and left. He jumped over the ocean and changed himself into a golden dragon. After seven days and seven nights he came to the hall of the king of Yen. When the king saw the unusual dog he became very interested and took him in. He gathered his soldiers together for a great celebration, and everyone drunk until all were intoxicated. When he was lying completely drunk on the bed, the golden dog came in and bit off the head of the king of Yen. Then he returned secretly to our country and reported his deed. The emperor heard about the dog's abilities and was very happy that he had pacified the people and had such merits. And he adorned a girl as princess. But the strange dog just barked and didn't want her. He went straight to the main hall of the palace and bit the hem of the dress of the third princess.... The emperor commanded.... He was able to change into a human being, except as yet for his head. The princess wanted to become his wife. Then they served wine, the flute was played, and there was singing.... Then, at the command of the emperor, he gathered together horses and 14,000 warriors, built several warships, crossed the river and set out against the northern enemies. They chastened and captured the dissolute tyrant, and won victory. When he returned and reported this to the emperor, the emperor was very pleased and arranged the wedding for the same day. The

4. Hsia-min woman in simple
dress, Li-shui, Chêkiang, 1934.

5. Hsia-min woman in traditional headdress with
child in front of the ruins of a village temple,
Yün-ho, Chêkiang, 1934.

country was at rest, the empire secured, the people at peace, the animals flourishing. All the countries brought tribute year after year, and came year after year to be received in audience. Our ancestor, however, was granted the title of a son-in-law as an imperial favor, and received his seal as...king P'an-hu. He carried a golden shield and governed our country under imperial grace. He had three sons and a daughter and requested at that time... heaven and earth, if his sons and grandsons would rise up to heaven, then the sun and the moon.... And the heavens and earth really did turn around. Then he went with his three sons for an audience.... In the second year *chien-yüan,* in the twelfth month, on the eleventh day, the secretary in the Ministry of the Interior Chang Ling-ch'ung, the Tuan-hsüeh P'eng Kuang-yao, the professor Chü Chih and the censor Fan Chih, and other civil and military officials, entered a petition, whereupon the oldest son was granted the surname P'an and the first name Hsün-neng, and make Hu-wu-kuo count by authority of the emperor. The second son received the surname Lan, and the first name Kuang-hui, and he became the Hu-li-kuo count. The third son was called Lei Ch'en-yo and was Li-kuo count. Then one of the daughters had a husband from the family Chung, by the first name of Chih-shen, who became the Ti-jung count and was made a third-grade official. . . . They lived in Mt. K'ui-chi and were free of all taxes. . . .

Ta-sui, fifth year, fifth month, fifteenth day...
ninth year Chia-ch'ing, ninth month, fifth day.[8] Chung Yüeh-ch'i.
Written by Sun Tsao-liang and Sun Tso-k'un.
K'ai-t'ien-huang. — K'ai-ti-huang. — P'an-ku-huang.
T'ien-huang. — Ti-huang. — Jen-huang.[9]
The emperor Kao-hsin...
The empress Kao-hsin had a large ear-women,
who got earaches.
The doctors opened it with a knife and an animal came out.
They nourished it on a golden plate, and it became a dragon.
The emperor Kao-hsin issued a decree in the palace.
The emperor Kao-hsin sat in the palace, the dragon went to the
      enemies.
In the second year...
In the third year the dragon bit off the head of the enemy king.
The enemy king was drunk with wine, and the dragon went across the sea.
The dragon returned to the court.
...

The ministers gave the head to the king.
And emperor Kao-hsin was very happy.

He enfeoffed P'an, but he didn't want this and shook his head.
Then all the ministers said: Your majesty had a decree,
which promises the princess.
Then they had the dragon go under a bell tower
and let it be covered seven days by the bell so that it would be
     transformed.
Then it was supposed to marry the princess.
And get her two sisters in addition.
The dragon had been six days under the bell,
when the princess secretly opened up the bell and took a look.
By then only the body had changed, but not the head.
The dragon P'an was enfeoffed as king P'an-hu
and led the third princess home as his bride and was imperial son-in-law.
The emperor granted him his favor.

...

P'an-hu produced three sons and one daughter...
Emperor Kao-hsin enfeoffed the oldest son P'an, the second son Lan,
     the third son Lei
and a brother-in-law Chung...

****

II.

The genealogy given by Ho Tse-hsing[10] likewise does not describe the descent from a dog as clearly as our own chronicle.

Regarding the settlement of the Hsia-min in Chêkiang, a report in the Yün-ho gazetteer is of interest:

"The filiation of the Hsia-min is unknown. Some are of the opinion that they came from Kuangtung and the islands in the sea. Under the present dynasty, at the beginning of the K'ang-hsi period (1662), they moved into the county of Ch'u-chou. They build their huts in the mountains and engage in agriculture. In summer and winter they wear clothes made of hemp. The women wear a cloth headdress covered with pearls and jewels. Together with the men they carry burdens. Their language is peculiar. The local inhabitants don't intermarry with them, but they make use of their energies for plowing, weeding, and other work in the fields. In the eighth year Chia-ch'ing (1803) the governor Jüan Yüan and the commissar Wen Ning allowed them to take the examinations. Among the Hsia-min in Yün-ho there are now some who want to take the examinations, and some now have passed them."[11]

But in the chapter XV, 32a of the gazetteer it is stated that already during a flood in 1648 some Hsia-min drowned. Thus, they appear to have been in the Yün-ho district even earlier, yes, even prior to the date that Stübel gives for their initial settlement (1580) on the basis of the genealogical chronicles which he examined. The question of their initial settlement is actually made more complicated by references to the Hsia-min in sources from the Sung and Yüan periods to which Hsü I-t'ang refers.[12] According to these sources, Hsia-min were already settled in the area of Li-shui as well as in Fukien by the time of the Sung and Yüan periods (1276-1284 are given as dates). Perhaps even statements from the T'ang period which place the Hsia-min in Chêkiang can be applied to them. According to this, then, a tradition which I heard in Yün-ho is apparently correct. This tradition has it that the Hsia-min who live there now did not migrate to the area until the beginning of the Manchu period, just like the Chinese inhabitants of southern Chêkiang, after nearly the entire former population had been almost totally wiped out by this time as a result of wars. But according to this tradition the Hsia-min had already been living here even before these people. As a matter of fact, all the genealogical chronicles place the first arrival of the Hsia-min in Chêkiang only at the beginning of the Manchu period. But the present-day Chinese population, according to its genealogies, did not migrate here again from Fukien and Kiangsi until the Manchu period, and many even not until after the T'ai-p'ing revolt. Both groups thus appear to have resettled in the area for a second time simultaneously, and, according to the sources, we would have to place Hsia-min in the area by the thirteenth century at the latest. This results in certain difficulties regarding the explanation of the migrations of the Hsia-min.

One would have to assume that their emigration out of their previously determined homeland (according to Stübel) in Kuangtung went at a faster pace, and that they arrived at a very early date in Fukien and Chêkiang. But Stübel himself mentions the other possibility, namely that connections might well exist between the Hsia-min, who are undoubtedly a branch of the Yao, and one of the tribes mentioned in the ancient literature. Now it is really odd that, with about the fifth century A.D., the Yüeh people, who in antiquity had occupied great areas of Chêkiang, Fukien, Kuangtung, Kuanghsi, Kiangsi, and for a time even more northerly areas all the way to Shantung, almost disappear from the literature, and that in the following period entirely new names appear in place of them. The really heavy settlement of these areas by Chinese began especially during this period (ninth century A.D.).

For the Yüeh, Mt. K'ui-chi was always a particularly holy mountain, and in the course of their history the Yüeh had many close connections with this mountain. It plays such a role in our genealogy as in all the others. Mt.

K'ui-chi is located in Chêkiang, northeast of the limit of the present-day distribution of the Hsia-min. In order to make sense out of the migrations reported in the genealogies, Stübel is obliged to look for this mountain in Kuangtung province. He keeps another possibility open for himself, however, by pointing out that the genealogies draw their material from various sources. It appears likely to me that in the legend contained in the genealogical chronicle, we have an older legend which connected the Hsia-min with Mt. K'ui-chi in Chêkiang. This legend was closely related to the dog myths of southern peoples in the ancient literature, and merged with a later legend of the new diffusion of the Hsia-min. This would then mean that Chêkiang and Fukien were settled by ancestors of the Hsia-min even before the Chinese settlement. At that time these Hsia-min were probably not very different from the Yüeh. It would further imply that later on Hsia-min settled again in both provinces, proceeding out in various waves from Kuangtung after the decimation of the older population as a result of the wars during the Ming and early Manchu periods. This hypothesis would furnish a good explanation for the numerous divergent and special customs which can still be found today in southern Chêkiang, namely, bullfighting, tree temples, certain forms of folktales about the world conflagration and sibling marriage, and, perhaps, certain survivals of the phallic cult and the cult of female deities. The new Hsia-min settlers, who came in the migration period sketched by Stübel, thus added a new legend, namely the embroidered history of their new migration from south to north, and their confrontation with the Chinese, to the old tribal legend common to all Hsia-min and Yao. This old legend is mentioned in the ancient literature as a Yao legend. Our genealogical chronicle reports almost nothing about this. Like many other genealogies, it contains only the first part.

For the time being we still cannot furnish any conclusive evidence for the suggested possibility of a relationship between the Hsia-min and the Yüeh. The notion that the Hsia-min are direct descendants of the Yüeh is definitely excluded. The only real possibility I can see is a tribal relationship. As far as can be judged from the sources, their material culture was probably not very different from that of the Yüeh. Linguistically, however, one matter is very striking: the name of the Yüeh is actually Yü-Yüeh according to the ancient literature. And the name of Wu, a related tribe in Kiangsu, is actually Kou-Wu. The name of Ch'u in Hunan and Hupei is actually Ching-Ch'u. The name of the small state Su is actually Ku-Su. Such double names, which were later shortened, also appear among several old tribes in Shantung. And according to everything we know today, Shantung was partially inhabited by southern peoples, particularly in the coastal area. But the name of the Yao is really Mo-Yao. Thus the entire group of non-Chinese peoples in the south, including the Yao, belong to a group with double names of a similar structure. Since we know practically nothing about the ancient languages of the south, it remains impossible for the present to expand on this idea.[13]

PART TWO / *Essays on the Folklore of China*

12. POUNDING SONGS FROM PEKING*
collected by Ho Feng-ju

The Pekinese masons can be divided into three groups. The first group consists of the brick-pattern makers, who produce the brick rosettes and figures on the ridge of the roof. The second group is made up of the pounders, and the third group of the actual bricklayers. The pounders pound the foundations until they are solid. Some pound with a block of iron approximately thirty centimeters in diameter and six centimeters thick. Others work with a hand-pounder made of wood. Now, when these pounders are working, one man sings a song and the others join in at the end of each verse. These songs are paid for by the owners of the building under construction — the going rate at present is about ten cents a song — so that the workers will pound down the clay as long as possible in order to render the foundations more solid. Some of these songs are very lengthy, and have already appeared in print. These represent a sort of novel in song. Most of them, however, are quite short. They are rhymed according to the rhyming pattern of folksongs and folk dramas (*shih-san chê*). This type of rhyme differs sharply from that of poetry, since it is not the T'ang rhyme. There is no recognizable division into stanzas, and the length of the songs is not prescribed.

The songs which are sung in Peking can be divided into four categories: (1) songs which take their subject matter from novels and dramas, and tell a story; (2) songs which enumerate heroes of novels; (3) moralizing songs; (4) songs about the ten numbers. In respect to type, these songs can be classified as worksongs, but they have nothing in common with the usual type of worksongs especially well-known from southern China. They are more related to the novel and folk play. Thus, we find many parallels to them in the planting songs of Ting-hsien from Hopei province.[1] In other cities, the songs also appear to be quite different. Thus, in Hang-chou, I always heard the pounders singing songs which sounded more like the songs of Pekinese ballad-mongers, (i.e., they were improvised; made reference to passers-by in the street, to the employer, or a similar theme; and always had very humorous lyrics).

*Revised and translated version of "Pekinger Stampferlieder," *Zeitschrift für Ethnologie* LXVII (1936), 232-248.

I do not know of any publication of similar texts from other parts of China. A modern folk drama from Anhui province mentions that the soldiers who built the Great Wall of China sung a "Four Season Song" while pounding the wall,[2] and this song may be regarded as a genuine pounding song. The only other song which is similar in style is the Chê-tan-ko of Hsi Yung-jen,[3] but since its author is known, it can hardly be regarded as a folk poem. I have found no other references to this type of worksong in the literature.

Mr. Ho Feng-ju had the following songs sung to him by masons he knows on the east side of Peking. He wrote them down immediately, and what follows here is a translation of his manuscript.

Song 1: *The Praise of Kuan Yü.*

One mustn't despise the writing of K'ung-tse,
All must understand the ritual prescriptions of Chou-kung,
Master Ts'ang created writing, and all can use it,
But Master Kuan left behind integrity, humanity, rites,
prudence and trust, in order to give the people moral examples.
Humanity: that was the union of the three in the peach garden.
Integrity: that was his trip of 1000 miles to seek out the emperor.
Rites: that was his instruction given to Chang Fei in Ku-ch'eng.
Prudence: that was his killing of Hua Hsiung even before the wine was cold.
Trust: that was on the Hua-jung road, where he let Ts'ao Ts'ao get away
and Ts'ao Ts'ao was able to escape death under the sword of the blue dragon.
That is Kuan Yü's fulfilment of the five great duties of humanity, integrity, rites,
            prudence and trust.
through which he received the honorary title of the most faithful man in the world.

Notes to Song 1: The content of the song comes completely from the novel *San-kuo-chih,* and alludes to deeds of Kuan Yü described there. – Chou-kung supposedly lived in the twelfth century B.C.; he is believed to have written the *Book of Ceremonies (Li-chi).* – Ts'ang Chieh is a mythical figure. – Chang Fei is one of the oath-brothers of Kuan Yü who guarded a pass when Kuan Yü came to Liu Pei on his flight from Ts'ao Ts'ao. Chang Fei didn't want to let him through, because he still considered him to be a follower of Ts'ao Ts'ao, until Kuan Yü had killed the pursuer from Ts'ao's party, and had thus proven his honesty. – After the battle at the Red Cliff, all roads were occupied by followers of Liu Pei. Ts'ao Ts'ao fled on the Hua-jung road, which Kuan Yü was guarding. Kuan Yü let him pass through under his sword without striking him, as an expression of thanks for the decency with which Ts'ao Ts'ao had treated him earlier.

Song 2: *Warships Sail to I-chou.*

At the end of the Han era there were wars for over ten autumns,
When did the wars between the North and the South cease?
Six times they went to Chi-shan and bowed down unto prostration.
Nine times was war waged against China, but the plan did not succeed.
Until the second lord came and subjugated Sihch'uan again,
and only the Nanking empire of the Suns, called East Wu, was left,
and they stepped down and left the throne to the family Sih-ma, the "Great Chin."
Only the censor Wang Chüan stayed on in I-chou.
Then Wu-ti had the warships readied,
and let them sail against the city of I.
The warships stood in rows along the shore,
they wanted to destroy Wu quickly.
But the mighty name of the censor was Wang Chüan,
he had brave warriors in the capital of Shu.
He had the order to proceed east in ships painted with strange animals.
One saw only the sails reaching down from the heavens,
the city loomed lonely and abandoned.
The rudders flew with the waves, the banners towered above the straits.
The wind chased the ships, and the waves tried to outrace them.
They arranged the metal halberds,
the iron cables hidden in the river were no more.
One only saw the ships being destroyed in numerous attacks,
during the battle one heard the swans and cranes crying.
You still can see the ancient shore implacements.
A sound of autumn fills the reeds.

Notes to Song 2: The content of this song is also taken from the *San-kuo-chih,* this time from the last section of the novel. This is probably the best of all the songs.

Song 3: *The Praise of the Mulberry Tree*

The sun rises out of the eastern sea like a disk.
It shines on the house of our ruler, the emperor.
There the mother of the country, the empress, has born a crown prince
and all the officials receive rewards.
They are golden and silver flowers.
All the officials take the gold and silver flowers and wear them,
only Pao-kung takes a small mulberry branch
and puts it on the flaps of his official's cap.
When the empress saw this, she flared up in anger,
and said: "The brave Pao-kung, he's making fun of me."
Pao-kung knelt down, and crawled forward a little
and said respectfully: "Mother of the country!

hear my praise of the mulberry tree!
People eat the fruit of the mulberry, they are sweet as honey.
The silkworms eat the mulberry leaves and make silk.
When the silk comes into the skilled hands of a man,
then they weave crêpe and cloth in the winter, gauze in the summer.
The first is a dragon-and-phoenix robe for the empress,
and a dragon robe for the master of the 10,000 years.
From mulberry bark they make paper, needed by all men,
from its wood a bow for the general to shoot with."
When the emperor heard this, he was pleased
and called out to Pao-kung: "Listen!
I will give you an imperial sword,
and along with it a golden and silver, a copper and guillotine with designs of tigers,
          dragons and dogs.
With the dragon-head you will kill the minister and the imperial sons-in-law,
and with the one with the tiger-head kill the insuborbinate civil and military
          officials,
and with the one with the dog's head, the common people.
All within my palace are subject to you! "
Then Pao-kung fell to his knees, thanking him, and rose again quickly,
had Wan Ch'ao and Ma Han quickly bring the sedan-chairs.
I won't tell anymore about how Pao-kung went home to the *yamen*,
I'll stop and will continue the story after I've rested.

Notes to Song 3: Pao-kung is the Salomonic judge of China, also called
Pao Lung-t'u. His official name is Pao Ch'eng, and he lived 999-1062. His
deeds are described in the novel *Pao-kung-an (The Cases of Pao-kung),* and
are glorified in numerous dramatic plays.

Song 4: *The Eighteen Black Men.*

The tyrant had a black face from birth.
He serves Li Ta with a meal.
Now the famous general Wang Chien has the place of honor,
below as guests sit the brave Chang Fei,
Hu Yen-ch'ing and Hsüeh Kang have also all come.
Li Kang and Kao Wang are also present as guests.
Yang Ch'i-lang had asked Pao-kung.
The poor Chou Ts'ang becomes a robber,
and all three of them rob Chiao Tsan,
they steal from Cheng Tse-ming his helmet.
Ching Tê hears about the robbery,
Ch'ang Yü-ch'un pursues them eastward,
he pursues them as far as T'ang-shan east of the capital,
there he sees three men carrying coal,
he asks the three men their names,
and they say they are Hu Tai-hai and Wang Yen-chang
and, in addition, one called Yao Ch'i.

Notes to Song 4: Without any consideration of the chronology, this song groups together eighteen men, who, according to the traditional typing in the Chinese theater, are represented with a black face. They are initially thought of together at a banquet, then the scene shifts to the T'ang-shan near Peking, where coal pits are located. — I do not know of any other text in which eighteen people of this type are brought together. A standard series consist of eight black heroes. This series contains Hsiang Yü, Chang Fei, Chou Ts'ang, Yü-ch'ih Kung, Chung K'ui (not in the series of eighteen), Chao Yüan-t'an (likewise not in the series of eighteen), Cheng En (identical with Cheng Tse-ming), and Chiao Tsan (drama *Chien-tan chi,* seventeenth century). — The tyrant is Hsiang Yü, commander-in-chief at the beginning of the Han period. His battles are related in the drama *Ch'i Ying Pu* (fourteenth century), and in the later drama *Yü-lin fu.* — Li Ta is a figure from the novel *Shui-hu-chuan* from the Sung period. — Wang Chien is from the time of the Contending States, and is a hero in the drama *Ma-ling tao.* — Chang Fei is a confederate of Liu Pei and Kuan Yü, period of the Three Kingdoms, and is a hero in the novel *San-kuo-chih,* and in many plays based on this novel. — Hu Yen-ch'ing is from the T'ang period. — Hsüeh Kang was the stupid son of Hsüeh Ting-shan; he is the hero in the drama *Chü ting kuan hua.* — Li Kang was a general in the Sung period (see the drama *Ch'iu ju yuan*). — Kao Wang also lived in the Sung era, and lost his rank (*Kao Wang chin piao,* a modern drama). — Yang Ch'i-lang is from the Sung period, and is one of the main heroes in the novel *Yang-chia chiang,* and in many plays based on this novel. — Pao-kung is from the Sung period (see Song 3). — Chou Ts'ang is from the time of the Three Kingdoms, and is mentioned in the novel *San-kuo-chih,* and in many plays, such as *Shui-en ch'i-chün.* — Chiao Tsan is from the Sung period, and was a friend of the Yang brothers (see above the novel *Yang-chia chiang*). He and a number of the above-mentioned heroes occur together in a phantastic-religious play *Chien-tan chi.* — Cheng Tse-ming is from the beginning of the Sung period. He was one of the main helpers of the founder of the Sung dynasty, and was originally an oil-seller. A hero in plays such as the *Chien-tan chi, Chan huang p'ao*, and *Chang Cheng En.* — Ching Tê is from the T'ang period; his full name is Yü-ch'ih Ching-tê or Yü-ch'ih Kung. He is a hero in the drama *Chien-tan chi,* but also in many other plays, such as *San-to sho, Ch'i-lin ko,* and *T'ou T'ang chi.* He is now one of the door gods of China. — Ch'ang Yü-ch'un is from the Ming period. He became famous for his fight against the Mongols (see the dramas *T'ien-sui-ko* and *Yao ch'ang chi*). — Hu Tai-hai is likewise from the Ming period. — Wang Yen-chang is from the time of the Five Dynasties. — Yao Ch'i is from the later Han period, and is a hero in the plays *Shang t'ien-t'ai* and *Ta Wang Ying.*

Song 5: *The Eighteen Red Men*

Wu-sheng had a red face from birth;
Chao-pa became famous by pilfering grain;
Wu Han murdered his wife and joined Kuang-wu,
The general of Lung-hsiang was Kuan Hsing.
Yao Pin stole the red rabbit-horse.
Wei Yen had the bone of unreliablity in the back of his head.
Kuan So married a southern barbarian.
Chiang Wei went out nine times into the field against the Wei,
Chao T'ai-tsu struck, whenever he lost, and demanded when he won.
Ts'ao Pin again marched for the wine against the south,
Meng Liang helped general Yang.
Kuan Sheng led troops and conquered the Liang-shan moor.
Sun Hsing-tsu let his golden knife fly.
On the Cattle Head Mountain Kuan Ling had his revenge.
Ts'ao Liang-ch'en disturbed China several times.
K'ang Mou-ts'ai fought in a red robe.
The one-eared Ma Fang brought distress to the cities.
And also Kun T'ai, with the name of Hsiao-hsi, had a red face.

Notes to Song 5: This second of the enumerative songs no longer attempts to make any connection between the various figures, but rather just disconnectedly strings together eighteen persons who are represented on the stage with a red face. I know of only one other set of red-faced heroes, namely in the drama *Pao ch'uan chi,* written in the seventeenth century. This set contains only seven heroes, and only one of them, Kuan, the God of War, also occurs in the set of eighteen. – Wu-sheng is the God of War, Kuan. – Yü Chao-pa is unknown to me. – Wu Han lived at the beginning of the later Han period, and served the first emperor Kuang-wu. This event, which most likely comes from the novel *Tung-han yen-i,* is mentioned on a set of oracles found in temples of the deity T'ien-hou (oracle text No. 35). – Kuan Hsing is a son of Kuan Yü. – Yao Pao is from the time of the Three Kingdoms, and stole the horse of Kuan Yü. – Wei Yen is from the time of the Three Kingdoms. – Kuan So is a figure from the novel *Shui-hu-chuan* from the Sung period. – Chiang Wei is from the time of the Three Kingdoms; his story is related in the drama *T'ien-shui kuan.* – Chao K'uang-yin was the first emperor of the Sung dynasy, T'ai-tsu of the Sung. He liked to play, and struck down his opponent whenever he lost. Otherwise he demanded his winnings. – Ts'ao Pin was a general during the tenth century (see Doré, *Recherches,* IX, 510, and the drama *San hsing chao*). – Meng Liang was a general of the Sung era, and is a hero in the plays *Meng Liang tao ku* and *Hsiang lin chien.* – Kuang Sheng likewise. His exploits are related in the novel *Shui-hu-chuan* and the drama *San hu hsia-shan.* – The Liang-shan moor was the seat of the "robbers of Liang-shan moor," the heroes of the

novel *Shui-hu-chuan.* — Sun Hsing-tsu was a robber during the Ming
period. — Kuan Ling is from the Sung era (see Doré, *Recherches,* XVII 139,
154). — Ts'ao Liang-ch'en is from the Ming period. — K'ang Mou-ts'ai is from
the Ming period. — Ma Fang likewise from the Ming period. — Kun T'ai is
from the Ch'ien-lung period.

Song 6: *The Eighteen White Men*

A treacherous hero with a large white face was Chao Kao.
He made a terrible line of battle and brought distress to Ts'ao Ts'ao.
Wang Mang asked Tung Cho to watch it,
but on the way they saw the three Ma eating together from a manger.
Sih-ma I pretended to be rich and took Ts'ao Shuang's life,
Shih and Chao murdered Fang and Mao.
Wang Lang, who had not died from insults, came to watch the battle.
Emperor Yang-ti of the Sui arrived on a dragon ship,
and Yang Su, the king of Yüeh, trembled with fear.
Yü-wen Hua-chi again acquired troops.
The treacherous plans of Lu Ch'i went quickly.
They called Fan Jen-mei, whose art of war was not so great,
called Ou-yang Fang, whose teeth had been knocked out.
But it was also in vain that P'ang, the master, came.
In addition, they invited Ts'ai Ching and T'ung Kuan,
the two acted as if they were brave and watched the battle.
Then Ch'in K'ui took Li Liang by the hand,
and these two soft people defeated the army.

Notes to Song 6: White, ordinarily the color of mourning in China, or
the color of the dress of commoners in certain periods, indicates a
treacherous hero on the stage. I do not know any other set of eighteen
white-faced men. Our songs mixes heroes and periods, completely disregard-
ing historical fact. Thus, Chao Kao lived about four hundred years before
Ts'ao Ts'ao. Most of the heroes mentioned in this song are very well known
from popular novels and/or plays. — Chao Kao was a treacherous minister of
the emperor Shih-huang-ti of the Ch'in. — Ts'ao Ts'ao was commander-in-
chief and a hero during the time of the Three Kingdoms. — Wang Mang
overthrew the western Han dynasty, and founded his own dynasty. — Tung
Cho was a treacherous minister of the eastern Han period. — The three Ma
are Sih-ma I, Sih-ma Chao, and Sih-ma Shih, and lived at the close of the
Three Kingdoms. —Ts'ao P'i had a dream in which he saw three horses eating
from a manger. — Ts'ao Shuang is from the Chin period. — Sih-ma Shih and
Sih-ma Chao murdered Ts'ao Fang and Ts'ao Mao at the close of the time of
the Three Kingdoms. — Wang Lang was a minister of Ts'ao Ts'ao, and died
from cursing. — Yang-ti was the second emperor of the Sui dynasty. — Yang
Su lived in the Sui period; he was responsible for the selection of Yang-ti as

emperor instead of the correct successor, a crime for which he was punished by the deities *(T'ai-shang pao-fa t'u-shuo,* III, 50a). – Yü-wen Hua-chi lived in the time of the Six Kingdoms, about the same time as Yang Su, and fought for Yang-ti against the new dynasty (see dramas *Chin-yang kung* and *Ch'ih lung hsü*). – Lu Ch'i likewise. He is another rebel who is punished in hell for his crimes (dramas *T'an-hua chi* and *Yeh-kuang chu*). – Fan Jen-mei and Ou-yang Fang lived in the Sung period. – P'ang is unknown to me; his full name is not mentioned and therefore cannot be determined. – Ts'ai Ching and T'ung Kuan lived in the Sung period at the time of Wang An-shih. The actions and reforms plans of these men are mentioned in many plays, always in a completely negative way (dramas *Tang jen pei, Pai sui yüan,* and others – Ch'in K'ui and Li Liang likewise lived during the Sung era. Ch'in K'ui is the archetype of the traitor in popular Chinese thought. His actions are described in many plays, such as *Ju shih kuan, Hsiang nang chi,* and *Hu Ti pang Yen*). Ch'in K'ui murdered the general Yo Fei.

Song 7: *The Eighteen Blue Men*

The face color of men is not the same,
There are black, white, red, and yellow ones according to the five elements.
Now, the East belongs to *chia* and *i* and to wood.
Now listen, as I tell about those with a blue face:
There have been persons with a blue face and a red beard since antiquity.
At the meeting of Lin-t'ung there was Liu Chan-hsiung.
Mao Pen made a five-part line of battle.
Chou Ch'u made a big name for himself after he had removed the three evils.
Chi Tsun became a robber and saw Ma Wu.
Ch'eng Hsiao-chin caught Yü-ch'ih Kung three times.
Shan T'ung from the village of Erh-hsien became a robber on horseback.
Ko Su-wen caused unrest in Yüeh-hu-ch'eng.
In the Yu-kuan Pavilion Meng Chiao-hai was captured.
The one quarreling about the imperial coat was Chu Ch'üan-chung.
The one dwelling in the Two-Dragon Mountain was called Yang Chih.
Lo K'ai-tao cleaned up the city of Ku-yang with his stick.
The one saved by the eleventh youth is the blue-faced tiger.
Smoke of clouds in the wind has the name of Lei-ming.
The War Plague God is called Ku-ch'ing.
Yü Chin-piao aided Hung-wu in the collection of volunteers.
Yü Kao stole imperial things and became a rebel.
Tou Erh-tun had a big name in the *Lien-huan-t'ao*.

Notes to Song 7: I do not know of any other set of blue-faced heroes. – *Chia* and *i* are the first two characters of the series of ten which are associated with the East and the color blue. – Lin Chan-hsiung lived in the T'ang period; Lin-t'ung is a place with hot springs near Hsi-an-fu. – Mao Pen lived in the in the time of the Three Kingdoms. – Chou Ch'u in the Chin period was a good-for-nothing who improved himself later on by killing an evil dragon and a wild tiger. He improved himself so that he conquered the three evils of the area. His change is described in the drama *Shuang jui chi.* – Chi Tsun and Ma Wu in the eastern Han period. Ma Wu's story, from the *Tung-Han yen-i,* is told in the plays *Liu Hsiu tsou-kou* and *Ch'ün hsing fu.* – Ch'eng Hsiao-chin and Yü-ch'ih Kung at the beginning of the T'ang period, figures from the three large novels which tell about the beginning of the T'ang period, such as the *Sui-T'ang yen-i.* – Shan T'ung a robber of the T'ang period. – Ko Su-wen a robber in Korea, T'ang period. He is a hero in the drama *Hsüeh Jen-kui jung hui ku-li.* – Meng Chiao-hai lived in the T'ang period. – Chu Ch'üan-chung is the first ruler of the Hou-Liang dynasty; he murdered the last emperor of the T'ang dynasty, tenth century. – Yang Chih in the Sung period plays a role in the novel *Shui-hu-chuan.* – Lo K'ai-tao lived at the close of the Sung period. – The blue-faced tiger cannot be determined, since I am unfamiliar with the play. Cloud-smoke in the wind is a figure from the novel *Chi-kung huo-fo.* – Ku-ch'ing likewise. – Yü Chin-piao lived at the beginning of the Ming period and helped the first emperor Hung-wu. – Yü Kao was from the Ming period. – Tou Erh-tun, a robber during the Manchu period, whose exploits are the theme of the drama *Lien-huan-t'ao.*

Song 8: *The Eighteen Threes*

Three times I Yin was invited to protect T'ang of the Shang dynasty.
Three times Hun-wang of Ch'i was warned by the playing of the zither.
Yen P'ing-chung killed three warriors with two peaches.
Three times Pien Ho came to Chin-yang in order to offer the stone.
Three times Chang Liang, who could bear disgrace, learned the art.
Three times Yao Ch'i was asked to protect the king of Han.
Liu, Kuan and Chang, the threesome, made the pledge of brotherhood.
Three times T'ao Kung-tsu offered Hsü-chou to Liu.
Three times Hsü-chou was defeated, and the brothers were scattered.
In the three demands at Mt. T'un-t'u they showed conscientiousness.
Three times they went to the straw hut to ask Chu-ko Liang.
The triple division of the empire lay determined in his hand.
Three times the prince in the city of Ching-chou asked for advice.
Three times they went to Yen-shang-tao and got provisions.
Three passes were stolen during the day, and eight camps.
Three times Hsüeh Ting-shan caused the downfall of Han-chiang, fallen in
      punishment.
Three times Ch'en Yo-liang robbed Chin-ling.
Three times they looked to Kuang-t'ai-chuang to get heroes for the empire.

Notes to Song 8:   The song brings together eighteen events in which people did something three times. Once again, the various lines have no internal connection with one another. — I Yin was the minister of the first king of the Shang dynasty, T'ang period. — Hun-wang of Ch'i lived in the time of the Conflicting States. — Yen P'ing-chung, better known as Yen-tse, lived in the time of the Conflicting States. He distributed only two peaches to three heroes through his prince, so that the heroes who had received the present first committed suicide out of magnanimity, and then the third killed himself out of sympathy with the other two. — Pien Ho, in the time of the Conflicting States, found a jewel and offered it at the court. The first time the stone was declared to be a fake, and one of Pien Ho's legs was cut off. The second time ditto, and his second leg was hacked off. Only the third time was the genuineness of the stone recognized. — Chang Liang, in the earlier Han era, tied the shoe of an old man in the street. The old man later gave him the *Book of Huang-shih-kung,* a work on the art of war, which proved very useful to Chang Liang. There is now a monograph by W. Bauer on the Huang-shih-kung (in *Oriens Extremus,* III (1956), 137-152). The *Book of Huang-shih-kung* was first cited in an edict of the emperor Kuang-wu of the later Han period *(K'un-hsüeh chi-wen,* X, 21b). Huang-shih-kung had several temples in western China (Yünnan; see *Sou-shen-chi,* IV, 3a, and *Fa-yüan chu-lin,* LXII), and also in Yün-yang and Sihch'uan (see *Chien-hu chi,* VI, chap. II, 13b). Chang Liang's deeds are described in plays such as *Ch'ih-sung chi, Shuang ch'ui chi,* and others. — Yao Ch'i protected the first emperor of the later Han dynasty, and is described in plays such as *Shang t'ien-t'ai* and *Ta Wang Ying.* — Liu, Kuan and Chang are Liu Pei, Kuan Yü, and Chang Fei, the three main heroes of the novel *San-kuo-chih,* who drank to their blood brotherhood in the peach garden. — T'ao Kung-tsu offered Liu Pei the city of Hsü-chou several times (see *San-kuo chih*). — The scattering of the blood-brothers after the attack on Hsü-chou is also reported there. — Kuan Yü was encircled on Mt. T'un-t'u. He made three demands which ensured the safety of the relatives of his blood-brother Liu Pei, and only then did he surrender. — Chu-ko Liang, the most important advisor of Liu Pei, has to be asked three times to enter Liu's service. This event is the topic of one of the most popular temple paintings on the walls of Chinese temples in Taiwan today (note also chap. II, sec. 3 of this volume). He predicted the triple division of China by reading his palm. — The prince Liu Ch'i in Ching-chou asked Chu-ko Liang three times for advice to use against his wicked stepmother. The *San-kuo-chih* reports all these events. — Yen-shang-tao alludes to events which took place in the T'ang period. — The story about the passes alludes to events at the beginning of the T'ang period. These events are described in the popular novel about Hsüeh Ting-shan, the *Hsüeh Ting-shan cheng hsi.* — Ch'en Yo-liang lived in the Ming period. His actions are the topic of dramas such as *Hu fu chi* and *Hua Yün tai chien*. — Kuang-t'ai-chuang was a village in which Chao P'u lived, whom the first Sung emperor wanted to have as his helper. His story is the subject of the drama *Feng Yün hui*.

Song 9: *The Eighteen Small Men*

> Yen P'ing-chung was small by nature.
> Mao Sui, who stole the elixir of life, looked at Sun Pin.
> Chih Chün-chang also fought once in K'un-yang.
> The three-foot-high Chiang was wearing a red robe.
> Hou Chün-chi stole the Hu-lei panther three times.
> Tou I-hu became very famous because of the So-yang blockade.
> Feng Mao was very small from birth.
> And the height of Wu Ta-lang was also not great.
> The nickname of P'i Lung was "three-foot-high spirit-faced ghost."
> P'i Hu was the three-foot-high short-lived one.
> The "short-foot tiger" Wang Yin lived in the Sung period.
> The short-legged Taoist is called K'ung Kui.
> The "short T'ai-shan peak" Pao Lei was actually called by the name of Pao.
> The short Hsü Fang protected Hung-wu.
> He locked up Chao Kun so that he couldn't escape.
> Han Meng was one-legged from birth.
> And Sung Ch'ien-ts'ê was also only three feet high.

Notes to Song 9: Yen P'ing-chung, see Song 8. — Mao Sui lived in the time of the Contending States (see the drama *T'o nang ying*). — Chih Chün-chang fought against Wang Mang at the beginning of the later Han period. — Chiang lived during the Sung period. — Hou Chün-chi is unfamiliar to me. The problem here, as in other cases where identification was not possible, is that the heroes are often not mentioned by their official name, but rather by a special name or even a nickname. In other cases, the trouble is that the heroes are not historical personages at all, but rather figures in popular novels or in plays which I have not read. — Tou I-hu plays a role in the novel *Chi-kung huo-fo*. — Feng Mao appears in the novel *Chin-p'ing-mei*. — Wu Ta-lang is a hero in the shadow play *Wu-hua tung* (W. Grube, *Chinesische Schattenspiele*. Munich, 1915. p. 4). His name is very common in proverbial sayings, as the symbol of a slightly questionable character. — P'i Lung, P'i Hu, Wang Yin and K'ung Kui appear in the novel *San-hsia wu-i*. — Pao Lei lived in the Sung period. — Han Meng was a robber during the Ming period. — Sung Ch'ien-ts'ê is unknown to me.

Song 10: *The Eighteen Beautiful Men*

To the great generals with a beautiful appearance belong from ancient times Tse-tu.
And Chi Pu, who was once a slave.
Ts'en P'eng, who took the Chuang-yüan seal.
Chia Fu, who pushed back in his entrails three times, and whose entrails came out
     again three times.
Lü Wen-hou, who had an argument in the Feng-i pavilion.
Chao Tse-lung, who protected the young emperor on the Ch'ang-pan slope.
Sun Po-fu, who mightily defeated Yen Po-hu.
Ma Meng-ch'i, who with his Hsi-liang people made the Chiang and the Hu tremble.
Lo Ch'eng, who destroyed the line of battle in the form of a snake.
Wang Po-tang, who met an immoral woman on his campaign.
Hsüeh Jen-kui, who deceived the emperor and crossed the ocean.
Lo T'ung, who cleaned up the North and killed the princess.
Kao Sih-chi, with a white horse and a silver lance.
Kao Hsing-chou, who was the equal of eight warriors.
Yang Tsung-pao, who fought in the Mu-ho-chai.
Hua Jung, who astonished the people by shooting a wild duck.
Kao Ch'ung who overthrew the wagons and there found his death.
As well as the petty tyrant Kuo Ying, who was brave and clever.

Notes to Song 10: Tse-tu was a general at the time of the Contending
States. – Chi Pu, a general of the earlier Han period. – Ts'en P'eng, at the
beginning of the eastern Han period, passed the warrior's exam. – Chia Fu
was wounded in battle at the beginning of the eastern Han period. – Lü
Wen-hou, known as Lü Pu, fought for a woman in the pavilion of Tung Cho.
The story about the pavilion is in the play *Pai-men-lou.* This scene is
represented as a wall painting in the Ts'ih-sheng-kung Temple in Taipei,
Taiwan (seen March 30, 1964). – Chao Tse-lung protected the son of Liu Pei
at the time of the Three Kingdoms. His real name is Chao Yün. The story is
the topic of the drama *Ch'ang pan p'o.* This scene was represented as a set of
figures made of paper and wire, moveable by means of a hidden motor, and
decorated with lights as a New Year's decoration in the Lung-shan Temple in
Taipei (seen March 11, 1964). – Sun Po-fu is known as Sun Chien in the
state of Wu, time of the Three Kingdoms. – Ma Meng-ch'i is known as Ma
Ch'ao, a general in Shu, at the time of the Three Kingdoms. – Hsi-liang
refers to people living in the present-day province of Kansu. The fights
against Ts'ao Ts'ao and his defeat are described in the drama *Ch'ing Kang
hsiao.* – Lo Ch'eng lived in the T'ang period, mentioned in the drama *Nao
hua teng.* – Wang Po-tang married a woman already married once before. He
lived at the same time as Lo Ch'eng, and is a hero in the drama *Hung i
kuan.* – Hsüeh Jen-kui, in the T'ang period, brings the emperor by trickery
across the sea to Korea when the emperor is afraid of the waves. The
activities of Hsüeh Jen-kui are described in the popular novel *Hsüeh Jen-kui*

cheng tung. He is also the hero of many plays. The event mentioned here is in the folk play *Cheng tung chi.* – Lo T'ung is the son of Lo Ch'eng. – Kao Sih-chi and Kao Hsing-chou lived in the Sung period. – Yang Tsung-pao and Hua Jung lived in the Sung period. The former is one of the famous generals of the Yang family, late tenth century. His actions are related in the popular novel *Yang-chia chiang,* and in plays like *Pai-sui kua-shuai* and *P'o Hung chou.* His proverbial beauty is mentioned in a folk ballad from northwest China (see J. Trippner, "Das Lied von Ma Wu-ko," *Folklore Studies,* XVII (1951), 148. Hua Jung is a hero of the novel *Shui-hu chuan.* – Kao Ch'ung overturned iron wagons which were rolled toward his army, became exhausted, and was killed by the last wagon – Kao Ch'ung, in the Ming period. – Kuo Ying, in the Sung period.

Song 11: *Exhortations to do Good*

One shouldn't seek fame and advantage,
when will the struggle for fame and advantage finally cease?
For fame one labors over the study of the classics and reads thousands of books.
Merely to get a name and pass the state examination.
And for the sake of advantage one gives up house and profession, and wanders
    about evermore as a foreigner in strange places,
doesn't think that the mother is sad when the child is 1000 miles away.
That is fame and advantage.
And now about wine, women, riches and anger:
The drinker falls down drunk after three cups
and says that in drunkeness all cares vanish.
The lover of women finally dies of syphilis,
and says he can still enjoy himself as a ghost too.
The greedy man forgets everything for the sake of a cash coin,
and comes into conflict even with his brothers.
The angry man wants there to be no peace among men,
and in the end he wears a cangue with a lock and sits in jail.
That's what wine, women, money and anger are.
I'll pause now and then continue on with my story.

Notes to Song 11: The cangue is a wooden board worn around the neck as a punishment.

Song 12: *The Ten Connected Numbers*

One letter, a hand full of snow, the only maiden Mêng Chiang.
Mt. Erh-lang, the lord of Erh-lang. Ask the monkey-king twice.
The novel of the Three Kingdoms, three times ask Chao P'u, three times beat Yang
    Ling.
Four horses join up with the T'ang, four phoenixes greet the son, the four great
    vajras.

The Five-Tiger Mt., the five human duties, with a five-colored stick kill Yang-ti of
    the Sui.
Go forth six times from Mt. Ch'i, six countries enfeoff him as minister, the sixth
    son of the family Yang.
The seven-star terrace, the seven-star sword, seven times capture Meng Hu.
The eight great mallets, the eight great strange ones, the eight saints wish the
    queen-mother of the West happiness.
The Nine-Mile Mt., the Wang Ao with the nine mountains, the Niang-niang Temple
    on the Nine-Peak Mountain.
The ten great evils, the ambushes on ten sides, enfeoff ten kings in a single day.

Notes to Song 12: The text of this song is a concatenation of titles of
theater plays, or refers to events in plays. — *One Letter* is the drama *I-feng
shu,* seventeenth century. — *A Hand Full of Snow* is the drama *I p'eng
hsüeh,* seventeenth century. — Meng Chiang is a virtuous bride, whose tragic
fate is the subject of numerous popular books and dramas, such as *Meng
Chiang-nü hsün fu, Sih-liang ch'i,* and *Ch'ang ch'eng chi.* —Erh-lang is a
popular deity and hero in several novels. — The king of the monkeys refers
to Sun Wu-k'ung, the main hero in the popular novel *Hsi yu chi.* — *Novel of
the Three Kingdoms* is the *San-kuo chih (yen-i)* which has been mentioned
many times. — Chao P'u, late tenth century, was mentioned above. — Yang
Ling lived at the same time. — The sixth son of the family Yang is Yang
Liu-lang. — The eight saints, refer to the popular text *Pa-hsien ch'ing-shou,*
and so forth.

Song 13: *The Song of the Ten Numbers*

The *1* looks like a gun.
In the *2* the stroke on top is short, long on the bottom.
In the *3* the middle one is short, and the other two long,
and if you stand it up, it looks like the character 'river.'
In the *4*, all four corners are present, and the mouth is wide open.
The *5* looks like the character *ch'ou.*
The *6* has three dots, and a long diagonal stroke.
The *7* looks like a wing of a phoenix.
In the *8* one stroke goes this way, one that way, like Yin and Yang.
The *9* looks like the golden fishing rod with which Chiang T'ai-kung fished.
And in the *10* there is a diagonal stroke and a vertical stroke right in the center..
And if you add a stroke to the *10* on top, then it's a *1000:*
Chao Kuang-yin led the Chin-niang for 1000 miles.
If one leaves off a hook from the *9*, and adds an arch, then it's a 'strength.'
The man with great inexhaustible strength was king Hsiang of Ch'u.
If one adds a half-stroke to the *8*, then it's a 'human being.'
Among those who are human, Sung Chiang from Mt. Liang is the greatest.
If one adds a 'white' to the *7* on top, then it turns 'black.'
The third sister-in-law Tien divided the household and defeated the 'black king.'

If one adds a half-stroke to the *6* on top, it is 'great.'
The great king in the seventh heaven is the king of the monkeys.
If one adds a standing man to the *5* in front, it is still a 'wu.'
Wu Tse-hsü whipped king P'ing of Ch'u.
If one adds a stroke to the *4* on top, it becomes a 'west.'
In the west room Ying Ying asked Chang Lang
If one adds to the *3* a vertical stroke, a stroke which doesn't face toward the
    outside, then it's a 'king.'
Wang Hsiang lied down on the ice and caught fish, and in this way taught his
    mother.
If one adds a vertical stroke to the *2*, then it becomes the character 'earth.'
Among the two earth-workers, there was one called Ting-lang.
If one adds a hook to the *1*, it becomes the character *ting*.
Ting Hsiang cut off some of her flesh in order to honor her mother-in-law.

Notes to Song 13: The song first describes the shape of the numerical characters, and then it forms new characters by modifications of the numbers, and tells about these new characters. – *ch'ou* is the second character in the twelve-cycle. – Yin and Yang are the two principles of nature. – Chiang T'ai-kung was fishing at the river when the ruler of the Chou dynasty appointed him to be his advisor. This scene occurs as a painting on the walls of many Taiwanese temples, and allusions to it are made in at least four oracle slips which I have seen (Lung-shan oracle, No. 13; T'ien-hou oracle, No. 15, 17, 22). – Chin-niang was loved by the first emperor of the Sung dynasty, Chao K'uang-yin, with whom he had no sexual relations, according to tradition (drama *Pai ts'ao p'o*). – King Hsiang was Hsiang Yü at the beginning of the Han period. – Sung Chiang plays a role in the novel *Shui-hu-chuan.* – The third sister-in-law is a figure from the collection of short novels *Chin-ku-ch'i-kuan.* – The "Black King" is the name for the God of the Hearth. – The king of the monkeys plays a role in the novel *Hsi-yo-chi.* – The character for *5* is read as 'wu,' the newly-formed character likewise as 'wu.' – Wu Tse-hsü was a minister at the time of the Contending States. – Ying Ying and Chang Lang are main figures in the operetta *Hsi-hsiang-chi.* – 'King' is read as 'wang,' and the name Wang Hsiang is also written with this character. He was one of the twenty-four models of childlike piety. – On Ting-lang, see below. – Ting Hsiang cut off some of her own flesh in order to heal her mother-in-law.

The notes to our songs have been kept as brief as possible. Our intention has been to give only enough information for the reader to arrive at an approximate understanding, in so far as that is feasible, without relating the entire content of the novel or play alluded in the song. Some names could not be identified, and some are uncertain. Sometimes the transcriptions we give of the names are also questionable.

The astonishing thing about these songs is the immense knowledge they display of the novels, novelle, and dramatic literature. This fund of knowledge, which undoubtedly far surpasses what we might expect to encounter among our own masons in the West, can be accounted for by the popularity of the theater among the Chinese. All the personages, even those who often played no particular role at all, are quite familiar to every Chinese through the theater. His historical knowledge is therefore very large, even if it is not completely free from one-sidedness and distortions.

Now, where do these pounding songs come from? Among the masons in Peking there is the tradition that they were invented by Ting-lang, and this Ting-lang is considered to be the actual ancestor of the pounders. A particular pounding song tells only about Ting-lang. This song is contained in a novel entitled *Hsiao-T'ang ch'u chien chuan*.[4] This novel, a folk novel whose action takes place in the Ming period, relates the story of a holy man gifted with magic powers, who destroys the evil in the world and helps the distressed. In chapters XXXV through XLII, the story of Ting-lang is recounted, the most important section of which we would like to present in translation. First the story relates how a scholar by the name of Kao Chung-chü went to the capital with his wife to take the exam. There the vassal of a powerful courtier, Nien-ch'i, fell in love with his wife, implicated him in a murder, and had him brought to trial. Kao is spared from the death penalty by the intervention of a friend, but is forced to go into exile in Han-k'ou. He separates from his wife, who puts out one of her eyes as a token of eternal loyalty, and who gives him a half-mirror to take along as a sign of recognition. The last thing she tells him is that she is expecting a child, and he decides that the child should be named Ting-lang. Then he goes off into exile. He goes to Wu-ch'ang, and there he is taken in by a state secretary called Hu; Hu almost treats him like his own child. He also marries the daughter of Hu, and she presents him with a son.

Meanwhile, the former wife of Chung-chü gives birth to a child and raises it in secret. But later on at school the boy Ting-lang is scoffed at by his fellow pupils, and finds out about the story of his father. During the lantern festival he breaks into the house of Nien-ch'i, his father's enemy, and stabs Nien-ch'i several times. After a long while Nien-ch'i accidentally learns who the boy was, and he tries to have him murdered by hired killers. The boy is saved through the intervention of a holy man, and at the advice of this holy man he goes with him to Wu-ch'ang to look for his father and escape the danger in the capital. The saint tells him that there in Wu-ch'ang he should ask everybody he meets about his father, and the the 108th person he will ask will be his father. The following section (chapters XL-XLI, pp. 150.) is given now in translation:

After he had asked 107 people, the 108th man was a scholar dressed in fine clothes and followed by servants. He was probably a little over thirty, and looked just like the way his mother had described his father to him. So he no longer felt any shame, went right up to him, and said: "Please, just a moment, sir! Aren't you my father? " When Chung-chü was addressed in this fashion, he had to laugh, and replied: "Boy, but you're a stupid child! You've never even seen me, so how can you call me father? " Ting-lang said: "I only dared to do it because you look the way you do. But now I see that you're probably not my father." Chung-chü noticed that he was speaking the dialect of Peking, and that he was somewhat similar to Yü, his wife, in appearance. Then he felt emotions stirring in his heart, and he asked: "Boy, you seem to be from Peking. Tell me, what's your father's name, what is he, and where do you come from? Just tell me, and then I can ask around for you." Ting-lang was no longer afraid to tell him the whole story, since he was three thousand miles from Peking now. So he told him where he lived, that his father had been punished and condemned to military service, and how his father had escaped. Chung-chü found that everything coincided completely with his own situation, and he wanted to reveal his identity. But then he became afraid that Mr. Hu could hear about this through the servants, and that then he could be found guilty of bigamy.[5] For this reason he suppressed his good sentiments and thought: "Children and grandchildren have their own fate. Why should they stay so attached to their parents? I'll separate from him today. Maybe there'll be another opportunity again some time later on." And so he said to Ting-lang: "My child, I haven't been able to understand a single sentence of your story. Don't take up any more of my time. Just go someplace else and ask around some more." Ting-lang, his eyes full of tears, said: "I have to tell you one more thing: you see, a holy man guided me to this place and told me I should ask everyone I met, and that the 108th man I would meet would be my father. Now, I had already asked 107 and they all had said they weren't my father. Finally I asked you. So you must be my father. And that's the only reason I told you the whole story. How was I to expect that despite everything you still wouldn't admit the truth? " And then Ting-lang started to cry. Chung-chü too was no longer able to hold back his tears; his face became pale, then turned red, and secretly his eyes filled with tears. After a while, though, he pulled himself together again and said: "My child, I feel very sorry for you. Let me give you some advice: if someone asks you later on, don't tell him your whole story, so that you don't run into some wicked man and put your life in danger again." And then he went away. Ting-lang noticed that the man spoke Shantung dialect, and on top of this he had left him with a warning: then he really began to suspect that the man might be his father, and wanted to run after him again. But then he paused and thought: "After all, he doesn't want to recognize me, so there's really no point in chasing after him." So after a while he headed south out of the city.

But the Taoist Ch'eng-kuang, who had brought Ting-lang to the city, made himself invisible with his invisibility magic, and went to Shuang-yang street. Here he met the Taoist I-chih-mei,[6] and said to him: "I have carried out my task, and so I've come to see you. Now I'd like to go back to Peking again." With this he said good-bye and left. But I-chih-mei quickly took the magic letter which the holy man Hsiao-T'ang had given him, and opened it. It said that he should wait outside the south gate of Wu-ch'ang at the river for a child by the name of Ting-lang. The child is nine years old now and would be wearing a Taoist dress. When the child is about to jump into the water, the letter said, he should grab hold of him and give him something to eat, and then teach him the pounding song. As soon as Mr. Hu starts work on his buildings, he should join in and take along the boy Ting-lang. Ting-lang should sing the pounding song there in order to see his father again, the letter concluded. And the pounding song was written at the end of the letter.

When the holy man Miao (I-chih-mei's family name) had finished reading all this, he put the letter back in his pocket and went to the river. Ting-lang came crying out of the south gate. He was terribly hungry and didn't know what to do. So he went crying to the river, and he thought to himself and thought — his misery was great — and finally decided to put an end to his life. I-chih-mei had been waiting for him there, grabbed him quickly and said: "Ting-lang, you mustn't do that. I want to give you some good advice! " When Ting-lang heard someone calling out his first name, he turned around, saw the Taoist, and said: "Listen, monk, I want to put an end to my life. Why do you want to stop me? Hurry up and be on your way! " I-chih-mei said: "Whoever is dead will never come back to life again. Follow me and my words, and then things will be good for you." Ting-lang refused: "Don't you trick me again. There was one Taoist already who brought me here and told me I'd meet my father. I went to the city and searched for a long time, but found no trace of him. So he must have deceived me. Now maybe you want to trick me again too." I-chih-mei said: "There is something that you can't know about. This Taoist was my friend. But he was only supposed to bring you until here. If you want to see your father, then you're going to have to turn to me." Ting-lang replied: "So when can I see him? " "Within three days! " Then he took Ting-lang along to a restaurant, and after eating, they went to a Kuan-ti temple, and rented an empty room. Toward evening, after they had lit the lamp, I-chih-mei taught Ting-lang the pounding song. Now, Ting-lang was a very fast learner. He had scarcely finished reading it through three times, when he was able to sing the song so that it sounded wonderfully clear and pure. But we don't want to talk about that anymore.

Now we want to relate that Chung-chü had to think of Ting-lang at home in his study, and tears involuntarily came to his eyes when he thought of him. Now, at that very moment his wife Feng-ying came in through the door-curtain, and when she saw him she said to him: "Why is my husband so sad? Is there something troubling him? " Chung-chü declined: "I've spoiled my eyes these last few days by reading too much, and when I went out a while ago to visit some friends, the wind blew both my eyes full of sand, and that's why I have these tears." Feng-ying objected: ' "Lai-ying, your servant, just came and told me you had met a boy on the street who was looking for his father. He said that you spoke with him a long time, and that then you two started to cry. I can't figure out the reason for this." But Chung-chü was quick to answer: "Oh, that was a child from Shantung who was having a very difficult time of it here in a strange place. That moved me very much." The wife was just about to continue with her questioning, when the old court supervisor Hu Ting came in and said: "The master of the house would like to speak with you about when to begin building, and is waiting in the garden." Kao Chung-chü was angry, took leave of his wife, and went out into the garden. Then his wife had to withdraw to her chambers too. But we don't wish to talk about this. We do want to relate that when Chung-chü appeared in the garden, Hu said: "Didn't we decide to build a flower-hall in the garden? Now, the geomancer has calculated the day, so that we can start the work tomorrow. You can ask the manager Hu Ting to hire some masons, the kind who pound the earth." Chung-chü agreed, and went quickly to arrange everything. But he was afraid his wife would question him some more about why he had cried, and so he spent the night in the outer study.

Now, the earth-workers who did the pounding all lived outside the south gate. I-chih-mei disguised himself as a master pounder, when he heard about the job, and took over the building contract. To Ting-lang he said: "Work in the Hu house starts today. You have to come along, and when I have the men start pounding, then you should sing the pounding song. Then you'll meet your father." After this he took Ting-lang along, and went together with the workers to the Hu house. Ting-lang stood on a high wall and said to them: "Comrades! I'm going to sing you a pounding song in which I tell about something very sad. I'll sing, and you listen, and you can all try your very hardest together at pounding." All the workers agreed, and they prepared their pounders and waited for Ting-lang to start singing. Ting-lang beat the rhythm-board with his hand and sang in a loud voice:

On the fifteenth of January[7] is the lantern festival,
people kneel down and burn incense for heaven and earth.
My father is a scholar with a good education.
I, his child, am looking for him, and my name is Kao.

In February Tu Fu[8] goes walking in the spring weather,
an inch of light is an inch of gold.
Yüeh-ying from the family Yü is my mother,
through whose beauty the evil was evoked.

In March the whole garden blooms full of peaches,
the bees come in swarms.
She wanted to burn incense in the East Mountain Temple,
but Nien-ch'i saw her and concocted his plan.

In April people go out with baskets to pick mulberry leaves,
in order to raise the silkworms.
The wicked fellow had an evil heart,
he planned to kill my mother.

In May, at the Tuan-yang festival,[9] the landscape is new,
the dragon-boats race against each other on the rivers
He made a plan against my father,
pledged brotherhood with him, to get into his house.

In June are the dog days; how can one stand the heat?
The swallows fly in pairs among the rafters.
He flirted and my mother scolded him,
then he devised a murder plan at home.

On the seventh of July, people look for their fate in needlework,
weaver and shepherd boy join in wedlock.[10]
He had someone killed, and blamed it on my father,
he was unjustly condemned. How can this wrong be righted?

In August comes the mid-harvest festival[11] with beautiful weather,
the moon is round like a disk, but not yet our family.
My father had to go as a soldier to Hu-kuang,
my faithful mother put out one of her eyes.

On the ninth of September is the double-Yang festival,[12]
the asters are in bloom, and all is fragrant.
My mother gave birth to me, Ting-lang,
but even before I could take my revenge, trouble descended upon
          me.

In October Meng Chiang sends the clothes of winter,[13]
cries at the Great Wall, and her blood drips down.
I went looking for my father, and left my mother,
in Wu-ch'ang-fu I cried.

In November people count the cold nine-days,[14]
the water drop turns to ice, and makes us freeze.
Ting-lang is destined to suffer,
The father doesn't want to recognize his son.

In December the plum blossoms are like dust,
winter approaches its end, the sun returns, we think of home.
Ting-lang finally came a-pounding,
and sang this to voice his sorrow.

You people who can hear, listen,
be sad where it is sad.
If my father does not wish to recognize me,
then he'll kill his child, and his wife too.

Thus, Ting-lang sang, and all those who heard him cried. Chung-chü watched the pounders and heard this pounding song. Vehemently he thought to himself: "Just who taught this song to this person who has suffered so much injustice? And who brought him here? If my adopted father should hear of this, what on earth should I do then? I will force him to go away, and afterwards I'll figure out a plan." He was just about to utter this aloud, when a servant came up and said: "Say, boy! You over there, the one who just sang the pounding song! The lady of the house would like to speak with you." Chung-chü quickly interrupted her: "How can a boy who sings pounding songs here be allowed into the chambers of the lady? I'm afraid that won't do." The servant said: "Excuse me; madam heard the song, thought it was sad, and wishes to speak with him." Then I-chih-mei called out: "Comrade! Inside you can tell the whole truth! " So Ting-lang accepted and went with the servant into the room. Kao's wife Chang thought that Ting-lang was a good-looking boy, and said to him: "My child, you have recited such a terribly sad song. Is that an old song or a new story? " Ting-lang could see that this woman was elegant and very nice, and so he told her the whole truth, just as I-chih-mei had advised. After she had heard this, she felt very moved and said to Ting-lang: "You were not yet born when your father left the house. That's why it will be difficult for you to recognize each other when you meet. Do you perhaps have some object that might serve as a token of recognition? When Ting-lang was asked this, he drew a half-mirror from his pocket, and gave it to the woman: "This was once a whole mirror, but it was divided into two when my parents separated. Each of them has half of it as a token of remembrance. But I simply have no idea where the other half might be now." When his wife Chang saw the half-mirror, she remembered that she had often seen her husband secretly taking out a half-mirror and crying over it. She had never known why. Now she thought she should go and get this half-mirror out of the book-chest for once, and compare the two. She had the servant bring the chest, opened it herself, found the mirror, and saw that it matched the one of Ting-lang. It matched perfectly. Full of inner emotion, she reached out her hand to Ting-lang: "My child! When your father came here, he married me. That was nine years ago now." Filled with joy, Ting-lang ran up to her, knelt down and thanked her.

But then Chung-chü stormed into the room. He had been secretly listening outside in front of the door-curtain, and had heard everything. He knelt down when he saw that his wife Chang had recognized his son. Now, if you want to find out what he said, you'll have to read the next chapter.

Chapter XLI. We related that Chung-chü had knelt down. He said: "Have thanks, my wife, for having taken in the orphan. The reason I didn't want to recognize him was not that I was so cruel, but rather that I was afraid of father and you! That's why I didn't want to reveal my identity." Quickly his wife raised him up: "Be quiet, my husband, and don't worry, I'll take care of everything when my parents find out." Chung-chü thanked his wife, went to embrace Ting-lang, and cried. His wife Chang comforted both of them, and then had the boy take a bath. She gave him some of Hui-lang's clothes. You see, Chang had gotten a son by the name of Hui-lang in the mean time. He was two years younger than Ting-lang. He had the maid call Hui-lang, and introduced him to Ting-lang. Then she had the meal served, and they all ate together. Suddenly a servant came in and said: "The foreman wants to know from the master of the house whether the boy is staying with you or is supposed to go." Then Ting-lang interrupted and called out: "Thank the man for me, and tell him he was right." The servant promised to do this and left. But Chung-chü asked Ting-lang: "My child, what do you mean, he was right? " And Ting-lang told them how a Taoist had brought him there, and how another posing as foreman had taught him the song. Then Chung-chü ran outside to see him, but I-chih-mei had already gone...

The story of Ting-lang who searches for his father is also known to us from another source: as a folk play in Ting-hsien (Hopei province). The plot of the folk play runs as follows:

The twelve-year-old Ting-lang, while searching for his father, is brought by a holy man to Wu-ch'ang, where his father is located. When he sees Ting-lang at a festival, and Ting-lang speaks to him, he refuses to acknowledge his son, because he is afraid of his new father-in-law and wife. But Ting-lang becomes familiar with his father's new wife. She recognizes him, and identifies him by means of a broken mirror, right before the eyes of his father. After this his father acknowledges him as well.[15]

It is interesting to note that this folk play does not contain the pounding song. The entire passage in the novel gives the impression as if the song were something which had been slipped into the novel, and was not an absolutely integral part of the text. The novel is regarded by the editor to be a product of the Ming period, and thus probably dates back to the sixteenth century. The song it contains is therefore the oldest pounding song with which I am familiar up to now. It cannot be much older than this, since the type of rhyme it contains makes its appearance only with the Sung period. Consequently, it is impossible that this is a considerably older song which was later incorporated into the novel.

The song differs completely, however, from the present type of pounding songs encountered in Peking. This is hardly astonishing, since it is clear from the one line which mentions the dragon-boat festival, that this must be a song from central China, due to the fact that the dragon-boat festival was not celebrated in the north. Even nowadays the central Chinese pounding songs differ from the Pekingese songs. The fact that this song is also sung today in Peking is irrelevant here.

The song belongs to the type of so-called "twelve-month-songs" which are widespread in China today. This type of song can be divided into various sub-types:

(a) The monthly festivals: The songs describe the festivals celebrated in various months. Due to the peculiarity of the Chinese yearly festivals, the eleventh and twelfth month are often excluded, or the song is sung altered in some way or other for these months. Thus, a play song of children in Peking only goes up to the tenth month;[16] there is a song going up to the 12th month, which simultaneously describes the amusements in Peking.[17] A song which likewise goes through twelve months is sung by the candy-sellers in Chi-ning (Shantung province).[18] There is a song only going up through the tenth month, which is sung during a New Year's game called "dry ship" in K'ai-feng-fu.[19]

(b) The "twelve-hour-songs:" Apparently the twelve-month-songs have more or less supplanted the twelve-hour-songs. I am familiar with only one example of a twelve-hour-song from modern folklore.[20] During the Sung period, to be sure, Ou-yang Hsiu (1007-1072) did write a twelve-month-song in the folk style,[21] But the twelve-hour-songs appear to have been more popular at that time,[22] and they are attributed to important poets.[23] We have the impression that these songs were originally of Buddhistic character,[24] and as such were already known in China before the T'ang period.[25] Similar in type to the twelve-hour-songs are the songs about the five parts of night.[26]

(c) The yearly flowers: These songs describe the flowers which bloom in the various months. In rare cases, these songs likewise go only up through the tenth month, like the song from Huai-an,[27] but usually cover all twelve months, like the song from Chin-hua in Chêkiang.[28] This type, mixed with that of the monthly festivals, also appears among the non-Chinese Yao in Kuangsi.[29]

(d) Altered type: Here we group together those twelve-month-songs which like the previous sub-types a and c, begin each stanza with the various months, but then continue on in a different fashion. The sub-type of the monthly festivals frequently undergoes this kind of modification. The most simple song of this group with which I am familiar is from Wu-hsing.[30] A humorous song from eastern Chêkiang describes the deeds of an itchy man.[31] Another from K'ai-feng-fu describes the sufferings of a prisoner over a period of twelve months.[32] A third treats the deeds of a shepherd, and comes from T'ai-yüan-fu.[33] A fourth song recounts the sufferings of Meng Chiang in connection with the tale of Meng Chiang. This tale is also alluded to in our song by Ting-lang.[34]

(e) Other "series-songs:" There seems to be an almost endless number of songs which enumerate sequences of events. Thus, the song about the ten months of pregnancy is very famous.[35] I have a copy of this song in a folk print from Taiwan,[36] to which another song describing youth and development up to the eighteenth year of life has been added. Another print of the same publisher (1958) sings about the "Twenty steps on which I am accompanying my sister."[37]

These twelve-month-songs are thus distributed throughout all of China. The various sub-types can also be found spread throughout China. Now, Ku Chieh-kang attempted to demonstrate in his study of the song about Meng Chiang, that the song was reworked from a twelve-month-festival song into a song about Meng Chiang at some later date. The same thing can be established for all the songs belonging to our sub-type *d* by means of a comparison of the various songs. The song of Ting-lang belongs to the altered type of twelve-month-songs *(d)*, and not to the type of twelve-hour-songs which we considered to be the oldest category. Added to the description of the festivals of the twelve months is the description of the sufferings of Ting-lang. It is simply a twelve-month-song which describes the sufferings of Ting-lang. It is impossible to find an original connection with pounding. I therefore prefer to think that a central Chinese folksong about the sufferings of Ting-lang only later became a song of the pounders. I believe this all the more strongly due to the fact that the style of the song is much more comparable to the style of the other twelve-month-songs than to that of the modern pounding songs. In my view, the song in question still dates back to the Ming period, but is probably scarcely much older than the novel in which it appears today.

The modern pounding songs are all uniform in style. But differences can also be found among them too. Thus, I consider the song about the "Eighteen Black Men" to be the oldest of the series of songs about eighteen things. A similar song appears as a Pekingese folksong, but it only contains ten persons, and is also somewhat different in style, although it has about the same content.[38] Mr. Ho also considered the song to be the oldest one, and regarded the others then as imitations or continuations. The number eighteen probably represents an attempt to link up with an older series containing eighteen members, in particular to the series of the eighteen Lo-hans in the temple.

In Chi-ning (Shantung province) we find a song similar to that of the "Ten Connected Numbers," but which is continued through number fourteen. This thus presupposes a certain age for this song too.

Tradition in Peking places the origin of almost all popular amusements and folksongs, such as the songs of the ballad-mongers, the *Shu-lai-po*, and many other phenomena, back in the Ming period. Thus, the pounding songs are supposed to have been invented by Ting-lang precisely in the Ming period.

However, I believe to have demonstrated that the song of Ting-lang initially had nothing to do with the actual pounding songs, and furthermore, that it represents a later development out of a particular type of folksong. The other pounding songs still sung today do not allow for any analysis of age, other than the general statement that a portion of the songs cannot be all too recent. Nevertheless, the novel again proves that pounding songs were already in existence during the Ming period, since otherwise the author would not have been able to have Ting-lang sing a pounding song. Now, it is impossible to decide whether the songs actually sung by the pounders at that time were, in fact, all still simple folksongs, and only later changed into a particular type, or whether we are dealing here with a special form found only in our novel, and that already in those days the pounders were singing songs which were similar to the type of pounding songs sung today. To determine this it would also be necessary to collect pounding songs from other parts of China, and to compare them more exactly with the songs from Peking.[39]

13. NOTES ON CHINESE PROVERBS*

A. *Notes on the Structure of Pekinese Proverbs*

During my stay in Peking (1934-35), I received a collection of 1119 proverbs made by Mr. Ho Feng-ju, and a collection of 34 proverbs made by Dr. Hellmut Wilhelm. I subsequently published these 1153 proverbs together with a brief introduction in 1941,[1] pointing out that existing collections at that time disregarded the place where the proverb had been collected, in the tacit assumption that proverbs were the same all over China. Today we know that this is not the case. Some proverbs are, indeed, known and used throughout China; many, however, have a limited geographical distribution.[2] For this reason, specific, local collections of proverbs have a certain value for folkloristic studies, even if many of the proverbs they contain are well-known.

To judge from my collection, the great majority of Pekinese proverbs are in rhythmic prose. Only about ten per cent of them are specifically rhymed, while the others may show other characteristics of rhythmic prose, such as rhyming of the first word of two lines, repetition of the first word of the first line in the second line, or repetition of a part of the first line in the second line. Many proverbs in this collection have the form of a *tui-tse*. In this typically Chinese form of composition, each word in the first line is related to the corresponding word in the second line grammatically as well as in content.

The proverbs can be divided into two classes:

> (*a*) Proverbs which consists of only one sentence or part of a sentence.
>
> (*b*) Proverbs which consist of two parts and can therefore be rhymed.

These classes may be further subdivided into the following types:

Class *a*:	Ho[3] %	Chu[3] %
1. Proverbs of four words (structure normally two + two)	8.0	8.3
2. Proverbs of five words (structure usually three + two)	10.0	8.0

*Based on the introduction to "Pekinger Sprichwörter," *Baessler-Archiv,* XXIV (1941), 1-43.

3. Proverbs of six words (structure normally three + three)	1.5	8.0
4. Proverbs of seven words (structure usually four + three)	24.0	8.0
5. Proverbs of eight words (structure usually four + four)	1.0	8.0
6. Proverbs of nine words	0.8	8.0
7. Proverbs of ten words	0.7	5.3
8. Proverbs of eleven words	0.3	—
9. Proverbs of twelve words	0.2	—

Class b:

1. Proverbs with three + three words	7.0	12.8
2. Proverbs with four + four words	19.0	8.0
3. Proverbs with five + five words	15.0	8.0
4. Proverbs with six + six words	2.0	8.0
5. Proverbs with seven + seven words	7.0	8.0
6. Proverbs with eight + eight words	0.4	—
7. Proverbs with ten + ten words	0.1	—

There are also proverbs with an irregular structure. Proverbs consisting of three lines (five + five + five) or even four lines (seven + seven + seven + seven) and similar ones are extremely rare. Of other irregular forms, only the two-line proverbs with four + five words (thirteen proverbs) and five + four words (seven proverbs) are more common.

Such a classification is not always simple. The difference, for instance, between sub-types a–3 and b–1, or between a–5 and b–2, is not clear in all cases. Our collection also contains proverbs which have word-couples (i.e., a word with full sound and meaning which is coupled with another word having no independent meaning and pronounced more as an addition to the main word than as an independent word). Such "fillers" are not regarded by Chinese as real words, and are, for this reason, not counted structurally. Thus, there are proverbs which are written with eight and even nine words, but which have sound values of only seven words.

In general, however, we can state that more than half of our proverbs consist of two parts or two lines, and the form consisting of four + four words (b–2) is the most common type. If a proverb consists of only one line, then the seven-word form is most common. Only about ten per cent of our proverbs have a final rhyme like that found in Chinese classical poetry. The rhyme system is that of Pekinese folk poetry, i.e., it is much simpler than the classical rhyme scheme, and is not based on historical pronunciation, but rather rhymes according to the present pronunciation. Only the proverbs in class b can, of course, be rhymed. Of these, b–1 has 17 per cent in rhyme, b–2 has likewise 17 per cent, b–3 20 per cent, b–4 15 per cent and subtype b–5 30 per cent. The remaining proverbs of type b are normally in the *tui-tse* form. Generally speaking, the most common forms of the Pekinese proverb are the subtypes five + five and seven + seven, if we regard the single lines of five and seven words as a part of a verse of two or more lines. These two forms are also the most common ones in contemporary folk poetry. However, the relative importance of the form four + four is of interest. This form likewise occurs in folk poetry, but was the dominant poetic form in the earliest period of Chinese poetry.

It is still impossible for us to decide yet whether our statistical data on Pekinese proverbs can be generalized, even as far as Pekinese proverbs are concerned. I compared the collection mentioned above with that of Chu Chieh-fan, the only other attempt at quantification in this field. Chu's statistics are based on some 376 proverbs coming from all parts of China. He seems to have more long proverbs (those consisting of more than eight words) than we do. I gained the same impression after examining his very recent publications of other portions of his very large collection.[4] Only a few of his proverbs come from Peking. This may account for the differences between our percentages and his. But it is equally possible that Mr. Ho Feng-ju had a personal preference for shorter proverbs and collected more of these. Such a personal bias is quite possible, since Ho's collection, as well as Chu's much larger collection, show evidence of some other biases. Both, for example, have completely left out erotic proverbs. We know that these are quite numerous. The prudishness of Chinese scholars may be the main reason for this omission.

Ho and Chu have also both omitted law proverbs. Very little attention has been paid to such juridical proverbs, despite the fact that Edwin Loeb and others have stressed their importance in societies which have no formal law codes. Chu has a few remarks on law proverbs, but uses as his sole source the same written collection which has been translated by Edward J.M. Kroker.[5] He seems to have no law proverbs from oral tradition. Chinese law proverbs are extremely interesting, due to the fact that although China had developed a codified, written law beginning about the sixth century B.C., the law codes, up until recent times, covered mainly criminal law. Students have often wondered why the Chinese never developed a full-fledged civil law code, although the ordinances of many emperors often dealt with matters of civil law. In practice, cases of civil law, such as the renting or mortgaging of land, houses, or other property, were decided by the judge on the basis of law proverbs. This was because such cases were considered not sufficiently serious to warrant official codification (i.e., not serious enough so as to endanger the state or the moral order).

A third possible bias is that both collections contain very few agricultural proverbs and proverbs dealing with the weather. Ho's collection is definitely "urban." Chu's informants were frequently soldiers or schoolboys, yet even he does not have as many agricultural and weather proverbs as one might expect on the basis of our personal knowledge.

This analysis of the structure of Pekinese proverbs can, therefore, be regarded as a first step, and as a hint that further research may establish regional differences not only in the text, but also in the structure of Chinese proverbs.

B. *Some Notes on the Use of Proverbs in Chinese Novels**

The Chinese language appears to be richer in proverbs than any other languages, judging from existing collections.[1] Two of the reasons for this wealth may be the concise style of the classical literary language which preferred short statements of a limited number of words (four, five, or seven are most common), and the predilection for statements structured in two parallel sentences. Thus, many sentences in the Chinese classics have a form that is very close to that of common proverbs, and, in fact, many quotations from the classical books can be used as if they were proverbs. Therefore, it is often not easy to determine whether a "common saying" is a quotation or a proverb, or if it is a proverb quoted by a writer of early times. This is, of course, a problem which also has occupied students of European proverbs, but research on proverbs in Europe already has a long history, while research on the history and the origins of Chinese proverbs has only just begun. Thus, for instance, until quite recently the existence of "juridical proverbs" in China was unknown. Now we know[2] that many laws which in our classification would fall into the realm of civil law, and which are not mentioned in the law codes, were orally preserved in the form of juridical proverbs and served as the basis for decisions of the judges.

But while we know that the earliest classical literature already contains numerous proverbs, many of which are still in use today, no systematic study of the development and spread of specific kinds of proverbs has been made. We do not even know whether certain proverbs are used only in specific parts of China and not all over China, though it seems safe to say that at least variants of one and the same proverb have limited regional distributions. Furthermore, we have no studies at all concerning the function of proverbs in China: we do not know in what situations they were used, by whom (social class? sex? age?), and for which purposes. Some of these questions can perhaps be answered by a study of the use of proverbs in colloquial literature (i.e., in novels and dramas). The following lines, based mainly on a reading of three novels — one of the seventeenth, one of the eighteenth, and one of the twentieth century —, may serve as an indication

*Reprinted from *Proverbium,* IX (1967), 201-209.

of the possible results of this kind of approach. The material is, of course, far too limited to allow definite conclusions but it may indicate some tendencies.

1. *Distribution of proverbs*: As far as I can see, all classical Chinese novels contain proverbs, but also modern novels which continue Chinese traditions and do not copy Western novels are rich in proverbs. The famous *Water Margin (Shui-hu chuan)*[3] has roughly one proverb in each 3,500 words; the 1929 novel *Wen Jou-hsiang*[4] still has approximately one proverb per 4,000 words.

Proverbs seem, however, not to be distributed evenly in the novels. In the *Shui-hu chuan*, chaps. XXI-XXXV contain more than twice as many proverbs as other chapters. Chapter XXIV alone has 23 proverbs, 15 per cent of the total of 154 proverbs found in the novel. In this novel, the last quarter has the smallest number of proverbs. On the other hand, in the novel *The Scholars (Ju-lin wai-shih)*[5] the third quarter has almost no proverbs while the first quarter has almost half of all (21 out of 44) proverbs. The modern novel has too few proverbs (11) to exhibit any pattern of distribution.

2. *Introductory phrases:* Fewer than half of the proverbs found in the three novels are introduced without any special introductory sentence. Our earliest novel, the *Shui-hu chuan,* has not only the greatest number of proverbs without introduction (49 per cent as against 30 per cent and 18 per cent in the later novels), but it uses only five basic phrases to introduce a proverb. Of these, the phrase "Since old (times it is) said" is the most popular one in all three novels (17 per cent *Shui-hu;* 23 per cent *Ju-lin;* 27 per cent *Wen*). Next common is in the *Shui-hu chuan* "This is just ..." (15 per cent). This expression does not occur in the other two novels. The *Ju-lin wai-shih* has the phonetically close form "This is truly ...", but only twice. Next in frequency we find the expression "A standard saying says" (12 per cent) which is changed in the *Ju-lin* to either "A standard saying says so well", to "An old saying says so well", or to "A proverb says so well". This last expression occurs also in the *Wen Jou-hsiang* once while, on two other occasions, the *Wen Jou-hsiang* just says "A proverb says". Comparatively rare in the *Shui-hu* are phrases like: "The people of old (times) said". "The people of old (times) had a saying", or "The holy men said". These expressions do not occur in the later novels. The closest form in the *Ju-lin* is "People say" or "Former men have said". *Shui-hu* and *Ju-lin* both used only once the phrase "How come you have not heard? ".

The preliminary impression is that the more recent novels show a greater variety of introductory phrases, and a need to indicate that what they are going to say is a proverb and not a phrase of their own coinage.[6]

3. *Context of use: Shui-hu* and *Ju-lin* both prefer to use proverbs in those parts of the novel in which the heroes themselves speak (84 per cent

and 91 per cent), while the modern novel uses the proverb mainly when the author describes a situation (63 per cent), and not in direct speech. In the *Shui-hu,* proverbs are not uncommon in descriptions of the thoughts of heroes, a usage which I did not find in the other two novels.

4. *Function of proverb in the novels:* For the purpose of analysis, let us first discuss those proverbs which occur in the regular prose text: As far as we can see from our novels, a proverb is most often used to summarize a situation or to allow the writer to describe a situation in the briefest and most concise form. The second function of the proverb in these parts of the text is to describe briefly typical behavior or a typical character trait of the hero. Occasionally, the proverb serves the author as a way of evaluating a situation or an action. Finally, the author attempts to explain that the hero's decisions are influenced by a proverb which he then quotes.

The proverb has a much wider range of functions in those parts of the novels in which conversations are given, including the sections in which a monologue of the hero is reported. We can divide the functions, on the basis of the persons involved, into three types: (a) The proverb is applied in relation to the partner with whom the speaker is in conversation, (b) it is applied by the speaker to himself, (c) it is applied by the speaker when discussing with the partner a third person or persons.

The most common way of using a proverb in the first type of application is to propose to the partner a certain way of action or behavior (in twenty-five places in the *Shui-hu* and in nine places in the *Ju-lin,* none in the *Wen*). By doing so, the speaker proposes a standardized action or behavior form and, implicitly, advises against an individual attitude to the problem facing the partner. Often this advice takes the negative form, when the speaker quotes a proverb in order to warn the partner against unwise actions or behavior, or – rarely – to prove to the partner that he, the partner, already acted in a wrong way. In the modern novel the speaker twice uses a proverb in order to prove his own point and to induce the partner to act as he, the speaker, wants him to act.

Another use of the proverb is to simply describe to the partner the situation in which he, the partner, is, or to explain the general situation to him. In a few cases the proverb is used by the speaker to generalize about a situation or to draw general conclusions from a situation. As we saw, this function of the proverb seems to be more typical for the author than for his figures whom he lets speak. In the *Shui-hu chuan* – but in none of the other two novels – the speaker quite often (twenty times) uses a proverb in order to criticize, curse, or denigrate his partner. The *Shui-hu chuan* also often lets the hero use a proverb in order to flatter the partner, a kind of use which also occurs in the *Ju-lin*, however not often.

The second type of use of proverbs most often takes the form that the speaker justifies his own ways of behavior or action by referring to a proverb (thirteen times in *Shui-hu,* five times in *Ju-lin*). This function of the proverb is very similar to the speaker's quoting a proverb in a silent monologue to himself: here the proverb tells him how to act or to behave. In the modern novel only one case of the second type occurs: the speaker quotes a proverb in order to justify his adherence to a superstition. This could perhaps be compared with the use of a proverb by the speaker in order to reject a criticism uttered by another person or by a partner (one case in the *Ju-lin*). Finally, some speakers quote proverbs in order to characterize themselves or to make a statement about their person toward the partner.

The third type of use of proverbs in our novels is similar to the use of proverbs in the general text: the speaker quotes a proverb in order to describe briefly and clearly the behavior of a third person, or to explain the behavior of a third person to the partner. Similar to this function is the quoting of a proverb in order to simply describe the situation of a third person.

Two more particularities in the function of proverbs may be noted: in none of the novels under discussion is a juridical or a weather proverb quoted, even though numerous juridical scenes are described and at least a number of descriptions of the weather are found. Secondly, the main body of the *Shui-hu chuan* consists of actions of male heroes, females not playing a prominent role. However, the chapter in which the action deals with male/female interactions (chap. XXIV) is richest in proverbs. Here, clearly, the proverb has the function of avoiding that the conversation between the sexes could become too personal or too intimate. By conducting the whole discussion in the form of proverbs, each partner can show his wit and mental abilities, can express criticism or praise without producing embarassment, because all that the proverb expresses overtly is standardized and expected behavior or action, standardized wisdom. Yet, when used at the right moment, they can function as rigorously as a personal remark. As women in Chinese society are regarded as persons of lower rank, we could hypothesize saying that proverbs in general are more often used in conversations between persons of different social status. This hypothesis is not easily testable because, although classes and class status are well established in traditional China and known to everybody, a novel like the *Shui-hu chuan* describes numerous situations in which these ordinary classifications do not operate, for instance, a woman is of lower status than a man, but the wife of the head of a group of bandits is assigned a higher status than a man when she talks to one of the subordinates of her husband. In general, however, I have the impression that proverbs of the type *a* are more often used in conversations in which there is a clear status differential between the discussants.

5. *Form of proverbs:* As mentioned above, Chinese proverbs are normally in the form of the classical literary language, or close to it. The *Ju-lin wai-shih* presents a clear exception to this rule, as it has a fairly high number of "irregular" proverbs (i.e., proverbs in colloquial language). We can conveniently divide the proverbs into (a) those consisting of one line, and (b) those consisting of two (and, very rarely, of two times two or three) lines. For comparison, I will add the distributions as found in a collection of 1,161 proverbs collected by Mr. Ho Feng-ju in Peking around 1934:[7]

	%Shui-hu	%Ju-lin	%Collection Ho
One line, 4 words	7	11	8
5 words	7	9	10
6 words	10	2	1.5
7 words	6	9	24
Two lines, 3:3 words	6	—	7
4:4 words	38	16	19
5:5 words	9	16	15
6.6 words	3	2	2
7:7 words	9	7	7
Other and irregular forms	5	28	7

The two main irregularities which the *Shui-hu chuan* seems to show are its preference for proverbs consisting of six words (normally 2:4 words), but in this category one single proverb is six times repeated: and in its preference for proverbs consisting of two four-word lines. Here the percentage is slightly raised because proverbs with three and four lines of four words are included (without them it is 34 per cent). The collection of Mr. Ho shows an unusually great number of seven-word proverbs. Such irregularities cannot, at this moment, be explained satisfactorily. I have the impression that proverbs which occur in the main text of a novel are more often the longer forms while those which occur in talks are more often the shorter forms. In general, the most favorite types of proverbs in novels as well as in colloquial use seem to be the two-line proverbs with four words and the one-line proverbs with seven words (which are structured as 4:3 word sequences).

Conclusion: This brief note seems to indicate that the study of proverbs in Chinese popular literature shows some promise. Although the formal differences between literary and colloquial proverbs are not great and probably reflect personal tastes of writers, this question should be further studied to see whether there are long-term historical trends. Secondly, there seems to be a trend to decrease the use of proverbs in recent times and to introduce proverbs in a colloquial form rather than in the standard, more classical form. There also seems to be a tendency, in recent times, to attempt a greater variety in the introductory phrases and more often to use an introductory phrase than in earlier works. Thirdly, the novels indicate clearly the three different functions which proverbs fulfill in conversations between people. It will now be much easier to attempt to find out whether proverbs used in everyday talk still have the same functions or whether the functions of the proverb in China have changed.[8]

14. CHINESE FOLK LITERATURE IN CHINESE FOLK TEMPLES*

Unfortunately, the study of Chinese temples and the representations they contain has been neglected. We have approximately ten descriptions of temples which could be considered more or less complete. But these are always temples of a special character, usually the kind that are of particular artistic value, or are especially old. Still extant folk temples were not studied, because they were regarded as uninteresting and artistically worthless. Today it is hardly possible for us to make up for lost time in this area of research, since in contemporary China most of these temples have been destroyed, and the remaining ones, as far as we can ascertain, have been transformed. Research today must be limited to the examination of temples in Taiwan, Hong Kong, in Chinese communities in Southeast Asia, and in California. This cannot result in a complete picture, since the temples in these areas, as we are well aware, have a particular form which deviates from that found in other parts of Mainland China.

One can examine a multitude of problems in connection with Chinese temples. How is a temple and the cult practiced in it financed? How much capital and investments does a temple possess? Which deities and groups of deities are worshipped in the temple? What kind of people feel themselves as belonging to a specific temple? What differences exist between temples located within settlements and those outside settlements (i.e., in the mountains)? The question to which I have addressed myself is this: what meaning do the representations on the walls, beams and altars of contemporary Chinese folk temples have? [1] By "folk temple" here I mean a temple in which deities are worshipped which are generally, although not quite correctly, called "Taoistic" deities.

I am concerned with three hypotheses in connection with this question: (1) About forty years ago Alfred Conrady gave a new interpretation of the poem *T'ien-wen (Questions to Heaven)* attributed to the poet Ch'ü Yüan.[2]

*Revised and translated version of "Chinesische Volksliteratur in chinesischen Volkstempeln," a paper originally read at the Congress of the International Society for Folk-Narrative Research, Athens, Greece (September, 1964), and published in *IV. International Congress for Folk-Narrative Research, Lectures and Reports,*ed. Georgios Megas (Athens, 1965), 100-105.

He maintained that the poet had wandered through a temple, had looked at the paintings on the walls and had described their content in the form of questions. This explanation has never been completely accepted, principally because we have no information as to whether such temples even existed at the time of the poet in the third century B.C., and, if so, whether these temples contained any paintings. (2) Some ten years ago, A. Bulling interpreted the reliefs which are found in graves of wealthy people from the Han period (mainly the first to second century A.D.), and which portray very vivid and often phantastic scenes, as representations of scenes from the theater.[3] This interpretation has likewise never found complete acceptance, largely because we have no information as to whether there was already such a well-developed theater in existence at that time. (3) The purpose of representations in a temple is to communicate certain values to the visitor. They are also supposed to satisfy him aesthetically, or at least stimulate him. Where does the painter get his motifs?

In an attempt to shed light on these questions, I visited a large number of temples in Taiwan (*illustrations 7,8,and 9*) and in the New Territories (Hong Kong) in 1967 and 1968, and gathered information on more than one thousand paintings. This research revealed the following points: (1) Not only folk temples, but also Buddhist temples, and even the Great Confucius Temple in Taipei are decorated with paintings of the same type. Buddhist temples, however, limit themselves to fewer pictures. Some are without pictures entirely, and have only abstract or non-abstract symbolic representations. (2) The wealthier a temple is, the more pictures it contains. Some temples had only four, others up to one hundred pictures. (3) Most of the temples show several types of representations. On the beams which support the ceilings and gates, one can usually find brightly-colored paintings. The walls often have the same paintings, but frequently they will also be covered with half-reliefs carved out of stone or concrete, or even engravings. On the roof one generally sees fully plastic scenes in the round made from plaster and colored glass. In all cases, the representations are of similar character and content, and the only differences are stylistic ones.[4] (4) Only in a few instances could paintings be found which were thirty years old. Most of them were just a few years old. The paintings do not last long due to the effects of the incense and the weather. Stone carvings and reliefs were often considerably older. (5) The various paintings or reliefs were contributed by different citizens, but are usually the product of the same artist.

On the basis of content, these representations can be divided into the following groups: (a) Representations of a purely symbolic character, such as the swastika, maeanders, and flowers of the four seasons. (b) Various persons with companions. There are only a few pictures of this type. These portray famous scholars of the ancient period. (c) Pictures from the series of the "twenty-four examples of filial piety." (d) Mass scenes.

The last two categories are of interest to us here. The twenty-four examples are a very well-known folk text which is quite frequently printed in folk calendars. These consist of twenty-four stories about children who demonstrated their love for their parents through unusual, sacrificial deeds. We can already find several of the "examples" on the above-mentioned grave reliefs from the Han period (and the hall graves at that time did have the character of a grave temple), but we still do not come across one of the several twenty-four story sets as they are found in the contemporary chapbooks of today. And similarly, only a few of the present-day temples have the entire series. They prefer certain pictures, to an extent the same ones as the Han reliefs. By far the most popular is Shun, who is plowing with an elephant when the emperor Yao invites him to become minister. Then there is Lao Lai-tse, who at the age of over sixty plays like a baby on the ground in order to give his much older parents the illusion that they are still young. And then there is the daughter-in-law who lets her baby go hungry in order that she might feed her mother-in-law, who otherwise couldn't eat anything, with her own milk!

But by far the majority of the representations belong to the fourth group. Now, these mass scenes are based on Chinese folk novels. Representations from the novel *History of the Three Kingdoms (San-kuo chih yen-i)* are by far the most popular *(illustration 8)*. Here we find that it is those scenes which are most dramatic which have been selected from this very voluminous novel. For example, the way the main hero Liu Pei goes three times together with his companions to Chu-ko Liang, who lives in solitude, in order to ask him to become his advisor. Twice Chu-ko Liang refuses to see him, in order to test Liu Pei's sincerity. Or the scene in which the antagonist Ts'ao Ts'ao surrounds the heroes at a moment when they are nearly without troops, and the heroes station themselves on the city wall at the advice of Chu-ko Liang and start up a drinking party. Ts'ao Ts'ao then concludes that the city must be full of soldiers, since otherwise the leaders could not remain so calm.

The second most frequent sort of representations are from the mythological novel *Feng-shen Yen-i (The Enfeoffment with the Dignity of the Gods)*. Next in popularity comes the novel *Hsi-yo-chi (The Trip to the West)*. Other folk novels are *Sui-T'ang yen-i (History of the Sui and T'ang Dynasties)*, *Yang-chia chiang (Generals of the Family Yang)*, *Tung-Han yen-i (History of the Eastern Han)*, and *Yo Fei chuan (History of the General Yo Fei)*. Representations from the novel *Shui-hu-chuan (Brothers of Liang-shan Moor)* and the operetta *Hsi-hsiang-chi (The West Room)* are very rare. I did not find any scenes from the novel *Hung-lou-meng* or other literary novels in the temples.

Now the interesting thing about all this is that (1) No temple specializes in just *one* novel and gives the entire series of pictures. One always finds

6. Scene from the novel *Hsi-yo chi:* The monkey Sun Wu-k'ung attacks heaven. Temple is in Taipei, 1964.

7. Scene from the novel *Pai-shê chuan:* Madame White Snake and her servant attack the Chin-shan temple. Painting is exhibited during the *chiao* ceremony in Chung-li, Taiwan, November, 1967.

8. Scene from the novel *San-kuo chih yen-i:* The "plan of the empty city." Illustration is on an incinerator belonging to a temple in Kuan-tu, Taiwan, 1964.

9. Scene from the folktale, "The Shepherd and the Weaving Girl": the couple is reunited each year on the seventh day of the seventh month. Painting was exhibited on one of the sacrificial buildings for the *chiao* ceremony in Chung-li, Taiwan. The style clearly shows the influence of modern motion pictures. November, 1967.

representations from various different novels. Frequently, however, a certain parallelism is preserved, and representations from the same novel will appear at the exact same spot on the right and left sides of the temple. If Conrady's hypothesis were correct, you would expect to find entire complete series. (2) The scenes selected are always ones which appear in dramatic works. There are many more than a hundred dramas which treat themes taken from the novel *San-kuo-chih.* We now know that some of the dramas are older than the versions of the novel popular today. Early versions of the novel appear to go back to still older single stories of public story-tellers, and the early dramas appear to be based on these stories too. In the historical novels the story-teller apparently drew his main motifs from the official historical works, but in many cases he appears either to have added free inventions or to have used other oral sources. Thus, the temple painter made use of novels, but he stuck to those scenes which were also familiar from the theater. From interviews I conducted with painters it became clear that contemporary painters work partially on the basis of oral tradition, and in part on the basis of stimuli provided by illustrated editions of novels. (3) The persons depicted are dressed in the manner familiar from the theater, and in the way they are also represented in the illustrated novels. One recognizes the main heroes from the theater costumes, physical details (such as skin color and hair), or from the symbols they carry. The organization of the picture and the representation of the secondary figures or the surrounding landscape is left completely up to the discretion of the artist. In this he works according to his taste and the amount of space available.

Together with the folk novels and folk theater, the temple representations thus form a unit which can probably be traced back historically to the narratives of the story-tellers. This conclusion could be used as support for the hypothesis of A. Bulling.

The representations have basically nothing to do with the deities worshipped in the temple. Deities are sometimes represented (in accordance with the novels *Feng-shen yen-i, Hsi-yo-chi* and *Pai-shê-chuan* [*illustration 7*]), but even in such cases the deities represented have no relation to the gods worshipped in the temple. The ethical values which the pictures attempt to transmit are quite clearly not religious values, but rather patriotic ones, such as loyalty to the military leader, loyalty to the ruler, selfless service to the ruler, and the punishment of those who revolt against the ruler or the gods. Second in line of importance, we find social values, such as filial love, devoted loyalty of women, and chastity, as well as service to the parents-in-law. Warlike scenes glorifying heroic deeds are in the vast majority. Hero worship and patriotism are major motifs in temples whose deities preach submission and withdrawal from the world. These clearly represent values of the Chinese lower classes, and are also historically demonstrable in the literature from about the tenth century on. But traces of the same attitude also appear in the literature of the upper classes beginning about the same time. The most popular folk novels and folk dramas are likewise heroic-patriotic, while the upper classes preferred the essay and poem to the novel and drama.

15. ORACLE AND THEATER IN CHINA*

The Chinese theater was always one of Eduard H. von Tscharner's main areas of interest. He enjoyed it as an aesthetic spectacle, but at the same time also recognized its great importance as a source of entertainment and education for broad masses of the people. The following brief study will attempt to show the extent to which the Chinese theater has influenced another sector of Chinese life.

In most Chinese temples you can find a bamboo box containing a large number of small bamboo rods. Each of these oracle-rods has a number. Whoever wants an oracle, shakes the box after saying a prayer until a rod falls out. Depending on the number of the rod, the inquirer takes a slip of paper from a stand. This slip (*illustration 10*), on which an oracle text is printed, usually measures seventeen by six centimeters, but is sometimes only seventeen by three centimeters. Normally one finds a poem in the form of a quatrain with seven words per line written on the slip, and sometimes there is a second poem which is called an "explanation." The main poem is composed in a rather flowery language and, for this reason, has many possible meanings. The so-called "explanation." which may be written in prose, gives the inquirer information about pertinent details phrased in a much more simple language. Generally the "explanation" consists of direct information, such as: "wealth: can gradually be acquired," "trips: favorable," "rain: comes at the end of the month," etc. Some oracles contain a general evaluation, such as "very favorable" or "average," but others do not. Some supply astrological information, and many bear the name of the person who paid for the printing of various slips of paper or of the whole series. Every slip of paper has either a number or cyclic signs corresponding to numbers, and most of the slips have the name of the temple in which they can be found written at the top.

There are various series of this type of oracle. The most important one consists of one hundred oracles and is usually associated with the god Kuan-ti (*Kuan-sheng ti-chün ch'ien*). This series is very common today in

*Revised and translated version of "Orakel und Theater in China," *Asiatische Studien* XVIII-XIX (1965), 11-18; this is a special memorial number for Eduard Horst von Tscharner (1901-1962), the noted Swiss Sinologist.

東和禪寺

臺北市上海路一段

觀音菩薩靈感籤

第十五首　上中

朱買臣求官

若是求謀多稱意　行人立至順風船

貴人接引友周全　爭訟年豐卻勝前

信士

張杜笑
張三桃　敬刊

解

功名：枯樹開花
婚姻：良緣月圓
運途：甘蔗之甜

家宅：有財有丁
失物：遲見不全
求安：不變即安

解

出行：吐氣楊眉
買賣：出入有利

貴人：煉鐵成鋼
年冬：秋收實際

10. Oracle slip from the Tung-ho ch'an-szu in Taipei, 1964. The text in the top right box refers to an event in the Han dynasty, the topic of a famous theater play.

Taiwan.[1] I also found it, however, on the Hua-shan in Shensi,[2] where it was known as the oracle of the god Chen-wu (*Chen-wu tsu-shih ch'ien*). In any case, the texts of this series were already in existence by the seventeenth century, since text No. 73 is cited twice in the literature of that period,[3] once with the additional note that this oracle comes from a temple of Kuan-ti in Kiangsu. According to another report, the city-god temple of Shanghai also had the Kuan-ti oracles in 1853,[4] but no text is given. I am convinced that many oracle texts have been cited in the literature, but up to now they have not received any attention, so that we do not know very much about the true age of the texts. For the Kuan-ti oracle on the Hua-shan, as in most cases, a supplementary book containing more information than was on the slip, was also used. This book, a manuscript, is consulted by the temple priest to supply the inquirer with details or furnish explanations, whenever the slip alone is not sufficiently understandable. The book mentioned above had a commentary attributed to the poet Su Tung-p'o (1036-1101). If this authorship were authentic, which is extremely doubtful in my opinion, then the texts would already have to have been in existence by the eleventh century. As a matter of fact, tradition ascribes this oracle to the temple of Chang Ya-tse in Sihch'uan, thus to Su's native area, and claims that it first appeared in the tenth century.[5]

Along with this series of one hundred oracles, there is another one widespread in Taiwan.[6] Up to now I have been unable to find this series mentioned in the earlier texts. Apart from these two series of oracles which are especially common nowadays in Taiwan, there are many others in existence. The Kuan-yin oracles (*Kuan-yin p'u-sa ch'ien*) are very popular,[7] and even appear in Japan[8] and California.[9] A series of fifty oracles of Wu-tang-shan has been found in California,[10] and I am also familiar with a series of Hua-kuang ta-ti Kuanghsi,[11] a series of Sheng-tsung ku-fo in Taiwan,[12] as well as at least four other series which had no name.[13] Since it is usually difficult to obtain complete series of these oracles, it is often impossible to establish just how large the series are, but 24, 28, 50, 60, 100 and 120 appear to be normal series lengths. Mathematically speaking, the consultant of an oracle does not have the same chances everywhere. In the above-mentioned Kuan-ti oracle, twenty-five oracles are very favorable, twenty-five are very unfavorable, and fifty are average.

Now what we find particularly interesting about these oracles are the sentences of five, seven, or occasionally even more or fewer words, which appear in the various oracles. They read, for example, "Chang Kang buried a wheel," or "Hsüeh Ting-shan asks the Fan Li-hua three times," or "Chuang-tse smashes the coffin." Since most of those who consult an oracle are simple people with little education, it is necessary to assume that these sayings, which often seem so difficult for us to understand, offer them few

11. Village theater built in the middle of a street
in Li-shui, Chêkiang, 1934.

or no difficulties whatsoever. If one examines these sayings, one finds that
most of them refer to historical events. These events, to be sure, are
frequently ones not recorded in the standard works, but rather in other
books which are much less known. A number of sayings, however, clearly
refer to non-historical events. The majority of all sayings are undoubtedly
allusions to historical as well as non-historical events, as these are treated in
the drama, and we can clearly establish that some of these sayings are the
titles of plays. The dramas are often ones which once enjoyed or still enjoy
great popularity, and we can be certain that most of those who consult an
oracle have themselves either seen, heard, or read about these plays. It
proved possible, by means of a comparison of approximately 750 dramas
from all historical periods, to find the corresponding plays for many of the
sayings. In a number of sayings, only the historical or literary reference
could be found, but not the drama itself. Yet I am convinced that the
matching dramas will also be found for the remaining sayings.

As the examples given above indicate, a single saying does not express
very much, and in itself is not enough to help the consultant of the oracle.
By means of the saying, the consultant must be reminded of the entire story
of the play in order to be able to divine his own future chances on the basis
of this knowledge. Let me give several examples. We will take a few of the
unfavorable oracles from the series of one hundred:

No. 4. "Chang Han remembers the perch." Chang Han, who lived at the time of the Chin dynasty, thought during the autumn of the fruit and fish back home, and decided to give up the civil service and return home (*Biographical Dictionary*, p. 971b). The consultant of the oracle is told by the saying that he should give up his position and his ambitions for fame and honor. The saying which accompanies the oracle expresses the same idea. The matching drama has not yet been found.

No. 6. "Hsiang-ju turns to Chao with the entire ring." The matching drama is called *Complete Ring* (*Wan-pi*) and was written during the Ming period. The state of Chao at the time of the Contending States had a famous jade ring which the king of Ch'in wanted to have. He was willing to give fifteen cities to Chao in exchange for it. The ruler of Chao was afraid that he would be cheated by Ch'in, and sent the ring together with Lin Hsiang-ju to Ch'in. Ch'in, in fact, wanted to take the ring without giving the cities in return. Under great danger, Lin succeeded in escaping back to Chao with the ring. During this time Lin's wife had to suffer very much and was nearly raped. The consultant is thus told here about dangers of all kinds lurking for him and his wife.

No. 10. "Meng Chiao passes the examination at fifty." Thus very late in life. Meng was a friend of the scholar Han Yü (768-825) (*Biographical Dictionary*, p. 553d). The oracle indicates that success will not occur until very late. No matching drama has yet been found.

No. 11. "Sun Pin meets P'ang Chüan." Refers to the drama *P'ang Chüan Flees at Night on the Ma-ling Road* (*P'ang Chüan yeh tso Ma-ling tao*) which takes place in the period of the Contending States. Sun and P'ang were students together. P'ang, out of envy, cuts off Sun's legs so that he can't serve as general. But Sun nevertheless succeeded in defeating P'ang when P'ang was serving another ruler, and P'ang was forced to flee in a disgraceful manner. The allusion is that plans may be successful at first, but later will lead to a bad end.

No. 14. "The exchange between Chang Erh and Ch'en Yü," who were close friends at the beginning of the Han period, but later broke up. Chang finally murdered Ch'en (*Biographical Dictionary,* p. 932a). No matching drama has been found yet. The text warns that even close friends can turn against a person.

No. 16. "The lily bush of the family T'ien is blooming again." Refers to a family in which the brothers wanted to split up their inheritance. Then the bush in the garden withered. It didn't bloom again until the brothers, warned by this miracle, decided to continue to live together as a single family. The story is described in *Hsü Ch'i-hsieh,* and no matching drama has yet been found. One shouldn't do anything thoughtlessly and without considering the family.

No. 17. "Yü and Jui quarrel about the free fields." This refers to two small feudal states at the beginning of the Chou period. The two were restored to harmony by the magic virtue of the duke of Chou. No drama text has been found. The text is already mentioned in the *Book of Songs* (*Shih-ching,* Ta-ya), and was cited frequently later on. A warning about selfishness.

No. 21. "Hsü Chia harms Fan Chü." This refers to the drama *The Vituperation of Fan Shu (Sui Fan Shu).* At the time of the Chou dynasty both men were sent as hostages to a neighboring state. Hsü observed Fan Shu (or Chü) and thought that he was collaborating with the enemy, and Hsü denounced him after their return. Fan was stripped of his honors and nearly beaten to death. Later on he took revenge and caused Hsü to suffer just as much. The oracle warns about revenge and slander.

No. 35. "Wang Chao-chün makes peace with the barbarians." Refers to the drama *Autumn in the Han Palace (Han-kung ch'iu).* During the Han period, as a result of an intrigue, the harem girl Wang was sent to the khan of the Hsiung-nu, since he had threatened otherwise to go to war with China. She went on her mission, but afterwards she committed suicide out of patriotism, in order not to have to live with a foreigner. The oracle warns that things may look good at first, but can later lead to catastrophe as a result of intrigue.

No. 38. "Kuan P'an-p'an and his swallow tower." This refers to the drama *Kuan P'an-p'an.* Kuan was the sweetheart of a high official and the poet Po Chü-i (772-846) fell in love with her. He wrote poems for her, but didn't obtain her. After the death of her lover, Kuan lived alone in a house, the "swallow tower," without ever having won Po. The oracle warns about separation and solitude.

No. 56. "Chang Kang buries the wheel." This comes from the drama *The Pavilion of the Buried Wheel (Mai lun t'ing).* At the close of the second millennium B.C. Chang discovered the crimes of a son of a powerful minister, and wrote them on a wheel which he then buried. The minister proceeded to slander Chang and tried to murder him and his whole family.

12.Marionette theater built on a harvested rice field in a village near Li-shui, Chêkiang. On the front posts there are bundles of harvested rice to indicate that the performance was held to thank the earth god for the harvest, 1934.

13. Marionette of the marionette village theater, Li-shui, Chêkiang, 1934.

This could only be prevented through the help of the gods and grateful friends. The oracle warns that even a good man can be in danger of life when he wants to bring foul deeds to light.

These eleven examples, all taken from the series of one hundred sayings, are, I trust, sufficient to show how these oracular sayings are worded, where they are derived from, and what they express for the reader who knows the story behind the sayings. The series of sixty sayings is perhaps even more typical than the one just treated, since it contains more non-historical figures which exist only in dramas – and probably, not infrequently, only in local dramas – than does the larger series. It is not possible to decide whether these sayings belonged to the texts from the very beginning, or whether they were only added at a later date. On some later-printed slips of the series of one hundred, the sayings have simply been omitted. Although we were not able to identify all the sayings, and although our series of one hundred oracles is not complete, a clear difference between the two series nevertheless emerges, as can be seen from *Table 2* below: The series of sixty takes its examples more frequently from more recent periods than does the longer series. Although both series do not refer to events which took place in the last four hundred years, and only very rarely to events within the past seven hundred years, the series of sixty stresses the period between 600-1200 A.D., while the one hundred series puts more emphasis on the years between 1000 B.C. and 600 A.D. In accordance with this, the dramas which the short series refers to are the more popular ones. Those referred to by the longer series are plays which are put on less often nowadays because they are of greater age. Neither of the two series contains references from classical literature, and both also avoid the manner of expression characteristic of classical works.

More than fifty dramas have been identified to date. We trust this proves that a knowledge of numerous dramas on the part of the common people must be presupposed, and that a commoner should know the plays so well that he is able to draw conclusions about himself on the basis of their content. This means that the plays are regarded as a guide for correct or false conduct, and that the values expressed in them are known or accepted.

Table I
Number of the identified texts in the series of 100
sayings and in the 60-saying series

	longer series	shorter series
Number of texts	100	60
Missing texts	10	0
Texts without a saying	3	0
Not yet identified	4	17
Identified	83	43

Table II
The historical periods in which the actions mentioned
in the saying are supposed to have occurred

Dynasty	Number of sayings (longer series)	%	Number of sayings (shorter series)	%
Shang	2	2.4	0	0
Chou	17	20.5	5	11.6
Ch'in	1	1.2	2	4.7
Han	18	21.7	0	0
Hou-Han	8	9.6	2	4.7
San-kuo	2	2.4	6	14.0
6 Kingdoms	10	12.1	0	0
Sui	1	1.2	0	0
T'ang	14	16.9	16	37.2
Wu-tai	0	0	4	9.3
Sung	9	10.8	7	16.3
Yüan	0	0	0	0
Ming	1	1.2	1	2.3

16. AUSPICIOUS MARRIAGES
*A Statistical Study of a Chinese Custom**

If we are honest, we have to admit that most of our information on folkways and customs of non-Western societies is unreliable. In many cases we read, for instance, "Among the X, the man pays a bridal price of Y cows." We are not, however, clearly informed whether (*a*) this is information gained from one, two or more informants in answer to a question like "How do your people initiate a marriage?," (*b*) information based on observation of one, two or more cases, or (*c*) information based on asking a number of individuals, "How did you get your own wife? " And even if the basis is given, we are rarely told how many persons have been asked this question, and who these persons were. If the statement is based upon a question similar to (*a*), we learn about the ideals and standards of some sector of a society (often not of all sectors); if the statement is based upon such a question as (*c*), we learn about actual practices. But to make the statement valuable, we must know the characteristics of the persons asked: their age, sex, social status, caste, etc. And if the statement is based upon the observational method (*b*), it is valuable, again, only if we know the details about the participants. But often we do not get the necessary details and can only guess that the writer has talked to one or two informants, yet the writer then often begins to "explain" the custom in functional terms to show the "equilibrium" in which his society operates. The "function" of the custom may turn out to be imagination, if the basic data are not well established.

The problem is not much different if the custom is taken from a written document in the case of literate societies: we have to establish whether the book reported what *should* be or whether it narrated what the author had seen or whether it told about a generally held belief.

In only a few cases are we in a position to test statements concerning customs statistically, so that we find out more clearly what the custom really meant. One such case is the "auspicious" marriage custom of the Chinese.

Books written by non-Chinese who describe the marriage customs of traditional China invariably mention that one of the first steps in initiating a marriage is to ask through the go-between the " eight characters" of the other partner. These symbols are the cyclical signs of the year, month, day

*Reprinted from *Sociologus* XIII (1963) 49-53.

and hour of birth. These symbols are then, we read, studied by an astrologer and if the symbols turn out to be incompatible the marriage is likely not to be concluded, because it would turn out to be a bad marriage. Of these eight characters, the first set is most important. One character in the first set is an animal of the twelve-animal cycle. Certain animals are incompatible, while others are highly compatible, according to a belief which really is familiar to almost every Chinese one can ask. If the "animals" are not favorable but not incompatible, the other characters become important. In some cases, for instance, the animals might indicate a successful marriage, but a bad outlook for a career: this, then, can be balanced by the other characters, it is believed.

There are twelve animals in the cycle, and each year has its animal, so that all persons born in the same year have the same animal. As bride and groom can be—and generally are—born in different years, a total of 144 combinations is possible. Of these, six combinations are regarded as highly inauspicious and six others as specially auspicious. This information is not only found in books written by outsiders, or heard from Chinese who have been interviewed, but also occurs in the one book which has the widest distribution of all books: the folk almanacs. The almanacs, which have a venerable history of far more than a thousand years, give the important calendric data, festivals, agricultural advice, and in addition the days which are lucky for some types of work and unlucky for other kinds of work. The almanacs also contain basic historical information, data on interpretation of dreams, interpretation of sounds, and other omina, among them much information concerning marriages. Such almanacs were available everywhere until the present (Taiwan), were extremely cheap and widely used. We are told that every Chinese would consult them before he started out on some trip, initiated an important business transaction, or thought of marrying.

We can therefore hypothesize that, on the average, Chinese will not marry partners whose "animals," or cyclical characters, are so incompatible with their own characters that an inauspicious marriage would ensue. Similarly, they will prefer to marry partners with highly compatible characters. We can add to this hypothesis another one: if not all Chinese behave in accordance with this belief, persons who are superstitious will strongly avoid inauspicious marriages, and if we find inauspicious marriages these will indicate persons who are not superstitious. In many societies, we think, there is a correlation between superstition and either social class or education: the higher the social class or education or both, the lower the incidence of superstition. We can, finally, set up a third hypothesis. Knowing that China has changed and strives towards modernization, we can hypothesize that in earlier times more Chinese will have followed the prescriptions of such a custom than today.

To test the first hypothesis, I used data about 2,329 couples from the Taiwanese town of T'ao-yüan. These persons were found in a sample selected for a study of attitudes towards family planning[1] which consisted of all females born after 1911 and of childbearing age in seven wards of the town. Their husbands were usually older than the women, the oldest being born in 1888, the youngest in 1941. Our 2,329 couples consisted of all the couples in the sample for which the necessary data were complete and without doubt. The sample represented different social groups and the data about the 2,329 couples could therefore be used also to test the second hypothesis. The data about the "animals" are found in *Table I.* The rows contain the twelve signs of the zodiac (i.e., the twelve "animals,"). These are the signs under which the husbands were born. The columns refer to the signs of the zodiac under which their wives were born. If husband and wife were born in the same year (i.e., under the same "animal"), the difference was zero years. But as the signs start anew every twelve years, a couple consisting of a husband with a wife twelve or twenty-four years younger than himself, would also show zero difference. If the wife is born one, thirteen or twenty-five years later than her husband, this would be found in column *1;* a couple in which the wife is one year older than her husband, or eleven, twenty-three, or thirty-five years younger than he, would be found in column *11*. Thus, the columns do not represent the age difference between husband and wife, although they are influenced by this factor. Therefore, the columns are not of equal size. The rows reflect the years of birth of the husbands, but men born in 1910, 1922, or 1934 would be found in the same row.

Table I
Zodiac signs of husbands and wives in T'ao-yüan, T'aiwan
(in percentages)

Husband's Sign	Difference between Husband's Sign and Wife's Sign											Total	
	0	1	2	3	4	5	6	7	8	9	10	11	No.	%
tzu	8.8	15.2	16.4	17.6	10.5	12.3	2.9	2.9	4.1	2.3	2.3	4.7	171	100.0
ch'ou	14.7	15.3	13.6	13.6	5.1	13.6	4.5	3.4	3.9	3.4	3.4	5.7	177	100.2
yin	11.7	12.6	9.2	15.0	12.1	10.2	3.4	3.9	5.3	4.4	4.9	7.3	206	100.0
mao	9.2	12.2	14.8	10.2	11.2	8.7	7.7	6.6	5.1	3.1	4.6	6.6	196	100.0
ch'en	8.2	10.3	12.0	20.7	16.8	9.8	2.2	2.7	3.3	6.0	3.8	4.4	184	100.2
szu	6.5	7.1	11.4	19.6	13.6	10.3	8.2	4.4	8.2	3.8	2.2	4.9	184	100.2
wu	8.8	11.1	17.2	16.0	13.3	7.7	6.6	5.5	4.4	3.3	2.2	3.9	181	100.0
wei	6.8	11.7	14.2	15.6	10.2	11.7	9.3	6.3	4.4	3.9	2.9	2.9	205	99.9
shen	6.1	10.3	13.1	13.1	14.6	15.5	9.9	4.2	3.8	5.2	3.8	.5	213	100.1
yu	9.0	9.0	15.4	14.4	12.9	9.9	6.5	4.5	5.0	2.5	5.0	6.0	201	100.1
hsü	7.7	9.5	15.8	18.9	13.5	6.3	4.5	6.3	5.9	3.6	3.1	5.0	222	100.1
hai	6.9	9.5	19.6	18.0	12.7	8.5	5.8	4.8	4.2	2.1	2.6	5.3	189	100.0
	8.7	11.1	14.4	16.0	12.2	10.4	6.0	4.6	4.8	3.6	3.4	4.8	2329	100.0

Combinations which according to two almanacs and popular opinion are auspicious, are indicated by underlining; combinations which are inauspicious are included in a square. A simple look at *Table I* shows that modern Taiwanese in T'ao-yüan did not care about this "custom": the variations which appear can safely be ascribed to chance. The objection could be raised that Taiwanese are not a good example, because the island had been under Japanese rule for a long period and this would have had an influence. A sample from Mainland China would certainly have been better, if it had been available. But on the other hand, in many questions of religious practices, the Taiwanese even now are more conservative than Mainland Chinese were before 1948.

For Mainland China, we have data for the period between 1600 and 1899; these data are all from the genealogy of the Jung clan of Kuangtung province and pertain to 3,709 couples.[2] Here, the objection can be made that a clan might have special clan rules influencing their attitudes towards marriage. On the other hand, it seems very unlikely that a clan with many independent houses could enforce a uniform attitude in all branches over three hundred years. The results of the inquiry are brought together in *Table II*, which is constructed like *Table I*. At first, we tabulated the data separately for the period between 1600 and 1799 and for that between 1800 and 1899, but when we noticed that the clan members apparently did not care about the "custom," we combined the information for both periods on one table.

A look at *Table II* shows that indeed in the last three hundred years, the Jung clan members in Kuangtung Province did not let themselves be

Table II
Zodiac signs of husbands and wives of the Jung clan between 1600 and 1899
(in percentages)

Husband's Sign	Difference between Husband's Sign and Wife's Sign												Total	
	0	1	2	3	4	5	6	7	8	9	10	11	No	%
tzu	9.7	_8.7_	10.7	11.0	6.5	9.1	8.1	8.4	6.5	6.8	5.8	8.7	309	100.0
ch'ou	10.8	8.0	9.1	11.8	9.1	10.4	10.1	5.9	5.6	3.5	8.7	7.0	287	100.0
yin	9.3	11.4	10.8	13.3	7.7	10.2	6.2	7.1	3.1	_6.8_	5.0	9.0	323	99.9
mao	7.4	12.1	8.8	10.7	10.3	8.8	9.6	_9.6_	5.9	5.9	4.8	6.2	272	100.1
ch'en	10.6	6.7	10.3	9.1	9.7	_9.1_	8.8	8.2	6.1	6.7	7.0	7.9	330	100.2
szu	8.7	7.3	11.1	_10.5_	9.0	8.4	9.7	7.3	6.3	6.3	4.9	10.5	287	100.0
wu	6.0	_10.7_	10.0	9.0	13.4	9.0	5.5	5.7	6.7	6.4	9.0	8.7	299	99.9
wei	9.5	9.5	11.1	11.5	7.5	6.9	5.2	8.5	6.6	7.5	9.2	6.9	305	99.9
shen	9.6	6.2	9.6	11.8	8.6	10.9	6.6	7.2	7.9	7.2	7.2	7.2	304	100.0
yu	7.7	12.5	12.5	10.0	10.9	7.0	8.0	8.7	6.7	4.5	7.0	4.5	312	100.0
hsü	8.8	11.3	13.5	9.7	10.5	5.8	9.4	5.6	6.6	4.7	7.7	6.4	362	100.0
hai	9.4	11.3	9.1	13.8	7.2	11.0	7.8	_7.8_	6.0	6.0	5.0	_5.6_	319	100.0
	8.9	9.6	10.5	11.0	9.3	8.9	7.9	7.5	6.2	6.0	6.8	7.4	3709	100.0

influenced by the auspicious or inauspicious combinations of signs in their selection of marriage partners. We feel that we can generalize on the basis of our two surveys to say that, in general, Chinese did not let themselves be influenced by astrology, at least not in the last three hundred years.

In order to test our second hypothesis, we constructed *Tables III* and IV. It is still possible that, although Chinese in general do not seem to let themselves be directed by astrology, some Chinese do follow the rules, while others do not. In *Table III* we selected those couples which married under auspicious or inauspicious signs and classified them according to the occupation of the male partner. The distributions were compared with the occupational distribution of all known males in the sample which we selected in T'ao-yüan. The table shows some differences, but these differences are the result of chance variation only.

Table III

*Preference for auspicious or inauspicious
marriages among T'ao-yüan citizens
according to occupations
(in percentages)*

	Couples selected auspicious data	Occupational distribution of total sample[3]	Couples selected inauspicious data
Farmers	33.9%	33.6%	27.2%
Business	23.4	18.9	15.2
Labor & Crafts	18.5	34.8	30.5
Civil Service	16.1	7.4	15.2
Other	8.1	5.3	11.9
Totals	100.0%	100.0%	100.0%
No. of couples	124	2373	92

For the historical data, we could not set up a parallel table, because we do not have information about the occupations of the Jung clan members. But between 1600 and 1899, 634 members of the Jung clan either received an official title or an official job. We think we are justified to assume that such titled persons represent the upper level, the most highly educated, sector of the clan; we assume further, that these persons are less bound by a belief in astrology. In *Table IV*, instead of repeating the full set of 144 combinations (as in *Table II*), we selected only the six auspicious and the six inauspicious combinations and compared them with the average distribution in the corresponding columns. The picture is the same as in *Table II*: auspicious as well as inauspicious combinations occurred often, inauspicious combinations even slightly more often than one would expect. But the result remains the same: the educated class between 1600 and 1899 was as little guided or as much guided as the rest of the population by astrological beliefs in the choice of marriage partners.

Table IV

*Preference for auspicious or inauspicious
marriages in the Jung clan between 1600
and 1899, among the titled members
(in percentages)*

	The six auspicious combinations		The six inauspicious combinations	
	titled	average	titled	average
1	9.1%	9.7%	16.6%	12.9%
2	6.1	5.2	2.1	5.2
3	8.3	6.0	7.1	6.0
4	7.1	7.1	5.3	7.1
5	8.5	11.2	20.6[4]	12.9
6	14.3	12.9	5.0	5.2

The result of this tedious investigation is: although Chinese, when asked, generally assert that the "eight characters" are studied in order to avoid combinations which are regarded as inauspicious; although the best and the worst combinations are expressly mentioned in almanacs which, according to general assertion, are in almost every house and are constantly consulted, the fact remains that the combination of astrological signs of marriage partners has played no statistically significant role in the last three hundred years. There is no change in this attitude over this time, nor is there any difference among different sectors of the society, as far as we could determine.

We might, therefore, be justified in concluding that the study of the "eight characters" during the process of planning a marriage does not indicate a belief in "fate." It rather seems to be a manipulation which normally is more or less playful or "ceremonial," but which can be used to call off marriage talks, if for other reasons the outlook for the planned marriage proves to be negative. We could call this, then, the "function" of this customary act; but we should remain clear about the fact that we constructed such a "function" on speculative grounds. Perhaps in the minds of the Chinese who went through this ceremony it had still another function or functions.

17. CHINESE TOGGLES*

While there exists a whole literature devoted to *netsuke* or girdle pendants in Japan, the mere presence of such objects in China is never so much as noticed, in spite of the fact that they may frequently be seen in current use. The collection of Miss Bieber, of Peking, which is now on exhibition at the Museum of New Mexico, is one of the first of its kind, and therefore deserves particular attention. Though small, it probably contains the most important types that we may expect to find; but when once an interest in such objects is aroused, doubtless many more examples, and possibly even more beautiful ones, will come to light. We know, at the present time, incredibly little about these objects, we are ignorant of their place of origin, of their age, and of who made them, and, in fact, we do not know what they represent. I am convinced that, just as in Japan at first very little was known about *netsuke*, and hardly the name of a single master, so too, in China we shall gradually arrive at more exact knowledge, and find ourselves in the position to publish the material in a scientific form. The purpose of this note is merely to call attention to the objects, to indicate the most important types known, and to explain them where this is possible.

The Chinese robe has always had a belt, even though it was only in certain periods, and clearly under foreign influence (on the one hand Turkish-Mongolian, and on the other hand, Tibetan) that it had a leather belt. Apart from this, all belts have been made of woven material. The old books of Rites describe all the objects that were hung at the belt: "On the right and on the left of the belt are hung the objects which are in use; on the left, a cloth for wiping things, a handkerchief, a knife and whetstone, a little ivory awl for loosening knots, and a metal burning-glass; on the right, the thumb-ring and arm-ring for drawing the bow, a reed and writing material, a knife in a sheath, a large awl for larger knots and a firedrill."[2] Besides this it is mentioned that a tablet for memoranda was stuck in the belt. The books of rites give representations of such belts, and explain that all the objects mentioned were carried as pendants. I am not entirely persuaded that this was always the case, since such pendants, which in some cases would have

*This article was translated from the German by John Hope-Johnson, Peking, 1939, and first appeared in *El Palacio* XLIX (1942), 91-104. It has been revised for publication here.

been very long, must have been extremely inconvenient in daily life; at the best, they could have been worn only on ceremonial occasions. The ordinary man must, even in ancient times, have stuck the most important objects in current use in his belt, since there were no trouser pockets, and the wide sleeves that might be used as pockets were to be found only in the ceremonial robes. The ordinary man, in everyday dress, must very seldom have worn these wide sleeves. But when objects were stuck into the belt, it was necessary to use toggles to prevent them from slipping out through. There are a great many small sculptures and plaques from Han times that could quite well have served as such girdle pendants. As soon as we get to know more about the later toggles, we shall doubtless be able to prove on grounds of comparison, that many of these small objects of the earlier time were also used in this way. At the present day the toggle is used principally, but not exclusively, as a counterpoise to a pipe. This usage cannot be older than the Ming dynasty, since presumably it was only in Ming times that smoking was introduced. Schuyler Cammann believes that toggles were already in existence during the Mongol period.[3] I have not been able to find earlier texts. In fact, any mention of toggles in texts seems to be quite rare.[4] O. Janse describes one object found in a Chinese tomb of the Han period in Indochina as a toggle.[5] I think it is quite possible that Chinese used toggles during the Han period, but we will have to wait for further discoveries.

It is also unknown from what region the objects in Miss Bieber's collection come. The greater part were found in North China, but the materials employed (bamboo, soapstone) would suggest that they originate rather, in Middle or South China. The centre of the soapstone industry, even today, is in southern Chêkiang. Possibly some came from Chêkiang or Fukien. There is not yet sufficient material for us to be able to make a division based on stylistic considerations into geographical regions or historical periods.

From an artistic point of view the toggles in Miss Bieber's collection are of unequal value, having been collected for different reasons, aesthetic, symbolic, material. All of them show clearly that they originate in popular art, but their differences in quality are great. Some have kept very close to the motives and forms of popular art and are entirely traditional, others have gone far beyond this, and, artistically, are of high quality. Popular art still lives on everywhere in China. The porcelain painter, who paints the common pottery, the wood-carver, who carves the posts and beams of new buildings, the image-maker, who carves figures of the Gods for the little village temples, the printer, who in his workshop prints amulets and prophecies, or the mason, who makes his tiles into ornaments — all are living examples of popular artists. Through the forms which, in their millenary development, they have produced, they have given inspiration to the aristocratic of China. So long as they have remained within the traditional limits their products have remained mere craftsmanship. But many of the girdle pendants represented rise far above these limits and are a contribution to art, made by popular artists of whose names and history we, as yet, know nothing.

From what source has the artist taken the motives that are represented in the toggles? Here again we touch on a question that hitherto has almost entirely escaped attention. It falls within the neglected domain of folklore. I think that they originate as little from pure playful and purposeless creative instinct as does any Chinese painting. When a Chinese artist paints a spray of bamboo, we can enjoy it in a purely esthetic way, but quite apart from this, we can raise the question, what did he wish to express? We can enjoy a picture by a Western painter, in which a woman with a child is represented, without knowing that it represents a madonna and child, and that the painter's intention was to depict the idea of motherhood. In spite of this, however, such knowledge leads us to a profounder understanding and so to a higher esthetic pleasure. This is a fact, which some may perhaps wish to dispute, but which can be proved and must be accepted.

If we look at the toggles from this point of view, we shall find that they all express a wish, just as do the greater part of Chinese paintings. They are not amulets or talismans; it is not believed that they have a magical influence on their wearers; but in the background may be felt that vague uncertainty characteristic of so much Chinese culture, that "it might be." The symbolism of the toggles is for the most part rooted directly in popular mythology, and is therefore of great antiquity. The peach, as symbol of long life, is known with this meaning as early as the Han period, and so is the pine tree as symbol of duration and of stability. Other symbols are, as far as we know at present, of less antiquity; the God, Liu Hai, standing on a three-legged toad and playing with coins, appears to have been first known in the Sung dynasty, even though the three-legged toad, as animal of the Moon, occurs in the earliest literature. The ape carrying peaches must be connected with the romance *The Journey to the West* (*Hsi-yo-chi*)[6] of which the earliest version can hardly be dated earlier than the Ming dynasty even though the peach, as symbol of good fortune, is much older. The great Chinese novels, which were seldom written by one man, but were made up and adapted from the most varied materials of widely different epochs, and the plays, which were closely related to them, were the common property of the whole people, and constitute a sort of encyclopedia of symbolism, from which modern popular art often draws its inspiration. I have seen altar-tables carved all over with scenes from the *Three Kingdoms* (*San-kuo-chih yen-i*), — scenes with absolutely no religious content, and without the slightest relation to the cult. Such things have implanted themselves into the repertoire of the craftsman.

Thus the novel has become the guardian of the folk-property; it brings this together, and gives it back, extended and transformed, to the people. In the case of toggles not only the object represented but, in most cases, also the material is symbolical. Any kind of material will not do. Very often soapstone, the modern substitute for jade, is used, exactly like the latter, to express the idea of purity and tranquility; often bamboo root is used to express constancy, or other woods are used to which medicinal qualities are ascribed. Metal and glass are more seldom used, but ivory, on the contrary, is very popular.

The Bieber collection of toggles may be divided into four great groups. These are represented by (a) human beings and gods, (b) animals, (c) plants and fruits, (d) implements. Among these the animals and plants play the most important part, and it is these two groups that the most valuable examples, from an artistic point of view, are to be found.

(a) Among the gods, there occurs one of the well known Eight Immortals (pa hsien), which are so often represented in popular art, only Li T'ieh-kuai – Li of the Iron Crutch. He is a bringer of good luck, as indeed are the other seven persons, above all, he wards off sickness. We next find Liu Hai, the god riding on a toad. He is said to have lived in the Sung dynasty, in the province of Shensi.[7] His personality is, however, far from clear. There was a general of this name of the Sung dynasty who fought against the Nü-chen (Liu, the sea-toad), who also is supposed to have lived in the Sung dynasty and who is mentioned in many sources of that date. He appears really to have lived, to have belonged to the southern school of Taoism, and to have been a pupil of Lü Yen.[8] It is possible that the representation originates in his name, Sea-toad, which is explained in modern Chinese folktales, though the motive in question is of extreme antiquity.[9] Today, Liu Hai is supposed to bring money and good fortune. The God of Long Life is also represented, another favorite figure of popular art.

When human beings are represented, then the wish expressed relates either to marriage or to children. A sleeping girl has reference to the marriage she is dreaming of: children; or a man with a child, are supposed to represent the wish for children, a wish that all Chinese people have, and which is represented again and again in thousand-fold variations. The equally common wish for official rank and honor is represented by the figure of an official or his attributes.

(b) Among animals, the monkey plays a preponderant role. It usually has a peach in its hand, and, in that case, brings long life. But there is sometimes a play upon monkey-love (a doting fondness for parents). The monkey with the peach appears to be the monkey Sun Wu-k'ung from the romance *The Journey to the West* (*Hsi-yo-chi*). In this story the monkey is a symbol of human intelligence, who, by his skill and resourcefulness, is always able to find a way out of the most difficult situations, and without whom the pilgrim, Hsuan-tsang, the symbol of the unthinking, believing man, would never be able to reach his goal.

Equally frequent is the lion, an animal foreign to China, which became known there through trade with Central Asia at the time of the Han dynasty. Since then it has played a large part in popular art. It is hardly ever represented alone, but mostly with the lioness and their cubs playing with a ball. This subject is found in the sculptures at the entrance of official buildings, even in early times. It probably originates in the lion dance which came to China in T'ang times, or a little earlier, from Central Asia. At the present day it is still performed by troupes of dancers. We do not know what this dance represented in its original home. Possibly it was part of a series of dances of the twelve animals of the animal zodiac cycle. It is a help to say that it was a fertility dance, which in some way must certainly be true. In the popular beliefs of today the gambolling lions still express the wish for children. The Pekinese spaniel is related to the lion, owing to its lion-like face (it is called the "lion-dog"). It also, like the lion, originates in middle or West Asia. In China it is the symbol of vigilance.

The horse occurs only twice in the toggles; here, as indeed in popular mythology in general, it plays little part. The horse here seems to symbolize the official, who may ride on a horse. The two monkeys represented with it come from a play on words. They must mean "noble rank" (*Hou*—monkey and *Hou*—Lord). The possessor therefore should achieve noble rank. Such plays on words are extremely frequent in Chinese symbolism, especially in later times. I am not persuaded that this was always so. In many cases philological history shows that they cannot be very old, or, in any case (owing to dialectal considerations) that they could only have occurred in certain districts of China; and this is so even in cases where they seem to be older and to occur universally. It is thus certain that a part of these plays on words go back in reality to older genuine symbols and to magical representations, though this may not be so in all cases.

The rat stands in a close relation to riches. It accompanies the god of riches. At the New Year's festival, one should neither sweep, nor kill rats, for one would be sweeping riches out of the house and killing them. Thus the rat, together with brooms, becomes a symbol of riches.

Although the bird plays a considerable role in popular mythology, it occurs in the girdle pendants but seldom. The crane is the symbol of long life, the companion of all pious Taoists, who desire to enter into the Elysian fields riding upon its back. The duck, as mandarin duck, alludes to married individual love. "Married people should separate from one another as little as the mandarin ducks."

Fish in all their forms are a symbol, on the ground of a pun (*yü*—fish and *yü*—overflow or abundance) of riches and overflow. But in its origin this symbolism possibly referred to the many eggs of the fish, and so to its numerous progeny. In the toggles it occurs as the goldfish (called dragon-silverfish), and, in this form, still more clearly symbolizes riches.

That the tortoise should still occur in these pendants is remarkable; for today in North and Central China it has taken an offensive meaning universally in popular belief. The beginnings of this symbolism are to be found as early as Han times. Here, it has clearly retained the older meaning which is still alive in South China: it stands for the wish for long life, because tortoises live for hundreds of years. At the same time a pun may be intended (*kui*—tortoise and *kui*—homecoming) when a wife sends her husband a tortoise. Both these meanings are ancient and at the present day are hardly in existence, since the newer meaning has almost entirely replaced them.

Like the tortoise the toad is one of the oldest symbolical animals of China; indeed for a long time it was a god in part of the south. It is the animal of the moon, especially when represented with three legs, and is animal of the night and of fruitfulness. It occurs alone, and also in company with the god of good fortune, Liu Hai, but also among lotus flowers in water. The wish which it expresses is everywhere the same.

Fruitfulness is also symbolized by the snake, which appears once in the Bieber collection. It is not a very widely distributed motive.

The bat is a particularly frequent element on carpets, clothes, and the pendants which are hung around children's necks. On account of a pun (*Fu*—bat and *Fu*—happiness), it symbolizes good fortune.

The cicada is a very old symbol. It occurs as early as the old ritual texts as an animal symbolizing rebirth. Even as the cicada, after an apparent death, slips from its old sheath and lives again, so, it is hoped, will man, too, live again. Thus in ancient times it occurs as a small piece of sculpture which is placed on the tongue of the dead. The cicada as toggle has the same meaning. The shell, on account of its form, is the symbol of continuity, of unending return, and so of the continuance of the family from generation to generation.

Among plants, trees play a small part; the pine tree stands for constancy, because it remains green even in the winter; the plum tree stands for purity. The pine tree is a very ancient symbol, but the plum tree, on the other hand, appears in literature just before the T'ang period. Before then its beauty had been as little noticed as that of the peony.

The chrysanthemum, however, occurs in literature before the birth of Christ. Its color is like that of sulphur, and therefore, like sulphur, it destroys all evil influences and prolongs life. The lotus, which has certainly obtained its important position in popular mythology owing to its connection with Buddhism, often occurs, both as leaf, flower, and fruit. The fruit holds many seeds, and is therefore a symbol for many children. Its blossom is a symbol of purity, since it emerges spotless from the dirty water of the pool; the long stalk with its many holes represents the opening of the mind. The peach has been referred to above. It means long life, though I have never been quite able to make out whence this symbolism comes.

The gourd, on account of its many seeds, stands for many children, and so do the eggplant, from a pun (*chieh-tzu*—eggplant and *to tzu*—many children) and the mushroom, owing to its rapid growth.

Pepper means near friends, possibly through a play upon words. All these are less liked as symbols than as useful elements of design, since they can be turned into many ornamental forms.

(d) Implements are almost all taken from everyday objects. They also have their symbolical meaning, and express the same wishes that are always to be found in the Chinese. Through a pun, the saddle means peace (*an*, saddle and *an*, peace). The winnow means, as already indicated, riches; the buckets, made of wicker-work, which at the present day are still used in North China, for drawing water, seem to be an emblem of the inexhaustibility and eternity of the life of the family; the dice in the shape of a coin plays upon the Chinese passion for gambling, and is supposed to bring luck in gambling.

Purely magical symbols are rare. In the Bieber collections, there is only one to be found. It represents the eight diagrams of the classical book, the *I Ching*, with the symbol for Yin and Yang, male and female, which are considered as the original forces of the universe. They are arrayed as on a Chinese compass and are supposed to preserve their wearer from ill.

Thus we see that the motives of the toggles are taken from the human, animal, and plant worlds, and besides these are others taken from daily life, without distinction, for no such distinction as we Westerners have made and as religion has still more strongly emphasized, really exists. Nature is one great being; we and the world around us are parts of her, the one as little in need of justification in its own sphere as the other.

Abstract forms, purely ornamental forms freed from all relation to reality, with the one exception mentioned above, are not to be found. All the things that are the most familiar to the Chinese occur, and they all tend to express something: the eternal wishes of the Chinese, for long life, the blessings of children, riches and high position. Everything turns round these four wishes; they are represented in ever-varying forms.

From a stylistic point of view, smooth forms are preferred. This is in the nature of the girdle pendant, for angular, sharp-edged hangers would cut the clothing. This is a concession on the part of popular art to utility, since popular art in China loves filling up and dividing the surface, and therefore likes to avoid smooth, rounded surfaces. Through this smoothness some of the single figures come to resemble those bronze small sculptures of the Hunnish ordos art, which have in recent years appeared on the market in such large quantities. I do not think, however, that any connection can be proved, but that this is a case where special accommodation to circumstances has led to an accidental resemblance.

18. A NOTE ON MODERN CHINESE NICKNAMES*

It is probably correct to say that the names by which we call other persons, or by which we talk about other persons, have two basic purposes. First, they must identify the individual who is addressed or talked about. At the same time, they have to clarify the degree of distance or intimacy existing between the speaker and the addressee, or between the speaker(s) and the person they are talking about.

Modern American society, as so often is the case, would seem to be something of an exception. In their more-or-less conscious desire to be, or to appear, "democratic" and "egalitarian," Americans try to avoid expressions which indicate that a speaker might not treat every person with whom he has some oral communication in the same way. In point of fact, of course, he doesn't. He might call his secretary "Peggy," the same way he calls his girl-friend or his cousin, but his secretary cannot automatically reciprocate by calling him "Fred," as his girl-friend or cousin do. She is obliged to wait until she feels she has received a signal indicating to her that it is all right for her to use the more intimate "Fred" instead of "Mr. Smith." It is well-known that it is often quite difficult to find out the true degree of intimacy or distance between speakers in the United States. In most other societies, the desired degree of intimacy or distance is known to the person addressed after the very first words have been exchanged, and thus, the whole tone of interaction between these persons is set.

While American society attempts to give the impression that each addressee is equally close to the speaker, Chinese society, right from its inception, has tried to stress the aspect of distance. This was true not only in the manner in which persons addressed each other, but was also expressed, for example, in the degree of physical contact permitted between persons. According to Confucianist rules, for example, not even husband and wife were supposed to touch each other in public, or in the presence of family members. "Touching" in this case even meant that a husband should not hand an object directly to his wife, because this might involve some contact of their hands, or an onlooker might think that there was contact between their hands.

*Previously unpublished.

The personal name (*ming*) of a person was considered to be so intimate that only the parents had the right to use it. Other family members would address that person by a kinship term. Nonfamily members would never even know the personal name of the individual, and would normally use his family name (*hsing*) combined with one or two words indicating his social status. A greater degree of intimacy between two nonrelated individuals would be indicated by the use of the *hao*, a name given to or selected by the person when he reached the status of an adult. An individual might also use his *hao* on his publications, where he would like to make his personal identity clear without revealing his personal name (*ming*). Another way to indicate intimacy between nonrelated persons was to introduce kinship terms, such as calling the other person "older brother." We cannot explore this topic here in greater detail, but we believe it is possible to analyze the principles and rules governing the ways of addressing others in classical China, certainly for the upper class and for relations between the upper and lower classes. There seems to be some problem about the rules governing the relations between members of the lower classes. However, we know from the novel literature that leaders and members of gangs always had nicknames. These nicknames were, perhaps, widely known, but they were supposed to be used to address a person only by members of the group.

There is a tendency to define a nickname as one used to designate an individual when talking *about* him, but not when talking *to* him. It would be difficult, in Chinese society, to keep the knowledge of the nickname secret from the person who has been given the name. Nicknames always seem to refer to members of a certain social group, such as a gang, a school class, a work crew, and so forth. We may surmise that even in traditional China students had nicknames which were used within the circle of fellow students, and which indicated the status or function of the individual within this special group. Nowadays nicknames appear to be widely spread among such groups as fellow students, workers or other persons commonly living in dormitories, and juvenile gangs.

To my knowledge, no one has yet attempted to collect or analyze Chinese nicknames. After I had realized that a direct approach was somewhat difficult, I undertook the analysis of one written source which turned out to be very rich in nicknames. The Taipei newspaper *Hsin-sheng pao* ran a column in 1964 in which readers reported about their life in dormitories. This column continued through the first half-year of 1964, and around two hundred letters were published. The contributors were mainly high school or university students, many of whom indeed live in private or public dormitories. But some contributions also came from soldiers, or from work crews, and even ship crews. All the contributors were young. Although the ages were not always given, it seems safe to assume that their ages varied between fourteen and thirty years. Both sexes were almost equally represented in the selection which was published, and the contributors were from either the middle or lower social class.

The 241 nicknames found in this series (128 male, 113 female)[1] can be divided into seven categories in respect to content, and five categories as far as their length is concerned.

More than 80 per cent of the nicknames consist of two or three words, and longer nicknames are unusual:

No. of words	% male	% female
two	46	42
three	36	42
four	13	11
five	3	4
seven	2	—

While the normal Chinese name today (*ming* and *hao*) has two words, and only rarely one word,[2] the high percentage of nicknames consisting of more than two words is interesting. I recall having found many three-word nicknames in Chinese novels starting from the Ming period on, but I could not say whether they were more typical then than nowadays. In spoken Chinese, a two-word combination is often not sufficient to express clearly what the speaker wants to express, while the meaning of a name (*ming* or *hao*) which is intended mainly for being read does not have to be clear when one hears it spoken. This may be one reason why nicknames are longer. Sex differences do not seem to play a role in the determination of the length of the nicknames.

An analysis of the nicknames according to their meanings is more interesting, and does show some differences between the sexes:

Nickname contains reference to	% male	% female
an animal	8	10
objects of nature	1	10
man-made objects	7	10

Nickname contains reference to	% male	% female
parts of the body	14	10
figures of history	12	8
social roles	29	11
personal traits	30	40

Girls or women seem to have nicknames which are much more often related to objects of nature than those of boys and men, and more rarely get nicknames indicating a social role. We might perhaps even say that female nicknames refer more often to nonhuman, impersonal objects (including animals) than do men's nicknames (30 per cent vs. 16 per cent). This may well indicate some fear of becoming too intimate towards women by using a reference to the human body or a role in society.

Within each category, the differences are even greater. Let me now give some examples. In male nicknames in which references is made to an animal, the dog plays a role: "Dog Number Two" (*erh kou-tse*)[3] "Wagging, Rolling Dog-King" (*yao-kun kou-wang*).[4] In Taiwanese folklore, the dog is a symbol of servility and obedience. Girls are never compared with dogs in our collection. "Old Ox" (*lao-niu*)[5] refers to a slow, lazy person, "Lying Dragon" (*wo-lung*)[6] to a strong, but inactive person, "Monkey King" (*hu-sun wang*)[7] to a cunning man, and "Field-Chicken" (*t'ien-chi*), referring to a snail, designates a person wearing glasses, because the eyes of the snail seem to look like those of a person with glasses. This nickname can be used for girls too.[8] Girls have names referring to birds such as orioles[9] or cranes,[10] or referring to beauty, but we find also less friendly names such as "Old Tigress" (*tz'u-lao-hu*),[11] "Rat" (*lao-shu*),[12] "Lazy Pig" (*lan-chu*)[13] and "Wild Calf" (*hsiao man niu*).[14]

Only one male name refers to an object of nature: "Burnt Island" (*huo-shao tao*).[15] In the eleven female nicknames in this group, we find four flowers, a melon, but also "Active Volcano" (*huo huo-shan*),[16] "Mars" (*huo-hsing*, the fire star),[17] "Venus" (*chin-hsing*),[18] probably with its European allusions, and "Star" (*ming-hsing*),[19] which may refer more to a movie-star than to a real star.

The category of man-made objects shows a great deal of humor, though the nicknames are often not very complimentary towards their bearers. A man is called "Food Barrel" (*fan-t'ung*),[20] because of the great quantities he likes to eat. Another is "Incense Which Comes By Night" (*yeh-lai hsiang*),[21] referring to the smell which his socks exude in the dormitory. There is a

"Little Trumpet" (*hsiao la-pa*),[22] a "Mr. Vitamin" (*wei-t'o-ming*),[23] and a "Meat Ball" (*jou-ch'iu*)[24] among others. Girls are "Sugar" (*mi-t'ang*), [25] "Butter" (*nai-yo*)[26] or "Bread" (*mien-pao*)[27] but also "Chamber-Pot" (*niao-t'ung*)[28] "Cess-Pool" (*hua-mi-ch'ih*)[29] "Earthquake Meter" (*ti-tung i*),[30] "Weather Station" (*ch'i-hsiang t'ai*),[31] which refers to the rheumatism which the girl suffered from, "Telegraph Pole" (*tien-hsüan kan*).[32] referring to her size and figure, and "Small Leather Ball" (*hsiao p'i-ch'iu*),[33] referring to her figure.

In the category of parts of the body, we have brought together mainly those nicknames which refer to physical characteristics. Thus, seven men are, in various ways, called "Fatty, and three "Bony." Similarly, there are five girls called "Fatty" and one "Leatherbag Bone" (*p'i-pao ku*),[34] two "Long Leg" and one "Pig's Feet."

Two features are of interest among the figures of history. Men are more often compared with movie stars than women. Among these, foreign actors, Americans such as Presley[35] and Yul Brunner,[36] as well as Japanese actors, are prominent. Among the girl's nicknames, we find Brigitte Bardot,[37] but more common are truly historical figures from the literature such as Napoleon,[38] Liang Shan-po,[39] Chiu-mei,[40] both from the same drama, and Su Tung-p'o,[41] the famous poet of Sung times. Here, one trait which can be observed fairly often in female nicknames is prominent: the woman is compared to a man, such as Liang Shan-po, Su Tung-p'o, or Napoleon, while we have not yet come across a male nickname which referred to a female person or a female characteristic.

Nicknames indicating social roles are not only much less common for females than for males, but the female nicknames are also much less imaginative: "Teacher's Wife" (*shih-mu*),[42] "Israeli,"[43] "Black Indian," [44] "Mongolian Fortune-Teller" (*Meng-ku suan-ming chia*),[45] are the best ones, but there are also the "Chief Advisor" (*ts'an-mou chang*),[46] "Lady,"[47] "Dance Instructor,"[48] "Director" (*tsung pu-chang*),[49] and "Patrolling Officer."[50]

Men go through the whole spectrum of roles: there are five "Poets," two "Detectives," two "Philosophers," two "Babies," three "Older Brothers," "Saint," or "Bare-Footed Saint" (*ch'ih-tsu ta-hsien*),[51] a "Librarian," a "Butcher," a "Pediatrician," a "Little Dictator," (*Hsiao pa-wang*),[52] a "Village Headman," a "Dead Ghost" (*szu kui*),[53] and others. In these names, three terms occur fairly often: *"Wang"* (King), *"sheng"* (Saint) and *"hsien"* (Immortal, or Saint). These three terms are commonly used in Taiwanese to convey the meaning "a person who is good at something," rather than to convey their literal meaning. Thus, there is in Taipei a "Great King Water-Melon," a shop which wants to indicate that they are specializing in selling water-melons, and others. Among the male nicknames in this class, only a single one is ethnic: "Chief of the Indonesian Chinese" (*Yin-ni ch'iao ling*),[54] In general, we get the impression that most of the male nicknames in this class are alluding to activities or behavior which are approved, while a greater number of the female nicknames express disapproval.

In the last and largest group, praise and blame seem to be expressed equally among women, while men seem to receive more criticism. There are six "Sleepers," one "Chain Farter," (*lien-huan p'i*),[55] a "King of Kings of Farters" (*p'i-wang-chih wang*),[56] a "Hen-Pecked One" (*chü-nei hsien*), [57] several "Love Experts," a "Mass Lover" (*ta-chung ch'ing-jen*),[58] an "Old Lover," an "Amorous Cheater," a "King of Smell," two "Mr. Toilet," (*kuai tung-tung, tung-tung-mo*; both Taiwanese terms),[59] a "Greedy One," given to a cook,[60] a "Lazy One," and two "Sour Ones."

The girl's nicknames seem to be less harsh and often express some praise. There are a "Cold One," a "Murderer Nazi," (*na-ts'ui sha-jen-wang*),[61] and a "Crying Iron Face" (*K'u t'ieh-mien*),[62] but there are also two "Sleeping Beauties," two "Handsome Girls," two "Sweet Sisters," a "Chaste One," an "Icy Beauty," "Miss Curiosity," a "Test Queen," a "Gentleman," a "Great Humor King," and a "Love Councillor," among numerous others.

Our collection does not indicate another source for nicknames which seems to be fairly common:[63] nicknames which have their origin in a pun on the name of the bearer. The reason for this is that the series which we used did not mention the real names of persons, only their nicknames. Our collection contains otherwise only a single pun. A man is called *chin-shih*, which means a man who had passed the highest examination under the old, imperial examination system. In our case, the nickname does not allude to the bearer's intellectual achievements, but rather to his nearsightedness (*chin-shih*).[64]

This brief note, we hope, will induce others to pay attention to this aspect of Chinese names. It may also serve as an inventory of what kind of nicknames are used today among the young nondelinquent groups. This inventory could now be compared with nicknames of criminals and juvenile gangs on the one hand, and with nicknames used in classical and modern novels on the other. We have the impression that nicknames in novels often have a deeper, literary or philosophical meaning, and that nicknames in gangs refer more often to heroes in novels.

19. MARRIAGE CUSTOMS AND FESTIVALS
OF THE MIAOTSE OF KUEICHOU*

Translated from the Chinese of Yü Chu-luan with an Introduction
by Wolfram Eberhard

The following is part of a study entitled "Reports about the Miaotse of Kueichou."[1] Under the name Miaotse, the Chinese group together a number of tribes which are very diverse in both race and culture. They formerly inhabited the entire southwestern part of China, but have now been pushed by the Chinese into the remote and inaccessible hill country of the southern provinces. The author, who spent five years in Kueichou as a government surveyor, presents a short description of some thirty-eight tribes, after referring in the introduction to the important role the Miaotse have played in Chinese history. He then turns to Miaotse culture. Although Chinese culture has made great inroads everywhere, the traditional marriage customs are still relatively intact. These marriage customs merit our particular attention due to the fact that they show many striking and detailed similiarities with the corresponding customs which Marcel Granet assumes for pre-Christian China.[2] In both instances, the large dance festivals at which the young people gather in groups for song contests alternating with dancing, play an important role in the joining of the marriage bonds. The real meaning of the festivals, which are undoubtedly a part of agricultural rites, has been almost completely forgotten in the process.[3]

We are fortunate enough to have older descriptions of the Miaotse of Kueichou which — for China — are quite detailed. These are the so-called Miaotse albums. For purposes of comparison with the modern tribal descriptions to follow, we will also present several older descriptions taken from a two-volume manuscript now in the possession of the Berlin Anthropological Museum. These older descriptions are all of tribes which were also visited by our author. The older material thus supplements the presentations of Yü Chu-luan, and it also shows that interesting changes have occurred. The Miaotse album is entitled *Pictures of the Miaotse of the Entire Province of Kueichou.* It is a folding album containing eighty-two pictures,

*Revised and translated version of "Heiratssitten und Feste der Miaotse von Kueichou," *Der Weltkreis* (Berlin) II (1931), 114-121.

each accompanied by a short text. The album thus seems to correspond to the general type of album commonly found among the Miaotse.[4] It is difficult to determine the age of the manuscript, but the material, like that of the other albums, goes back to about the middle of the eighteenth century. The watercolor illustrations have been tastefully executed, but lack artistry. The background has been somewhat neglected and left schematic so as to favor the figures.

This album contains the following information about the festivals and marriage customs of the Ch'ia-ch'ung Chung-chia tribe: "Every year, in the first month of spring, the unmarried men and women dance in the moonlight. They sing and dance in an open clearing. They make small round balls out of brightly colored cloth. These balls look like melons and are called 'flower balls.' If they like each other and fall in love, then they toss the balls to one another, and afterwards they secretly have sexual intercourse. Or if they happen to meet at marriages or funerals and come to an agreement, then they cut up their clothes and exchange sashes. They arrange a date and become one. Only after the girl is pregnant do they return to their parents' homes. Recently customs have changed somewhat, and in K'ai-chou (in Kueichou province) go-betweens are frequently used to arrange a marriage." —At the left in the illustration we see a couple from the tribe arriving at the dancing grounds, at the top of the picture a couple tossing a cloth ball, and in the center of the picture we see the ceremony of the loosening of the sash which is described below in such amusing fashion by Yü Chu-luan.[5] The men, as always, are much darker than the women, who are portrayed with white faces. The women's skirts are decorated with a star pattern, and have all the colors of the rainbow.

The following information is given about the so-called "Dog-Ears Lung-chia" (so named because of a head decoration which points straight up like the ears of a dog): "After the beginning of spring they erect a tree in some open clearing. It is called the 'post of the spirits'. The unmarried boys and girls dance around the tree and start up love affairs." — The Hua-Miao "prepare a flat spot to serve as the 'moon place' every year in the first month of spring. The unmarried men blow Miaotse flutes, and the women jingle bells. They sing, dance, play and have a good time all day long. When evening comes they secretly engage in sexual intercourse. More recently they have also started to make more frequent use of go-betweens." And in the tribe of black Miao of Pa-chai "every village sets up a house called a *Ma-lang*-house out in an open space. Here the unmarried boys and girls meet during the evening to amuse themselves with food and drink." Our second illustration shows the *Ma-lang*-house with its light construction and straw roof. The men are blowing large reed pipes. These pipes of various lengths — in the illustrations there are always three — are bound together and are blown through a mouth-piece mounted at a diagonal to the pipes.

But now to the report of our author. He narrates as follows:

The most striking thing about the Miao is their complete freedom of marriage. (They have no arranged marriages like the Chinese!). The parents give their children a brightly-colored sash. When they grow up later on and have secret relations with young men or girls from their own or a neighboring village, or when they gather together at festivals and reach a mutual understanding, they then exchange these sashes, the symbols of their freedom of choice. This means that they are engaged. Then they inform their senior clansman, set the wedding day, and decide on the presents. Even if they have both come to an understanding and want to marry, they are not allowed to exchange sashes in secret, but must wait for the opportunity to do so in public, in order to let everyone know that they desire to marry. Dance festivals provide such opportunities. Several thousand people attend every such festival. All those who are still single dress up in new clothes, and then walk around in groups singing songs and discussing their families and their own plans. Couples wanting to marry then publicly exchange their belts, clasp each other's hands and dance in the square while they sing a few songs. Then they separate again.

I witnessed the "dancing-grounds-festival" when I was in Chin-chin in Cha-wa-chi, and made the following notes: "They decorate their market-places for the occasion and invite everybody to the dance. All those who have heard the invitation leave their houses and come to the dance, since it provides an opportunity for a future marriage, and this is very important in the people's eyes. In Cha-wa-chi they decorated the horse-market and the cattle-market. In the morning the people swept the streets. They considered this to be a very important activity. Around noon the Miao started coming from every direction. Women, young and old, dress up in brightly-colored dresses, unusually attractive! Those who are still unmarried wear ten strands of false pearls or more in addition to their fine clothes, so that one can hear the sound of the pearls even from a distance. Then several hundred Miao arrive. They plant a pine-tree called the "brightly-colored tree" in the square. The men blow reed pipes, circle around the tree and dance. The women, one behind the other, accompany the men and sing Miao songs. The music rises and falls, and the text is impossible to understand. They dance for about two hours, and then amuse themselves and rest. Then come the engagements. The young men look around for young single girls, and the girls for young single men. If two meet who don't happen to take a fancy to each other, they shake hands, exchange a few words, and move on. If they happen to like one another, they clasp hands in a particular intimate fashion, and demand the exchange of the sashes. With this the marriage is official. I noticed an ugly girl who was asking a young man to exchange sashes with her, but he wasn't willing and refused. So she let go of his hand slightly and cried out in anguish. The young man was steadfast in his refusal, but she kept on asking him for his sash. And so they stood for one or two hours. Curious Chinese onlookers surrounded them like a wall and watched the spectacle. Some of the young men called on him to give up his sash, or on her to leave him alone. Others found the whole matter amusing. There was a gigantic confusion of voices, and the entire thing seemed quite picturesque. I stood and watched. The girl by now had become terribly sad, and since the young man refused to respond to anything she said, she turned her head away and her eyes filled with tears, as if she were grieved to death. But the young man felt sorry for her and unloosened his sash. And her tears were transformed to laughter. She ran to her parents and told them the good news. They too were glad, and they opened up their mouths and laughed. At the same time one of her girl-friends had asked a young man to exchange sashes. She was very beautiful and had very clear white teeth. He wasn't willing, but somehow or other she managed to get his sash and ran, radiant with joy, to show it to her girl-friends. He got ahold of her sash too. And so the two of them were happy and beside themselves with joy. They danced with their young men around the grounds several times, sang for a long while, and then departed."

There is even another way for a couple in love to arrange a marriage. Instead of personally exchanging sashes, the family of the man sends a go-between to the family of the woman. This go-between brings along several head of cattle and performs the rite of "entering the door." He lets an ox run loose at every gate he passes, one for each of the gates. After this rite has been completed, the woman's family recognizes the marriage. There is never a refusal, because an agreement has been reached between the man and woman beforehand, and their parents can't change anything now!

When the Black, White and Blue Miao and the T'u-chia and Chung-chia (tribes in Kueichou) marry, the family of the man sends five or six girls over to the family of the woman. These girls lead the bride back to the house of the bridegroom. She is not carried in the sedan-chair, but rather goes with her companions on foot. She doesn't put on any wedding clothes for the occasion, but does carry an umbrella. When she has arrived at the house of her future husband, she goes straight to the kitchen, washes the dishes, gets three loads of water, and then returns home (she doesn't stay overnight and has no sexual intercourse with her husband). The man often goes to the house of the woman after this, hides near her room, waits until she comes out, and then proceeds to have sexual relations with her. Only after a child has been born, is the bride formally brought home. And if no child is born, she must never again enter her husband's house! If the houses are located too far apart for the man to regularly pay his secret visits to his wife, the woman may have intercourse with another man without incurring the objections of her family. In this case too, the bride is not led home until a child has been born. If such a woman does not give birth to a child, then she buys one. The oldest son, however, has no inheritance rights then, since he is illegitimate — a bad custom, indeed!

The Ko-lo set up two high seats of honor after the bride has been brought home. Each family then invites a so-called "devil's master," who sits down at the seat of honor. Several taels of silver have been placed before each such seat, and a horse is also tied up there. Both devils' masters proceed to ask questions of each other, and answer in as witty a manner as possible. This goes on for several hours. Finally each one takes a horse and his portion of silver, and goes home. If one should be defeated during the duel of words, then he leaves secretly. The horse and the silver automatically then go to his opponent. This is a great disgrace for the family involved. Their marriage customs are unusually complicated. On the occasion of her first visit to her father-in-law, the young wife dons dresses with such an enormous amount of material that ten servants have to carry the train. This dress is not used again until she is buried.

The various Miao tribes do not all intermarry. The boundaries here are very distinct. If someone has sexual relations with a person from another tribe, he is attacked by his own clan. In this way they have been able to maintain the purity of the tribe until the present day. This is a good rule for the preservation of racial purity. Only the women of the White Miao and the Po-erh-tse marry Chinese. But the Chinese too avoid marriage with them, since, if they do happen to marry, their relatives will destroy their ancestral tablets and disown them. Such Chinese have actually rejected themselves!

Festivals and Amusements

The Miao are lovers of amusement. Their festivals are not everywhere the same, and their names are different as well. Several thousand Miao gather at all such festivals, and peddlers selling cloth, things to eat, etc. are also on hand. There are enormous crowds. Along with this there are amusements such as *Yao-ma-lang* and *Lao-ku-mang,* where people can have fun, rest up from the strenuous labors of the fields, and regain their strength. Such amusements, however, are not yet so generally widespread among the Miao.

1. *T'iao ch'ang* (a dance on the grounds). Common throughout western Kueichou. One clears an area of trees and invites the Miao for dancing: this is known as *T'iao ch'ang.* Everyone who hears about it comes, since this affords an opportunity for arranging a marriage. The women dress up in beautiful clothes, and all carry reed pipes and other instruments. People gather together in the clearing, and servants offer wine and pastry. A pine-tree known as the "brightly-colored tree" is planted there, and the men play flutes and dance with the women around the tree. They are laughing

and singing, and are in the best of spirits. The spectators clap in rhythm with the dance. The whole affair always lasts from noon until evening.

2. *T'iao chai* (dance on a fixed grounds). When the Miao of Kueichou wish to honor the spirits, they perform this dance. In the spring of every year a village sets a day and then invites all the Miao living within several dozen Li (about five kilometers) of the village. On the appointed day, men and women, dressed in new clothes and carrying flutes, appear in the open square. For two or three days they play the flute, dance, and sing all night long, and then they finally break up and go home.

We observed such a Miao dance festival in the village of Lo-wa several dozen Li from Kuei-yang. We took several photographs of the dance grounds. The people themselves were very afraid of being photographed and ran away. Later we got ahold of a few people and tried to persuade them to pose, but they didn't have an ounce of courage, wouldn't let us take their pictures, and disrupted the entire celebration.

3. *T'iao Yüeh* (dance in the moonlight). If an old man has died or there is a marriage, then the Miao get their musical instruments, sing and dance all night long, play ball, etc.

4. *Pa kao-p'o* (climbing a steep ledge). On the third day of the third month all the Miao of Huang-p'ing have a celebration. They gather together on a mountain. The men and women line up in pairs facing each other. Then they play the flute, sing, dance and compete with one another, everyone doing what he does best. The visitors set off fireworks and congratulate one another. Those who have been defeated in the contests go off to dance and sing with some other worthy opponent. Chinese who had come to witness the spectacle were cordially invited by the Miao to drink wine in every house during these days.

5. *Niu ta-chia* (bullfighting). Every Miao village in Li-p'ing and Yung-chiang keeps a pair of large water buffaloes (each village has a high tower in which these animals are kept). They are fed rice and are not used in the fields, but are reserved solely for bullfighting. The animals are extra large and fat. Their horns are covered with silver, and they wear cloth coverings. Every year after the harvest the Miao decide for themselves on a place for the event and make this known everywhere. On the appointed day they all arrive with their buffaloes. The appearance of the buffaloes is accompanied by trumpets and the beating of songs. The buffaloes are then let loose in pairs against one another. They jab at each other with their horns in wild hate. After a few clashes the weaker animal gives up. The victors light a fire and congratulate each other. Then they change the buffaloes and have another fight. Only after some two to three days of fighting do they go home. The victors are very proud, and the losers very abased. They slaughter the defeated buffaloes for the feast, or else they pay the winner more than ten taels an animal.[6]

6. *P'ao ma* (horse-racing). The Miao of T'ai-kung and Shih-ping have horse fights. They meet at a set time at a designated place. Those interested in purchasing a horse come early and look the animals over. Everyone rides a horse. They start at the same time. If the horse in question can pass five others, it's worth fifty taels. If it passes ten, then it's worth 100. Each one pays his price according to this. Even though the races are enjoyable, their main purpose is the performance test which determines the sale price.

These are the six general festivals. Local festivals are as follows:

Yao-ma-lang. The young men and girls from the Black Miao of Huang-p'ing and T'ai-kung meet in a clearing outside the village every evening after they are finished with their work in the fields and have had dinner. They take hold of each other by the hand, sing and do their best joking and mocking the other person. This is called *"Yao-ma-lang."* Their parents don't interfere at all in these activities. If you travel through Miao country at night, you can hear the singing almost everywhere. One year I lived for a time in the district office of T'ai-kung. Every night many Miao went out to the hill behind the office for *Yao-ma-lang.* The sound of their laughter and singing could usually be heard even as far as the district office. Every time I secretly stole into the woods on the mountain together with some of my office colleagues to watch them, they noticed us and left. But after we gradually became better acquainted, they stopped interrupting their *Yao-ma-lang* whenever we appeared, and even let us watch several times.

Lao-ku-niang. Among the Tung-chia around Yung-chiang three to five young men go over to a neighboring house where some girls live in the evening after dinner. They bring along stringed instruments, flutes, etc. The relatives of the girls have gone to sleep by then so as to make room for the visitors. The young men meet, play the violin and flute, and sing all night long. They are in excellent spirits. Should guests arrive, the head of the house invites them to the festivities. This is considered an honor. If a person accepts the invitation, he is received in a very friendly manner wherever he goes. The young start dancing then too.

Ch'ang shan ko (mountain songs). The men and women among the Chung-chia of Chên-ning and Lang-tai meet and sing mountain songs. The innumerable verses of a song are pleasant to hear. Among the local Chinese there are also some who prepare dinner, take the Chung-chia women out into the countryside, and sing mountain songs. But to do this they must have known each other for a substantial period of time.

One might suppose that it would be difficult to avoid a certain amount of wild behavior at these three festivals at which young people may meet and have fun without any limitations. However, although they are in good spirits, that's as far as it goes, and they don't become wild. These three festivals are very respected occasions, and no matter how much the young people may be in love, sexual excesses are extremely rare. Because these festivals are tests, trials for those who want to get married, the participants respect human dignity and don't get any foolish ideas. Whenever I witnessed these festivals, the thought came to me that we have been poisoned much too much by our own rituals and customs. Our social life is too solemn, the gulf separating man and woman is too broad, and the barriers between them are too great. Because of this, immoral behavior must be the result whenever we approach one another. In such interpersonal relations we might well take the Miao as our model.

PART THREE / Essay on Japan

20. SHIRAOI AND SHIKUKA
Notes on a Trip to Northern Japan in 1937*

Remnants of non-Japanese settlers still found in the Japanese islands include the Ainu, Orokes, Gilyaks, Tungus and Yakuts. Of these, the Ainu are living at present on Hokkaido, Karafuto (Sakhalin), and in the Kurile Islands. All the others live on Karafuto. A great proportion of the Ainu and many of the other groups are completely Japanisized by now. One frequently encounters Ainu women working as servants on Hokkaido. They can be recognized now only by their tattooed beard. The Japanese government places great importance on the settlement of the North, and likewise on the assimilation of the non-Japanese peoples who live there (this also holds true for the Korean, Chinese, Poles and Russians not mentioned here, who have recently emigrated to these parts of Japan). As the country is rapidly opened up, the non-Japanese are being forced to surrender their own ways and customs. In order to protect them from extinction and, at the same time, to accelerate their assimilation by means of better supervision, they have been brought together in settlements. I visited one of the Ainu villages in Hokkaido[1] which had come about in this manner, namely the village of Shiraoi in the southeastern part of the island, not far from the port of Muroran.[2]

This village is located adjoining to a Japanese village, but is about one hundred meters away from the latter and has a population of presumably some nine hundred Ainu. The houses all have the typical Ainu terraced reed-thatched roof, are rectangular in shape with a simple gable construction, have no posts or outlets for smoke, and are still being built without the use of nails.

The Ainu already all wear the simplest type of Japanese clothing in their everyday lives, and are outwardly, for the most part, indistinguishable from the surrounding Japanese. Only the old men are noticeable, due to their heavy beards, and women are conspicuous as a result of tattooing. Only three old families still wear the traditional dress and keep up the ancient customs. Today they probably do this mainly in order to earn money from

*Revised and translated version of "Shiraoi und Shikuka. Notizen über eine Reise in Nordjapan 1937," *Ethnologischer Anzeiger* IV (1941), 398-403.

vacationing tourists. It is also true that two of the old men played a special role in the bear festival, and because of this they were probably some sort of cultic leaders in the community. All of the Ainu already could speak fluent Japanese. Although the information obtained in conversations with one of the two old men and his wife does not contain any new ethnographic material, I would nevertheless like to sketch some of the main essentials here so that we can see what elements of the ancient Ainu culture are still alive in such settlements.[3]

The man says that the door of the house should be located on the south, the "gods' window" on the east, and another window on the south. His own house, however, had a second entrance on the narrow side facing west. This entrance went through a small front structure which served as a workroom. Other houses no longer had any windows facing south. The guest who enters a house, proceeds from the door eastward past the hearth in the center of the house, and sits down in the east section. The hosts sit to the north facing south, with the wife on the right next to her husband. The woman is supposed to perform all the duties relating to domestic economy. Nowadays, apart from pure housework, the only domestic job left is the weaving of mats decorated with very simple geometric patterns. The man is supposed to be occupied solely with hunting, fishing, and the bear festival. Today it has become almost impossible to hunt. The Ainu in the settlement are nearly all engaged in fishing, and in some cases already use small old motorboats. The larger fish caught are supposed to be brought into the house through the gods' window.

The women are tattooed in three places: around the mouth, between the eyebrows, and on the underarm and wrist. Tattooing was more frequent among older women and seemed rare among young girls. A sacrifice is made before every meal by squirting two samples into the hearth-fire with the 'beard-lifter,'[4] and then drinking initially from a cup (it was a lacquered Japanese cup) by means of a beard-lifter. The cult objects and vessels were preserved in round containers of Japanese origin. Even among these conservative families, the clothing is made of Japanese material which has been trimmed and embroidered by the woman. The patterns are supposedly free in design. By the way, the kind of trimming on a sort of vest the man wore shows a certain similarity to the type of trimming of Japanese peasant costumes from north Hondo which can be seen in the Folklore Museum in Tokyo. Numerous pieces of Ainu clothing on exhibit in the Toyohara Museum in Karafuto also revealed similarities with the Gilyak costumes likewise exhibited there. The man wore a headband made of wood, decorated in front with the small figure of a bear in three-fourths plastic relief, as well as wooden bear claws together with those wood chips that look like plane shavings, and which Ainu use just as much and for the same

14. Ainu hut and pig sty, Shiraoi, 1937.

15. Ainu couple in ceremonial dress, Shiraoi, 1937.

purpose as the Japanese their "gods' paper" (*gohei*). There was also a dress made of woven cowhide preserved in the house. The place to sleep was located in the house at the point where the *Tokonama* is located in the Japanese house, so that this is probably the old Japanese sleeping place, an assumption which we had made for other reasons as well. Arrows for the bear festival were brought out. They are short, and the point, formerly made of bone and now of bamboo, is separated from the shaft. The bow is simple, and is held horizontally. A lance with a mounted point is used in close combat with a bear. A harpoon with a point made of hartshorn or copper is used for fishing. Quite similar harpoons from excavations on Karafuto may be found in the Toyohara Museum. For certain large fish, they use a harpoon which can rotate around one of its ends and has a laterally mounted point in the shape of a half-moon. The fish is speared in the backbone with this instrument, and in its attempt to escape, it causes the point to rotate and thus become a kind of pole-hook. During the winter they wear shoes made of fishskin and woven snowshoes about fifty centimeters in length. They have simple sleds.

The settlements own two bear cages. One stood in front of the house to the south mounted on stakes about one and one-half meters high. Next to this there was a granary, likewise mounted on stakes. The heads of the sacrificed bears were impaled on poles to the east next to the house. There were wood shavings on the poles. The last bear festival was allegedly held in 1936. Judging from the appearance of the skulls, that did not seem impossible. All the skulls were from very young animals.

The museum in Toyohara, an exemplary well-ordered small-scale museum for the folklore and natural history of Karafuto (opened in the summer of 1937), is today the most important center for the study of Ainu culture. The museum exhibitions consist principally of the fruits of numerous excavations undertaken on Karafuto from 1931 to 1937. Without going here into detail, let me explain the major finds. These diggings bring three pre-historic cultures to light: First, a West Karafuto culture, which is pre-Ainu, has its center south of Hondo and extends to the Bay of Odomari. East of Odomari and extending as far north as Sakaihama is another culture, which for the present is believed to be Ainu. It is also represented on Hokkaido. In the north, located in the region of Shikuka, we find a third pre-historic culture, probably proto-Tungus in origin. It is even possible to extract a fourth pre-historic culture for Hokkaido. This culture is not Ainu, especially since the Ainu have always been and still are more coastal dwellers than settlers in the interior. It is of interest that the Karafuto finds show that influences of a higher culture were already felt there in the pre-historic period. These finds reveal that four-edged axes are frequent, and that the beginning of shoulder axes can be found, although there are no genuine rolled axes.

Shikuka (also called Shizuka, a non-Japanese word) is located on the Bay of Shikuka (formerly Terpjenje Bay) in the northern part of Japanese Karafuto. Originally a tiny settlement, it has grown in a few years to a town of about twenty thousand inhabitants, mainly due to the presence of a cellulose factory. The Japanese who settle in Karafuto come almost exclusively from Hokkaido and are seldom happy in this Siberian climate. The Japanese on Hokkaido, in turn, almost all come from northern Hondo and do not enjoy the Hokkaido climate, which is almost similar to that of Germany, either. On the other side of the large river which flows into the sea near Shikuka, likewise direct on the ocean, we find the village of Otasu. The dwellings in this village are almost all log houses built in the same style as those in the opposite Japanese city. This represents an adaptation of the Japanese house to the Siberian climate with borrowings from the Russian-Siberian log house. Two Yakut families live here. They live in a house almost completely Russian in character, with pictures of the Czar and Christian sayings on the walls. Ostensibly they emigrated here from the region of Yakutsk during the Czarist period, and they report that formerly such migrations occurred frequently, since the border control was not as strict as it is now.

In addition, four Tungus families live here during the winter. In the summer they move north with their reindeer, and were not around at the time of my visit.

There are six Gilyak families living here. They appear rather degenerated, most have physical maladies and they dress in rags according to the most simple Japanese style. They have preserved very little of their own culture.

Actually the Orokes are the only other people who still form a living cultural group. They also live somewhat apart from the others, and their settlement is the oldest. Today they nearly all live in the simplest wooden huts, and only two families were still living in pointed tents covered with cloth. In connection with the huts we observed that there is an iron oven in the center of the house, an adaptation of the hearth fire in the center of the traditional tent to the new conditions. They have not preserved any of their own traditional dress. Among their instruments I noticed a few traditional log canoes, one of which was even in the process of construction. It is made of willow. Dog's leather was used to make shoes. Otherwise we found that cheap Japanese articles, and, above all, gasoline cans reshaped in the most diverse forms, furnish the most important material for the house-hold. In fact, as far as I can judge, gasoline cans appear to be the most typical sign of cultures in the early phase of the process of Westernization!

Not far away from the settlement, located in a low wooded area, one finds the gravesites. They were rather crowded together, since the ocean and the settlement lay to the south, the river to the west, and immediately to the north and east the tundra began. I noticed a tree grave which the people in the settlement attributed to the Gilyaks. This grave was a small coffin made of boards about eighty centimeters in length, and was suspended some two and one-half meters above the ground in the branches of a pine tree. Next to the coffin hung a bunch of straw. The deceased (the grave could not have been more than four or five years old) must have previously been cremated or prepared in some other manner. I found a spot at which a burning had taken place not too long before (you could still see bits of skull in the ashes) near a house grave which was likewise attributed to the Gilyaks. It consisted of a small hut made of boards not more than sixty centimeters long. A board carved with typical Gilyak ornamentation had been placed on top as a gable, and the entire thing was held together by a cord. In front and to the rear of the grave were the broken household objects used by the deceased: dishes and sleds. Japanese influence could be seen in a wooden pillar, corresponding to a gravestone. The Orokes bury their dead in the ground. Like the Gilyaks, they put all the household objects broken on top of the grave, and, if they are Christians, they place a Russian cross with a Japanese inscription at the head of the grave. Otherwise they put up a wooden pillar with an inscription. In the near vicinity of all these gravesites the Japanese have erected a Shinto shrine. They are doing everything possible to introduce Shintoism here.

Close to the Gilyak houses I saw a "spirit-tree" about which the people could not supply any information. It was a young pine whose lower branches had been chopped off and trimmed with the wood shavings which are otherwise (as mentioned above) typical of the Ainu. I believe this was a Gilyak site. Finally, I saw a kind of tent made out of pine trees, open in front and hung with wood shavings. This was evidently a cult site, approximately similar to Siberian cult sites. Nothing could be seen inside the tent, but next to it a Japanese enamel ladle was hanging from a tree, and all around strewn on the ground one could see the gnawed-off paws of an animal, either a dog or a sheep. A Japanese I asked claimed this was the grave of an animal. However, this does not appear to be correct in any case. The work of the Japanese in this settlement consists in a kind of school they have set up in which the children are taught Japanese. There is also a kind of community center where people can gather and play. The relations between this settlement and the neighboring town of Shikuka, which lives off its cellulose factory and the lumber business, are not very extensive. Orokes live on fishing, Gilyaks for the most part likewise, and along with this they do some woodcutting. Tungus move around with their reindeer and live off these. The few Yakuts remaining are completely Japanisized. One Yakut is a teacher. There are no Ainu in the vicinity of Shikuka, and the majority of them live further south along the coast as fishermen. They are generally even more Japanisized than the Ainu of Hokkaido.

Unfortunately I had very little time for this trip, and my main interest lay in another field; I was busy at the time preparing for certain things that I wanted to work on in south China, and wanted to investigate parallel phenomena in Japan. Nevertheless, I believe that a more detailed investigation today of the non-Japanese in north Japan could still yield interesting results, both from the standpoint of ethnology and linguistics. The effects of these cultures on the Japanese also deserved more careful study. An interesting problem, for example, is how to explain the two completely different styles of ornamentation on the peasant jackets in north Hondo.

21. STUDIES OF NEAR EASTERN AND CHINESE FOLKTALES*

The comparative study of folktales is a somewhat discredited activity. Too often folktales which have only slight superficial similarities have been linked together; world-wide connections have been established on a purely imaginary basis. Since the days of Benfey, who was the first to trace most of our European folktales back to India, not even the basic question which method should be used in comparing folktales from different cultural areas has been solved. Against the "Finnish School," whose influence is widespread today, it can be pointed out that, although this method is well suited for comparisons within one cultural area, it is not safe for comparisons of folktales occurring in different cultural areas, because it only takes into consideration the folktale in itself, without first studying the situation of the folktale in general framework of each of the different cultures. Another method, newly developed by W. Ruben,[1] stresses the importance of sociological and historical factors but offers no safe criteria by which to determine relation or similarity. The classical method of Ehrenreich and Eisenstädter[2] demanded not only congruence of themes, but also of the sequence of the themes. Now, studies made by myself and P. N. Boratav on Anatolian folktales[3] have established the fact that, in areas where the folktale is still living and not yet petrified, there exists a certain stock of themes as well as of successions of themes which can within certain limits be linked together by the narrator. Therefore, (a) in cases where similarities are as clear as Ehrenreich's method requires, relation may be regarded as an established fact; (b) in cases where only some of the themes are identical or where the sequence of the themes is not the same, the situation of the themes or successions of themes in the respective cultures should be studied first, taking into consideration all available historical and sociological facts. Only if we are able to prove that the themes or succession of themes do not fit into the general framework of one of the cultures in question, but belong essentially to the other one, can we conclude that the folktale must have migrated from one place to the other. But in both cases we still have to study (a) the time at which and (b) the way in which the folktale came to its new home.

*Reprinted and revised from *Sinologica,* I (1947) 144-151.

To summarize the results of my studies on Chinese folktales, three different groups are to be found: (*a*) folktales of Eastern Asiatic origin, most of them already occurring in classical Chinese literature, (*b*) Indian folktales, imported from India since the first century A. D. by way of Central Asia, in the course of the propagation of Buddhism, (*c*) folktales existing only in the coastal part of southeastern China, never mentioned in Chinese literature before the fourteenth century. These folktales are of Near Eastern origin.

The folktale to be studied here belongs to the third group, but is an exceptionally clear case.

The modern forms of the tale in Anatolia and in China are as follows:

	A. *Near East*	B. *China*
1.	A poor man has (by predestination) to marry the daughter of the king.	A poor man falls in love with the daughter of a rich man.
2.	The king, in order to get rid of him, sends him to the sun, to collect taxes from the sun.	He goes to the Buddha to ask him how to get the three precious things required as marriage gifts.
3.	On his way the poor man meets (a) a priest who requests him to ask the sun when he may go to Heaven;	On his way he meets (a) monks, who request him to ask Buddha why nobody visits their monastery;
4.	(b) forty bandits who request him to ask whether they will ever go to Heaven;	(b) –
5.	(c) people who request him to ask why the fruits of an apple tree are so sour, the water of a well so bitter;	(c) people who request him to ask why their fruit trees never flower;
6.	(d) a fish lying half on the shore and half in the water who requests him to ask why he has to endure such hardship.	(d) a dragon who requests him to ask why he cannot yet go to Heaven.
7.	After the poor man has promised to ask this question, the fish bears the poor man on his back to the opposite shore of the sea.	After the poor man has promised to ask this question, the dragon carries him on his back to the opposite shore.
8.	The poor man meets an old man who tells him that:	The poor man meets an old man who tells him that:
9.	(a) the so-called priest will go to Hell, because he is avaricious;	(a) the monks are hoarding gold;
10.	(b) the bandits will go to Heaven, because they are repentant;	(b) –
11.	(c) the poor man must remove the treasures buried under the tree and in the well; then the apples and the water will become sweet.	(c) the poor man must remove the jars filled with gold under the tree;
12.	(d) a precious pearl in the mouth of the fish has to be removed.	(d) the dragon must give his pearl to the poor man.
13.	The poor man, now become rich, marries the daughter of the king.	The poor man is now able to give the marriage-gifts. He marries.

The congruence between the Near Eastern[4] and the Chinese[5] form is absolute. The only difference is the absence of themes *4* and *10* (which go together) in the Chinese form. In the Anatolian text four persons make requests to the poor man, not three, as is normal in folktales all over the world. But the question put forward by the bandits cannot be regarded as an independent theme; it is only the opposite of the question put by the priest, introduced only to point out the difference between the real and the false priests. So the difference between the Anatolian and the Chinese text is only a superficial one.

This means that — even according to the classical theory — the texts must be related; the folktale must have been brought from one place to the other. Now, we have to answer the questions: (a) where is the origin of this folktale and (b) when did it come to its second home?

In order to answer the first question, we must study the situation of the folktale in both cultures.

(a) The themes of the Anatolian version contain a great amount of local color: The theme that marriage is predestined reflects the general belief in predestination common to all Islamic countries; the theme itself occurs as the central theme in several other folktales[6] in a form in which the king, as soon as he knows the future fate of his daughter, tries to get rid of the poor man; another form, in which the king asks the poor suitor to fulfill three conditions, is even more common.[7] The collecting of taxes from the sun is connected with a proverbial expression occurring in Anatolia.[8] Variants simply say that the poor man goes away,[9] is sent to heaven,[10] to the moon,[11] to the "sunrise".[12] Several variants describe the poor man as a Negro slave to show that he is of the lowest social origin possible. These texts introduce the "theme" that he becomes white when he sees the sun.[13] The query of the impious priest and the pious bandit is to be found not only in Anatolia, but also in Palestine[14] and North Africa,[15] and belongs to a special folktale found in the whole Mediterranean area, and in Europe. Andrejew,[16] who has made an extensive study of this folktale, traces its origin back to the Near East. Bandits are always portrayed as a group of forty under the leadership of a big bandit; they are something like "gentleman-bandits" since they never rob the poor people but only bad, rich merchants. That means that they are not sinners in the ordinary sense, in spite of their bad social reputation. Undrinkable water is quite common all over the Near East, a question of the utmost importance for many villages. Hidden treasures play a role in many folktales[17] of different forms. As most of the rivers in the Near East dry up during the summer, fishes are often found in the situation described by the folktale; it should be remembered that the Turkish word for "sea" (*deniz*) often designates also a large "river," specially in the interior. A fish able to carry a man is of course something like a dragon, and the dragon (*ejderha*) or the dragon-king (*şahmeran*) is the holder of the great treasures hidden under the earth,[18] the theme of a set of folktales. Thus it is natural that the fish (dragon) should give a pearl to the poor man.

Not only are the single themes of our folktales deeply embedded in the general culture of the Near East, but also the tale itself is widespread in different forms. Up to now, it has been found in Anatolia and Iran in this special form, but there are two other very closely related forms that are even more popular:

(a) A poor man goes to the "fate" (*felek*) to ask it why he is so poor;[19] on his way he meets a wolf (bear, lion, snake) with a bad headache, two peasants whose trees or fields do not produce fruit, and a king whose commands are not obeyed by his subjects. The "fate" answers only the questions of these three (the king fails because he is a girl in disguise, a treasure is hidden in the field, the wolf must eat the brain of a very stupid man). As the poor man refuses to marry the girl-king, or to accept the treasure, he is the stupid man; the wolf eats his brain.[20]

(b) A king who knows that his daughter has to marry a poor man, buys the child and tries to kill it twice (three times). By exchanging a letter given to the child by the king ordering his decapitation for a letter ordering the marriage of the child with the princess, the poor man marries the daughter of the king.[21]

In some cases, form *b* is still more closely related to our folktale than in normal form related above. Folktale *a* contains a strong humorous element, but is so nearly related to our folktale that it could only be a variant of it if it were not so widely spread in Anatolia in this special form.

Altogether we can state that our folktale is so deeply embedded in the totality of Near Eastern folktales, that we should notice a perceptible deficiency if we took it out of this connection.

(b) The Chinese text too contains a certain amount of local color: The theme of the poor man marrying the rich daughter occurs quite often, but in accordance with Chinese social structure, the rich man is not a king, but normally a high official or a rich merchant. In many cases, the poor man is bald-headed as the result of scab, just as the poor man in Anatolia is also normally bald-headed (Keloğlan). The idea of visiting the Buddha may be connected with the famous novel *The Journey to the West*, based on the report of the journey of the monk Hsüan-tsang to India, written by Wu Ch'eng-en in the sixteenth century. Buddha is thought of as living in Hsi-T'ien-chu (Western India; sometimes shortened to Hsi-T'ien), changed into Hsi-t'ien (Western Heaven, Paradise) by folk etymology; so the poor man goes to Heaven.[22] The theme of the treasure hidden under a tree occurs in a different form in the tale of the "Conversation of the Animals,"[23] where treasures are hidden under the foundations of a bridge.[24] The monastery which is never visited can perhaps be compared with an episode in the above-mentioned novel, but this relation is quite weak. The dragon ascends to Heaven every spring according to Chinese folklore,[25] and normally has a pearl in or on his head,[26] or plays with a pearl. Journeys on the back of a dragon occur in Taoist stories, but are never met with in Chinese folktales.

In some Chinese variants a man asks why his daughter is dumb; in this case normally the poor man goes to the Buddha only to ask him why he is so poor, as in the Anatolian humorous variant. In a variant from Canton, the man in whose field the treasure is hidden excavates the jar by himself. He finds only snakes. He gets angry and throws the contents of the jar down the chimney of the poor man's house; there, all the snakes change into gold. This theme occurs in the same form as an independent folktale in the West.[27]

Our folktale as a whole is not embedded in the main body of Chinese folktales; there are no connections with other folktales found in China. Only some of its themes occur also in Chinese folklore, others in Chinese novels and stories. Furthermore, our folktale is to be found only in the coastal parts of southeastern and southern China.

Both versions, the Anatolian and the Chinese, have been collected in the last twelve years. Turkish folktales have only been collected systematically since 1944; only a very few tales, not including ours, have been translated into European languages. Chinese folktales have only been collected scientifically during the last fifteen years; only some of them have been translated into European languages and no translation into Turkish exists. So a transfer from one place to the other by means of written sources is out of the question.

As historical inquiries into Anatolian folktales have not yet been made – in fact they could not be made until the oral traditions had been collected – ,it is hard to determine at what time our folktale first occurred in the Near East. Only the fact that some of its essential "themes" spread over the whole of Europe in mediaeval times seems to prove that this folktale must have been in existence at least since the early Middle Ages.

The Chinese text is only to be found in modern oral tradition and not in literature. No mediaeval or ancient text contains this tale or parts of it. In my former studies on the novel *The Journey to the West*,[28] I accepted the possibility that our folktale influenced the general outline of the novel, but now this seems to me to be rather doubtful; on the contrary, it would be more logical to assume that the novel, today known to every Chinese and even to every child, influenced the special shape of theme two in the folktale.

To conclude: a relation between the Near Eastern and the Chinese folktale is undeniable. Its origin must be in the Near East, probably in Iran. As the Chinese folktale is told only in the coastal parts of China, it cannot have been introduced by way of Turkestan; it must have come by sea. It seems highly probable that it came to China during the fifteenth century, certainly not after the seventeenth century, since trade relations by sea between China and the Near East existed in the early Ming period (the expeditions of Cheng Ho!),[29] but were soon interrupted, never to be resumed after the appearance of European merchants in China. This conclusion is strengthened by the fact that this folktale is only one of a big set of folktales of the same character. These West-Eastern relations are only one link in a whole chain of mediaeval cultural relations between the Near East, including India, and the China coast. Studies by G. Ecke and by A. K. Coomaraswamy on Chinese architecture furnish further material.[30]

22. THE GIRL THAT BECAME A BIRD*
A Comparative Study

It is almost a generally accepted fact that many of our European folktales ultimately originated in India and reached Europe in the course of the medieval period. After a more thorough study of Near Eastern folktales, one can modify this statement by saying that tales originally Indian were transformed in the Near East and reached Europe in several different ways in this secondary form.[1]

It is also known that Indian folktales reached China via Turkestan in the course of the propagation of Buddhism. When a Chinese animal tale or any other tale can be traced as far back as the sixth century or earlier, it is almost certain that the tale is of Indian origin and that the origin can normally be proved by the Buddhist translations of Indian texts.

But there exists still another group of tales in China which never can be traced back further than the eleventh century, and these tales also normally are limited to a certain part of China, the southern and southeastern coastal provinces. It can be proved by comparison that this whole group of tales is of Near Eastern origin (i.e., these tales reached China not in their Indian form, but in a somewhat transformed secondary form). Three such comparisons are given here. The motifs of the Chinese tale are put side by side with the motifs of a tale which is rather common in Turkey. Turkish tales as a whole belong to the great Near Eastern tale circle which has its center in Persia. As Persian tales are not yet systematically collected, I prefer the Turkish tale, which is known by more than thirty different versions. All these versions are modern, as also are the Chinese versions.

CHINESE VERSION	NEAR EASTERN VERSION
(1) A man attacked by a snake is obliged to promise one of his daughters to the snake.	(1) A prince wants to win the three "Limon girls." He succeds only by the help of a witch.
(2) Only his youngest daughter is willing to marry the snake.	(2) By a mistake that he makes, only one girl remains alive.

*Reprinted and reviewed from *Semitic and Oriental Studies,* ed. Walter Fischel, University of California Publications in Semitic Philology XI (Berkeley, 1951), 79-86.

(3) In his palace the snake becomes a handsome man.

(4) When the bride visits her sisters and reports, one of them induces her to exchange dresses and then kills her by throwing her into a well.
(5) The jealous sister goes to the snake.
(6) The soul of the dead one changes into a bird and sings a song to her husband.
(7) The enchanted husband puts the bird into a cage, but the suspicious sister kills it.
(8) A broth made of the bird tastes good to the snake, but the sister dislikes it and throws it into the garden.
(9) A tree grows which the husband likes but which annoys the sister. She has it cut down.
(10) A bed is made of the tree. The husband likes it, but the sister is troubled.
(11) She burns the bed.

(12) The dead girl appears; everything becomes clear; the bad sister is killed.[2]

(3) He takes her to the outskirts of his town, asking her to wait until he comes back.
(4) She waits in a tree at the side of a well. A Negro girl sees her and induces her to exchange dresses; also climbs the tree and throws her down into the water.
(5) The prince takes the Negro girl.
(6) The soul of the dead one changes into a bird and sings a song to her husband.
(7) The husband likes the bird, but the Negro girl wants to eat it.

(8) When the bird is killed one drop of blood falls on the soil.

(9) A tree grows which the husband likes. The suspicious Negro girl has it cut down.
(10) A cradle is made of the tree. But one chip falls on the soil.
(11) An old woman takes the cradle home to burn it.
(12) A girl appears. The prince finds her; everything becomes clear; the bad Negro girl is killed.[3]

The parallelism is quite obvious if we leave motifs 1 to 4 out of consideration. Other Chinese versions even have the exact parallel of motif 11. Here the bad sister throws the bed away, an old woman takes it as firewood, and the dead girl appears out of the fire. The snake-man finds her one day in passing the house of the old woman.[4]

Only the difference in the introduction has to be explained. First it should be pointed out that nine out of thirty-six versions which I collected in Anatolia have a different introduction. Either the prince marries a poor girl or he finds a girl and marries her, and her sisters are jealous. Some of these introductions have motif 4; others omit this important detail.

Now, to speak of a relation between two tales occurring in different parts of the world should be admissible only when (a) the motifs and their sequence are really parallel, and when (b) other tales told in both places show a similar relationship. With regard to the second point it may be mentioned that in fact there are more than ten tales of the same type. [5] I hope to be able to publish my material on this problem soon. With regard to the first point, however, one fact should not be forgotten. A tale is not an abstract thing living a life of its own; wherever a tale is told it is in relation to the general pattern of culture. If a tale is introduced into a different culture, it is modified in such a way as to fit into the new pattern. A comparison of folktales, therefore, has always to consider the sociological facts. The Near Eastern text contains some details typical of Western Asiatic society, such as the Negro servant. Until recent times, rich families had Negro servants. And the well in villages is often just outside the village. Peasant women or servants come to it in the morning to get water, as the girl in our tale did. Very often a tall willow tree is beside the well, giving shade in a country where trees are rare. In China, however, such a situation is inconceivable. There, the well is within the village, no willow tree is beside the well, and Negroes are more or less unknown; at least, no one has a Negro servant. Moreover, the whole adventure of the prince is incomprehensible to a Chinese peasant. Owing to a curse by an old woman, the prince in the Western tale falls in love with girls whom he has never seen and who also have not been recommended to him by his parents. A Chinese man would either marry the girl chosen by his parents or marry a concubine of his own choice. But he would never bring her home; custom requires that the relatives of the girl bring her to his home. No Chinese girl would climb a tree and stay there for the night. According to Chinese custom, the bride has to leave her husband one month or earlier after the marriage and pay a long visit to her family. In a tale with the motif of a marriage this detail has to be mentioned.

Thus we find that, in the study of folktales, (*a*) the motifs must be compared and (*b*) the local "color" must be considered in its relation to the society to which the tales belong. In our tale the Chinese narrator had to substitute a new introduction, or he had to rely on one of the shorter introductions which also occur in the West, in order to make his tale understandable and acceptable to his public. The change is especially apparent in motif 4, where only the Western well with the tree is replaced by the Chinese well in the courtyard of the house.

But where does the "snake-man" come from? This is more difficult to decide, but it seems that the narrator substituted a set of motifs of a type "sexual relations with snakes," which is rather common in South China and serves as a basis for many folktales and artificial tales.[6] This solution is the best one, since there are other Near Eastern tales in which occurs a marriage with a ghost which takes various forms. The ghost always marries a girl in spite of the protest of the rest of the family and these marriages always bring great happiness.

Why is it improbable that the tale originated in China and thence migrated to the Near East? If the tale were indigenous, we should expect early quotations from it in Chinese literature. These have not as yet been found. On the other hand, the tale is so widespread in the Near East that it has to be regarded as old there, whereas it occurs only in a small part of China and did not spread over all that land, as other indigenous or early Indian tales did. And this is true also for all the other tales of this group.

Historically, we know that Persian and other Near Eastern merchants had many trading stations all along the southeastern coast of China.[7] We even know that Persians from Isfahan for a while ruled over the city of Zayton (Ch'üan-chou, Fukien province),[8] until they were defeated by the local army. It is highly probable that these merchants are to be held accountable for the transfer of this and similar tales.

In connection with our tale, one more detail should be mentioned. One Chinese version reads as follows (motif 3): "...The snake changed and became a very handsome, elegant man; he took the girl by the hand, and both entered the palace. In reality, this was the crystal palace of the dragon-king, and the big snake was the dragon-prince...."[9] The notion of a crystal palace is very unfamiliar to a simple Chinese. But in the Near East such fairy princes almost always live in a "crystal palace." The word "crystal" in Chinese is of Near Eastern origin; but it reached China much earlier than our tale.[10]

The change of details in a story when it is transmitted from one cultural area to another is a problem of great sociological interest, deserving much more consideration than it has hitherto enjoyed.[11]

In connection with our subject, I should like to mention two other tales which illustrate this very well.

The first follows.

CHINA	NEAR EAST
(1) A man by chance becomes famous as a fortune-teller.	(1) A poor woman wants to become rich and asks her husband to become a fortune-teller. He poses as a fortune-teller and by chance has great successes.
(2) He has several successes, such as finding a seal or saying the name of a thief.	(2) He finds a ring and traps thieves.
(3) ...	(3) He saves the life of the emperor.
(4) He is able to say what the contents of a closed box are. He says his own nickname, and thus names the enclosed thing.[12]	(4) He is able to say what the emperor holds in his hand by saying his own nickname.[13]

The parallel is even more striking when one reads the texts of the tale. In the Near East, the man supposedly practices the well-known form of oracle called "remil." In China, the introduction seems to be taken from another Near Eastern tale: The wife has a lover, for whom she always prepares chicken when he secretly visits her. Her husband observes this, and by taking an earthen pot and some chicken bones he pretends to make an oracle and "finds out" what happened to the chicken.[14] But other versions have still other introductions. The main stress lies on the next motifs. Here the man finds the ring of the emperor, whereas in China he finds the seal. The seal in China corresponds to the ring in the Near East as a badge of office. Motif 3, however, was inconceivable for a Chinese: In the Near East, the emperor visits a public Turkish bath. As soon as he is undressed the astrologer drives him out of the room. Minutes later the dome of the bath collapses. In China, the idea of an emperor visiting a public bath is unthinkable, and no man, except a eunuch, could be near the emperor in such a situation. In China, therefore, this motif is suppressed. Motif 4 is the same in both versions, only a box is substituted for the hand of the emperor; an emperor in China could not well hold an animal, such as a grasshopper, in his hand.

In China, this tale has not been found in the literature. It occurs only in southeastern China (with one exception: in Peking; but as a capital Peking is a place where people from every part of the country live).[15] Just as in some of the Chinese versions an introduction from another Near Eastern tale has been added, one Chinese version from Kiangsu province adds another end: The fortune-teller, now quite rich, visits the dragon-king. The king gives him a special ability, which he will lose at the moment he mentions it to another person. This motif, which is rare in China, belongs to another, quite famous Near Eastern tale in which instead of the dragon-king the snake-king Shahmeran is the hero. In this Chinese version the whole end part has no connection with the main tale; in the Near East this is a separate tale.[16]

The last example to be given here is a famous Near Eastern tale:

CHINA	NEAR EAST
(1) A man pretends to have things with supernatural qualities. He sells these one by one to his father-in-law:	(1) In order to take revenge, a man pretends to have things with supernatural qualities, which he sells to his enemy:
(2) first, a quick-cooking pot;	(2) first, a gold producing ass;
(3) then, a gold-producing ass;	(3) then, a hare which is able to run home and order a meal;
(4) then "several other things."	(4) then, a flute which resurrects dead people. The buyer kills his wife and tries to resurrect her.
(5) The father-in-law binds him and plans to throw him into the water.	(5) The hero is put into a bag. His enemy plans to throw him into the water.
(6) He manages to persuade a hunchback to take his place. The simpleton believes that he could be healed.	(6) He manages to persuade a shepherd to take his place. The simpleton believes that thus he would marry the daughter of the emperor.

(7) When the father-in-law sees the flock the man got from the hunchback, he asks how he too could get so many sheep.

(8) He says that he got them from the dragon-king in the sea. The father-in-law sits in an earthern jar, the hero in a wooden vessel. By throwing stones the hero sinks the earthen pot, kills the father-in-law, and gets his riches too.[17]

(7) The astonished enemy asks how to get these sheep.

(8) The hero says he got them from the sea. Both attach bladders to themselves and swim. The hero perforates the bladder used by the other and sinks him.[18]

This tale has several subtypes in the Near East, especially in its introductory part. Some texts replace the motif of the enemy totally. We are not yet able to say which introduction is the original one.

The motif 2–3 is only reversed in China; but the hare, which according to some texts[19] does not occur in south China, from which our texts come, or which has in Chinese folklore a special place that makes its appearance in this connection impossible,[20] is replaced. In both versions the guest is astonished to find a meal ready immediately after he enters the house — either by a "quick-cooking pot" or by the message of the hare.

Motif 4 does not occur in China, so far as my material is concerned. The texts I have indicate that a third trick is played, and this should be expected since three is the normal number in tales. Motif 5 is much more elaborated in the Near East: the intending killer visits a mosque or a marriage ceremony before going to dispatch the hero. Since a Chinese would not pray in a temple before such a deed, this motif usually is not elaborated in China; there, the enemy drinks tea or something similar. In motif 6 the simpleton is always a shepherd and the hero gets many sheep. In China, where sheep are much less important, some texts still preserve this motif, whereas others generally speak of "riches" only. But a shepherd as a simpleton is a concept foreign to a southern Chinese. He would conceive such a person as a young boy. And the idea that someone you meet on the street could be on his way to marry the daughter of the emperor is also inconceivable to a Chinese. So he inserts the motif of a hunchback, a man with an eye disease, or a merchant who wants to learn some new songs, and eliminates the shepherd and the marriage.

The same holds true for the last motif: the use of bladders to help swimmers is known in the Near East, but is foreign to a Chinese. So he substitutes the motif of the pots.

Like all Chinese folktales of this group, this one also is found in southeastern China only and never in Chinese earlier literature. Today this tale is famous and much treasured.[21]

Even though no other tales common to the Near East and southeastern China be cited, the strong influence of the foreign traders on the Chinese seems clear enough. On the other hand these few examples already show the social background of some of the differences between the Eastern and the Western texts. In the Near Eastern despotic empires, anything can be expected of the emperor. His deeds are incalculable, everything is possible. The hearer believes the storyteller if he says that a man is put into a bag because he was ordered to marry the emperor's daughter and was not willing to do so. No Chinese would believe him. In China, the concept of the emperor as a tradition-bound conventional high official is so deep-rooted that the hearer would expect a report on the attempts of the go-between to get a wife for the emperor, and the emperor would never think of marrying an ordinary man's daughter. The Chinese emperor would never hold a grasshopper or even a box in his hands: someone in his entourage would have to do it, and such a person could only hold a box, not an animal. In the Near East the despot can afford to be at the same time nearer to the common man and much higher: he can very well hold a grasshopper in his hand if this is pleasing to him, but he can also kill the common man without any real reason if he likes. Sociological analysis of related tales in different cultural settings can reveal interesting facts which sometimes cannot be got at through the more formal literature or by observation.

NOTES

FOREWORD

1. For a complete bibliography of my published works (1931-1965) see Eberhard, *Settlement and Social Change in Asia* (Hong Kong, 1967), 439-63.

2. Two vols. (Leiden and Peking, 1943); a revised and enlarged translation of the second volume is published as *The Local Cultures of South and East China,* (Leiden, 1968).

CHAPTER 1

1. This Chinese manuscript, as well as other manuscripts translated here, were deposited in the Berlin Anthropological Museum, and were destroyed during the War.

2. Temples with this name are mentioned, for instance, in the gazetteers of Huang-mei-hsien (Hupei), Tê-hua-hsien (Kuangtung), Chien-hsien (Hunan). In all three cases, they are located outside the city proper, and none of them is devoted to Ch'en Tao. They seem to be devoted to locally important persons. My edition of the Chin-hua gazetteer does not have this temple, nor the following one, because they were "unofficial temples."

3. In 1966 I received a manuscript by Mr. Feng in which he discusses the "Earth God Temples of Chin-hua." He tries to show that the tree temples are, in reality, earth god temples, and states that of the sixty earth god temples in Chin-hua, twenty one are named after trees. Any being or power considered beneficial to man was regarded as an earth god. Mr. Feng then continues: "Later people enlarged this concept, so that whatever was meritorious was given sacrifices at the *shê* (earth god altar), so that the earth god temples as well as the earth gods multiplied. Temples devoted to trees can carry three meanings: (1) When the people in ancient times set up an earth god altar, they planted a tree which fit the conditions of the place as "*chu*" (master, lord) just as the people of the Hsia dynasty planted pines, the

Yin people planted cypresses, the Chou people planted chestnuts (see *Lun-yü*, III, 21). The three states differed from one another, and so the trees which they planted differed too. *Chu* means 'god.' (2) They honored and remembered them, and let people see and esteem them, in order to make public their merits. A being which can show merits is supernatural. (3) Rural people believed that the trees were supernatural. They called the camphor tree 'Mother camphor tree' (*Chang-shu niang*). A newly born child recognized the tree as mother, so that (the tree) would protect it. Other trees also had similar powers. And from the ancient times on, people mixed up the tree and the earth god, so that later people honored either the one or both together. For instance, there is a legend that once during a war (the enemy) wanted to slaughter the people of the city, but would be willing to spare whoever was three feet away from the ground. So people all climbed the trees and thus were saved. Thereupon the trees got temples and sacrifices. This legend is recent, as it cannot explain the other temples. . . ."

4. Tree temples are, of course, also known from other parts of China, but they seem to be especially common in Chin-hua; they are also usually to be found outside the cities. Here they are inside. In the literature, tree temples are most often mentioned for the Chêkiang area and adjacent provinces. For example, *Shui-ching-chu* (VI, 40. 118) mentions one for Chêkiang; *Sou-shen-chi* (19, 1b) for Lung-shu in Anhui; *Chien-hu-chi* (I, 4. 5a) mentions that in the fifth century (i.e., approximately the time of our first source) trees in Chêkiang got official recognition as deities. We hear of a tree in Kiangsi province which received girls, sheep and pigs as sacrifices (*T'ai-p'ing kuang-chi* XXV, 315. 41a; tenth century). Many more examples could be given.

5. Chap. XIII, 14a-b of the new chronicle.

6. See *Min-chien yüeh-k'an*, II (Hangchow, 1933), 43.

7. See *China-Dienst*, III (1934), 941-45.

8. Couvreur I, 34.

9. Ia, 2b, under the heading "earth god."

10. Ie., *Lun-yü*, chap. 2, par. 21, in the R. Wilhelm translation, p. 27, form herinafter *Lun-yü*, II, 21=Wilhelm, 27; *Mê Ti*, 46 =Forke, 550; *Chou-li* = Biot, I, 193; *Han Fei-tse*, 34; *Po-hu-t'ung; Huai-nan-tse*, chap. "Shuo-lin;" *Chuang-tse*, IV, 4 = Wilhelm, 33; *Han-shu*, 27a-b; *Shih-shuo hsin-yü*, V and XXV; compare in particular E. Chavennes: *Tai-shan*, p. 371-467.

11. Yü-chang; *chang* is said to refer to camphor tree.

12. *Shui-ching-chu,* (chap. XXXIX).

13. *Chi-shen-lu,* as quoted in *T'ai-p'ing kuang-chi* XXXVIII, 354. 43b; and *Ming-chai hsiao shih,* III, 11a.

14. *Wu-chou fu-chih,* as quoted by *Yüeh-hsi ts'ung-tsai,* XI, 13a for Kuanghsi province.

15. *Kui-lin feng-t'u-chi,* quoted in *Yüeh-hsi ts'ung-tsai,* XIII, 7a, also for Kuanghsi.

16. See Matthias Eder in *Folklore Studies,* VI, 68.

17. For example, in Yang-chiang, Kuangtung province; see Lou Tse-k'uang, *Chung-kuo hsin-nien feng-su chih*, 1st ed., p. 46.

18. It was believed that the timely production of rain was a part of the duty of the local god. Magistrates, acting as representatives of the Emperor, who himself was the "Son of Heaven," could remind the deity of its duty, and we have many reports of officials blackmailing or forcing deities.

19. Temples all over China have to the present time served as unofficial hotels, but often developed into true hotels which charged fees. The motif of the temple dream is extremely common in Chinese folktales, theater plays and short stories.

20. I.e., they were formerly regarded as "unofficial" or "heterodox" deities. Wu is Kiangsu, Yüeh indicates here Chêkiang and Fukien.

21. Chap. XI, 1a-b.

22. *Chronicle,* XVIII, 5b.

23. See *Chung-kuo jen-ming ta-ts'ih-tien,* 429-30.

24. Ibid., 1409.

25. *Chronicle,* XVIII, 6a-7a.

26. Ibid., 10a.

27. See *Chung-kuo jen-ming ta-ts'ih-tien*, 435.

28. See *T'u-shu-chi-ch'eng*, chap. "City God."

29. See supra.

30. According to the *Sui Annals*, Wu-hsing-chih, and *Pei Ch'i-shu, XX*, The author of the *K'un-hsüeh chi-wen*, chap. XX, 12a, regards this reference of the year 552, mentioning a city in Hupei province, as the earliest. See also the discussion of this text in *Historical Annual*, II, 251ff.

31. It is not impossible that Chinese city god cults have some relation to Indian cults which came to China with Buddhism (mentioned in Surangama Sutra, *Taishô Tripitaka* text XIX, 945. 151a; and text XIX, 950. 193c).

32. Chap. V, 13b.

33. Chap. XV, 9a ff. of the *Yüh-ho-hsien-chih*.

34. Recorded by Mr. Yao in Yün-ho.

35. According to the Chronicle *Chin-yün hsien-chih*, V, 18a-b.

36. See *Min-chien yüeh-k'an*, I, no. 10, 79-80; Ku Chieh-kang in the book by Wei Ying-ch'i, *Fu chien san-shen-k'ao*, 67-77, with old sources; further ibid., 78-114; Jung Chao-tsu, *Mi-hsin yü chuan-shuo*, 222-28; R. Wilhelm, *Chinesische Volksmärchen*, 48; W. Eberhard, *The Local Cultures of South and East China* (Leiden 1968), 402.

37. *Chin-yün hsien-chih*, V, 3a-4a.

38. Information from Mr. Wei, Yün-ho.

39. *Yün-ho hsien-chih*, III, 20b. It is citing an older chronicle from about the year 1800; the printing at my disposal is of 1868.

40. It is interesting to note that early Chinese classical literature already associated the clan Liu with dragons (texts translated in Ed. Chavannes, *Mémoires historiques*, I, 168 and J. de Visser, *The Dragon in China and Japan*, 50-51), although I do not believe that this cult utilized the old tradition which was not too widely known in later times.

41. See *Zeitschrift für Ethnologie,* LXIII, (1932), 50.

42. See Jung Chao-tsu: *Mi-hsin yü chuan-shuo,* 199-200; see also ibid., 196-219 for more general treatment.

43. *Chung-hua ch'üan-kuo feng-su-chih,* II, chap. VII, 13-14.

44. For a further discussion of dragon mother cults, see my *Lokal-kulturen im alten China,* II.

45. *Chin-hua hsien-chih,* V, 21a.

46. See T. Mabuchi, "Spiritual Dominance of the Sister," in *Ryukyuan Culture and Society* (Honolulu, 1964), 79-80. Mabuchi has not studied the connections with China or with Japan.

47. To my knowledge, H. Stübel never got to publish this study and it does not appear to be in his files.

48. See Marcel Granet, *Danses et légendes de la Chine ancienne,* II, 55.

49. Special studies of shamanism in Taiwan are now in preparation, and should greatly clarify this problem.

CHAPTER 2

1. Some of the texts relating to Count Hu have been published in my *Volksmärchen aus Südost-China,* No. 85, Type 128. The remaining texts, not contained in this essay or the book, can be found in my *Erzählungsgut aus Südost-China* (Berlin, 1966).

2. A discussion of the mountains of the dead will be found in my *Guilt and Sin in Traditional China* (Berkeley, 1967).

3. All data are according to the Chinese (traditional) calendar in which the New Year occurred sometime between late January and late February.

4. I have not been able to find any information on the other four counts, who are supposed to be worshipped in this district. For a biography see below.

5. "Old Lord" is the term of address for Count Hu.

6. Among the people all gods are known as "Buddhas," even when they have no connection with Buddhism.

7. Among the people all gods are known as "Buddhas," even when they have no connection with Buddhism.

8. The three dots are also in the original. Apparently some text is missing.

9. Astrologically favorable days are determined for marriages far in advance. These are not so frequent that they can be easily changed.

10. Sentences and dots in parentheses are also in the Chinese original.

11. P'u-sa is actually a transcription of the word Boddhisattva; in folk belief this designates gods of the second level.

12. "Three Mornings" means New Year's Day.

13. See p. 60 of the edition of the Hsin-wen-hua Publishing House (Shanghai, 1934).

14. *Hou-tê-lu,* III, 2b; a Sung source.

15. *Fan Weng-cheng-kung chi,* chap. XII.

16. *Mo-k'o hui-hsi,* I, 1b; a Sung source.

17. See manuscript III, 199c; stories which are very similar to those about Count Hu are also reported for a deity on Mt. Ta-hua in Kiangsi province (see *Erh-shih lu,* I, 12a-b.).

18. See my *Lokalkulturen im alten China,* II, passim.

19. See my *Kultur und Siedlung der Randvölker Chinas* (Leiden, 1942), 220; they are identified there with the Yüeh peoples.

20. In most parts of China this ceremony has not been celebrated over the last few centuries. As weddings were performed earlier and earlier, the ceremony became a part of the wedding ceremonies.

21. See *Hsiao-tou-p'eng,* 83 and Wang Hui-chien in *Confucianism in Action* ed. D. Nivison (New York, 1959), 92; also K. Ch. Hiso, *Rural China* (Seattle, 1960), 230.

22. Already intimated by Ko Hung (4th century A.D.); see R.H. van Gulik, *Sexual Life in Ancient China* (Leiden, 1961), 104. Many Chinese texts have commented on the prevalence of prostitution at the centers of pilgrimages (see *T'ao-en meng lu* in *Li-tai hsiao-shuo pi-chi hsüan, Ming,* 408 and *Lu-shui-t'ing tsa-shih,* I, 4a). Others remarked on the illegal sex life of Buddhist nuns (examples in G. Schlegel, *Prostitution en Chine,* 30). Just to indicate the importance of pilgrimages, it might be noted that there were 6321 pilgrimages in 1935 in Taiwan (see *T'ai-wan feng-t'u,* No. 132, 1951).

23. See chap. I, sec. 1 above.

24. "T'ai-pei-hsien, Chung-ho shê-ch'ü-chih yen-chiu," anonymous B.A. thesis (1951), National Taiwan University, 41; see also the brief remarks by Lin Heng-tao in *T'ai-wan feng-t'u,* No. 132 (1951).

CHAPTER 3

1. See *Typen,* No. 100, and *Volksmärchen,* No. 62; also in my *Folktales of China,* No. 32. All texts not published in *Typen* or *Volksmärchen* can be found in my *Erzählungsgut aus Südost-China* (Berlin, 1966).

2. A 'shade-wall' is a small wall placed in front of a door or gate. This is supposed to prevent ghosts from entering, and also serves as an obstruction so that those outside cannot see into the house.

3. Chinese medicine has prescriptions against enuresis, but folk belief seems to connect enuresis with magic rather than regard it as a disease.

4. Chinese chamber-pots often have the shape of those aluminum water kettles which we often use in the kitchen, but they are made of clay or china, and because of the small opening they cannot be thoroughly cleaned. In Chinese folk belief, urine has the quality of fixing ghosts, spirits and even deities so that they cannot move any more. This seems to be connected with the concept of ritual impurity of urine. Lists of sins have many provisions of this type. It is, for instance, sinful to urinate so that the polar star can see it, etc. The tainting of the God of Thunder through contact with the chamber-pot or its contents is one of the most common stories.

5. A general term designating any deity, not necessarily Buddha. The text here introduces a motif which is known from all parts of China, namely that of the impostor, who, hidden behind a statue of a God, speaks for the God and influences the worshipper. In general, the scene is described as if there were an allusion to the motif of the temple-dream. This custom, still very common in present-day Taiwan, is to visit a temple with a powerful God, and to spend a night in or near the temple praying for a dream in which the God directly or indirectly gives an answer to the prayer of the worshipper.

6. This indicates that he made the figure of a spirit, not of a Buddha. Spirits do not dress their hair, just as native tribes do not, according to folk belief.

7. Such conduct is most highly improper according to Chinese customs. The bride is not supposed to even talk to her groom during the bridal night. I assume that the text here wants to indicate some resistance on the part of the bride against consummation of the marriage. Here and in other stories, one is tempted to make psychological interpretations, since the case seems (to us) so obvious.

8. See also my *Typen chinesischer Volksmärchen*, FFC No. 120, 150.

9. I am not sure about the symbolism involved. In general, ink frightens evil spirits away, because it symbolizes the superior man, the scholar who writes with ink.

10. This symbolism is based on a dialect expression.

11. See *Mê Ti*, 49 = *Forke*, 593-594; *Mê Ti*, 50 = Forke, 595; *Mê Ti*, 36; see also Giles, *Biographical Dictionary*, 1424, and Doré, *Recherches*, XI, 1031-1032 and fig. 299; further references in *Lun-heng*, etc.

12. *Shui-ching-chu*, chap. XIX = III, 108; *San-fu huang-t'u* and *Feng-su t'ung-i*, as quoted in *I-wen lei-chü*, chap. LXXIV.

13. *Yu-yang tsa-tsu*, as quoted by T'P'KCh. XVIII, 225. 6a-b.

14. On his present role as patron, see J. St. Burgess, *The Guilds of Peking* (New York, 1928), 91; his temple in Hong Kong is described by V.R. Burkhardt, *Chinese Creeds*, II, 117.

15. In *Min-su,* No. 113 (Canton, 1933), 13.

16. Published in Shanghai, n.d., Ching-chan Publishers; in 1964 in Taiwan I bought another copy of the same book: Taipei: Jui-ch'eng Publishing House, 1961.

17. A reference in the biography of the saint allows us to establish the time after 1420 as a date *ante quem non.*

18. Chap. LXIII, 1b; LXVI, 1b; XLV, 7b.

19. Attestations in *Typen chinesischer Volksmärchen.* 146; for a tale about a furnace foundation sacrifice, see *Folktales of China,* No. 60.

20. *Min-su,* No. 113, 14.

21. Ku Chieh-kang, *Meng Chiang-nü ku-shih yen-chiu,* I, 57-58; see also *Folktales of China,* No. 16.

22. Matignon, *La Chine hermétique,* 244.

CHAPTER 4

1. The stories are quoted, after a translation made by myself, in seven parts. The original Chinese texts were in the Berlin Anthropological Museum. It is not known to me whether they still exist. They were also organized in seven parts with the same numbers.

CHAPTER 5

1. See my *The Local Cultures of South and East China* (Leiden 1968), p. 185.

2. *Yung-hsien chai pi-chi,* V, 3a-b.

3. *Tung-p'o chi-lin,* IX, 3b.

4. *T'u hua chien wen chih,* VI; author Kuo Jo-hsü.

5. *Monumenta Serica* IV, note on p. 340 and plate 13e; W. Rudolph, "Bull Grappling on Early Chinese Reliefs," *Archeology* III (1960), No. 41.

6. References in my *Kultur und Siedlung der Randvölker Chinas;* see also I. de Beauclair, *Sinologica* V (1956), 29-31, with illus., and I. de Beauclair, *Bulletin of the Institute of Ethnology* X (1960), 130.

7. Choe Sang-su, *Annual Customs of Korea* (Seoul, 1960), p. 87.

8. Further literature on the general topic of bullfights in *Bulletin of Chinese Studies,* IVa, 174-175, and C.W. Bishop, "The Ritual Bullfight," *China Journal,* III: 630-37.

9. He died in 1689 (see A.W. Hummel, *Eminent Chinese,* I, 85). The line is from one of his poems.

10. This temple is not mentioned in the Chin-hua Gazetteer.

11. Six *mou* are equal to approximately one acre.

12. About the middle of September.

13. In the *Publications of the Academica Sinica.*

14. Or Li K'o in other sources; it's the same man.

15. Second dynasty, from the middle to the end of the first millenium B.C.

16. Commonly called "Count Hu". For material about him, see chap. I, section 2 above.

17. Philosopher and statesman in the third century B.C.

18. Historical work by Sih-ma Ch'ien, composed about 100 B.C.

19. Mr. Ts'ao refers here to an article by Chung Ching-wen in the journal *K'ai-chan yüeh-k'an* X, which discusses the Chin-hua custom (3-6, and earlier references).

CHAPTER 6

1. Since the tiger is regarded as a very strong animal, its parts, especially the fat and the liver, are valuable ingredients for many traditional Chinese medicines. The price given is in Chinese dollars, equivalent to approximately $50 in American currency at the time of writing.

2. This refers to her dowry which remains the property of the wife after marriage. A woman had no other personal property in traditional China.

3. The same story, but as an animal tale from Taiwan about a monkey and his mother, is reported by Chiang Chieh-shih, according to an article by Lou Tse-k'uang in the daily paper *Tse-li wan-pao* (Taipei, Taiwan. Sept. 8, 1967). Lou gives the full text of the fable.

4. The doll was probably of Japanese origin. Nationalistic propaganda was very strong in China at the time of writing.

5. The 'pigtail' was a custom introduced by the Manchu dynasty. After the Revolution of 1911, the pigtail became a symbol of reactionary attitude; therefore the governments of various periods often cut them off. I did not see men wearing pigtails in the area when I was there (1934).

6. I am not familiar with this custom. Presumably the sugar will change its color if the person was murdered.

7. The modern form in which opium is taken.

8. Undoubtedly inspired by a very similar story in a school book published by the Commercial Press, Shanghai.

9. The literary source of this story is mentioned in my *Guilt and Sin in Traditional China* (Berkeley 1967), p. 105, case no. 11.

10. The *Ch'ien-tse-wen* or "Thousand Character Text" is the second book which children were required to memorize in the old-time school. The line which is quoted is now a proverb. The whole story could come from a modern textbook, but I do not have any proof of this.

11. The custom of sleeping in a temple in order to get a dream which solves a problem the sleeper has, is widespread throughout China and occurs in many tales.

12. In reality, such an event could hardly ever happen, since the imperial princes did not play in areas accessible to the common people or beggars.

13. This story is puzzling. There is a widespread belief in China and in the Li-shui area that the lightning kills only persons who have committed

secretly a very grave sin, usually persons who have behaved in an unfilial manner toward their parents. Thus, relatives of such victims of lightning are very much ashamed, and nobody in the village would think of feeling sorry. This story is perhaps narrated in a corrupted form.

14. I do not know exactly what this means. Probably refers to a small stove to burn sacrificial paper.

15. On the importance of camphor trees, see chap. I, sec. 1. The farmer follows tradition when he was only interested in his son, but not in his daughter.

CHAPTER 7

1. See, for example, Li T'ai-po, *Mélanges chinois et boudhiques* I, 8; Hsü Wei, *Hsü Wen-ch'ang chi*, XI, 11ab.

2. See, for example, *Feng-shen-pang,* chap. VI (Grube, 67).

3. See Yüan Mei, *Tse-pu-yü,* I, 150.

4. Yüan Mei, *Hsiao ts'ang-shan-fang wen-chi,* chap. XII = II, 1; or Tseng Yen-tung, *Hsiao-tou-p'eng,* 59; Wang Shih-chen, *Ch'ih-pei ou-t'an*, II, 85; T'an Ch'ien, *Tsao-lin tsa-tsu,* I, 145.

5. *Hua-yüeh-chih,* IV, 19b-56b.

6. According to a personal communication of Mr. D. Parsons (London), who made photographs of inscriptions there.

7. This refers to the bound feet of Chinese women in former times; the feet were supposed to be not larger than three inches.

8. In Kiangsu province, quite far away from Yün-ho.

9. Quotation from *Shih-shuo hsin-yü,* XIX, 238.

10. This means: to the hells and to judgement there.

11. Last 2 words not clear.

12. Sentences like this one were formerly also found on the doorposts of the houses or shops of business men.

13. This is not a poem. Ordinary prose.

14. This poem refers to a story which also occurs in the drama, according to which the first emperor of the Sung dynasty (960-1268) had a meeting with Ch'en T'uan. According to tradition, he was called to court in 970, but retreated again into the Hua-shan. See H. Franke in *Zeitschrift der deutschen morgenländischen Gesellschaft* CIX (1959), 371; *Yü-hu ch'ing-hua* VIII, 1a; the dramas *P'an-t'ao hui, Ch'en T'uan kao-wo,* and *San hsing chao.* Ch'en is best known on the mountain as Ch'en Hsi-i, another name is Ch'en T'u-nan.

15. The first and last line (the latter with slight alterations) occur in a Peking folksong (*Pei-p'ing ko-yao chi*); the first and third lines occur in a folksong in Su-chou (*Wu-ko i-chi,* 75).

16. Last line missing.

17. According to a local legend, the deity was once a concubine of Emperor Shih-huang (3rd century B.C.), but she left him, ran away into the mountain which is not too far from the capital at that time, and became a saint. Her story is mentioned in many sources such as *Lieh-hsien chuan,* II, 6a-b; *T'ai-p'ing kuang-chi,* II, 29. 53b, and III, 40. 36a; also in *T'ai-p'ing kuang-chi,* IV, 59. 45a-b. The poet Su Tung-p'o wrote a poem about her (*Tung-p'o shih* XII; Shanghai edition, 234b).

18. As it is written, the word could mean 'bee,' but I assume that it is miswritten for 'mang,' a big snake.

19. Here, as in many other poems and essays, intercourse is thought of as a fight or battle.

20. This and the following riddles (Nos. 71, 72, 75, 76) refer to Chinese characters and the way they are written.

CHAPTER 8

1. Lou, who now lives in Taiwan, has recently republished this book, *Hsin-nien feng-shu chih,* with an introduction by Wolfram Eberhard (Taipei, 1967). He is also planning to republish his book on marriage customs.

2. *Min-chien yüeh-k'an (Folk Monthly);* a complete bibliography of its contents is given in *Min-su* (Canton), No. 115 (April, 1933), 26-32.

3. See, for example, *K'ai-chan yüeh-k'an,* No. 10/11 (July, 1931), and *The Adult Education Quarterly,* II, no. 1 (Feb., 1933).

4. In the famous series *Märchen der Weltliteratur* (Jena, 1921).

5. Introductory note by W. Eberhard and Alide Roemer; the essay which follows first appeared in Chinese in the journal *Min-chien yüeh-k'an* II no. 5 (Feb., 1933), 1-16.

6. For another view of the history of the Chinese folklore movement from 1918 to 1937, see Chao Wei-pang, "Modern Chinese Folklore Investigation," *Folklore Studies* I (Peking, 1942), 55-76, 79-88; a more detailed discussion of the development of Chinese folklore studies from their inception to the present, seen from a different perspective, is given by Richard M. Dorson in the Foreword to my *Folktales of China* (Chicago, 1965). A history of Chinese folklore on Taiwan still has to be written.

7. Brother of the famous writer and politician Lu Hsün.

8. He continued to work in Communist China, though mainly on ancient history, not folklore.

9. Written by Chou Tso-jen.

10. The weekly was restored in March, 1933, but in July it stopped again. Altogether it issued 123 numbers. A classified index to the content of the *Folklore Weekly* (*Min-su chou-k'an,* No. 1-123) is found in the *Journal of Chinese Folklore* I, no. 1 (Canton, Sept. 1936), 237-307.

11. No. 110 appears as a special number before No. 109!

12. See our reviews in *Sinica* VII (1932) 124; *Weltkreis* III (1932), 22, 87, 88, 153, 160; *Ethnologischer Anzeiger,* III, 80.

13. *Min-chien yüeh-k'an* (*Folk Monthly*); the final issue, II, No. 10, appeared before the Sino-Japanese War. Most of these journals and books are now extremely rare. Much of the data published in them used by Nagao Ryûzô in the first two volumes of his *A Record of Chinese Customs* (Tokyo, 1940-41). These two volumes deal with the New Year's Festival and other festivals of the first month of the year. Nagao, however, does not mention his sources. On Nagao's work, see Howard S. Levy and Ryooji Sasaki, *Unsung Hero. The Late Nagao Ryûzô. Conversations* (Yokohama, 1967).

14. See *Sinica* VIII (1933), 40.

15. See *Ch'iao-nü ho kai-niang-ti ku shih* (Shanghai, 1933).

16. See *Sinica* VII (1932), 124.

17. Compare already, for example, certain parts of Kuo Mo-jo, *Chung-kuo ku-tai shê-huei-shih;* and in particular the research program in *Min-su,* No. 113, 1933, 25.

18. See *Weltkreis,* III (1932), 88.

19. The three deities discussed in this book are very popular in Taiwan and much material on them can be found in Taiwanese folkloristic essays. I have never been able to locate a copy of Wei's book.

20. This is a mountain not very far from Peking, the center of yearly pilgrimages.

21. The essay appeared in *Min-chien yüeh-k'an* II no. 7 (July, 1933), 35-42.

CHAPTERS 9 and 10

1. In the "Ancient Chronicle of Shao-hsing," cited in Hsü Wei, *Hsü Wen-ch'ang-chi,* chap. XVIII, 7b-8a; Hsü Wei was a painter during the Ming period.

2. See my "Eine neue Arbeitshypothese über den Aufbau der früh-chinesischen Kulturen," *Tagungsberichte der Gesellschaft für Völkerkunde,* II (Leipzig, 1937), 90-107: see also my "Early Chinese cultures and their development: A new working-hypothesis," *Annual Report of the Smithsonian Institution* (1937), 513-30.

3. *Sou-shen-chi,* XII, 2a; quoted in *T'ai-p'ing yü-lan,* 888, 4b.

4. Died 238 A.D.; see Giles, *Biographical Dictionary,* No. 448.

CHAPTER 11

1. *The Hsia-min of Tsemushan,* Academia Sinica, Monographs of the Institute for Social Sciences, No. 6, (Nanking, 1932).

2. A word or two missing, probably something like "as follows." For a discussion about P'an-hu, the mythical ancestor of all Yao tribes, see my *Lokalkulturen im alten China,* II, 20 f.

3. Ch'u was a feudal kingdom before the 3rd century B.C. The date which is mentioned here is no true date. *ta-sui* (or more correctly *t'ai-sui*) is the Jupiter cycle of 12 years, not normally used for dating purposes. Mount K'ui-chi is located south of Hang-chou in Chêkiang province, a cult center connected with certain tribes. Nothing is known to me about the cave.

4. Yüeh-hsin hu. Not known to me from other texts.

5. A feudal state in present-day Kiangsu province.

6. All these animals with human family names are star deities. This part of the story seems like a special version of the story *Feng-shen yen-i.* Of all the animals mentioned, I am only familiar with K'ang Chin-lung. He is the youngest son of the dragon king Ao-kuang (drama *Shuang pao en,* Ming period. Quoted in *Ch'ü-hai,* I, 592).

7. Kao-hsin is one of the mythical emperors of China who supposedly ruled some 2000 years prior to the origin of the feudal states Wu and Yen. The missing part of the text relates that the hero, a dragon-dog, was born miraculously.

8. This refers to the year 1804.

9. Two sets of 3 "emperors:" "The Emperor who opens Heaven," "The Emperor who opens Earth," and "Emperor Pan-ku," another mythical figure related to P'an-hu; "Heaven Emperor," "Earth Emperor," and "Man Emperor."

10. See *Hsia-min wen-t'i,* in *Tung-fang tsa-chih* XXXI no. 13 (Shanghai, 1933), 57-65.

11. *Yün-ho hsien-chih,* XV, 10b-11a; from the year 1868.

12. *Chêkiang Hsia-min tao-yin,* in *Nan-ching hsüeh-pao* III no. 2 (Nanking, 1933), 427-42.

13. The problem of the Hsia-min is discussed in a larger frame of reference in the second volume of my *Lokalkulturen im alten China.* The

Chinese text of the genealogy, as copied, was deposited in the Berlin Anthropological Museum, and was destroyed during the war.

CHAPTER 12

1. *Plantation Songs of Ting hsien,* 2 vols. (Peking, 1933).

2. *Chung-kuo ti-fang hsi-ch'ü chi-ch'eng,* Anhui, 962-964.

3. Quoted in *Ch'ü-hai,* II, 1047-1050.

4. Ta-ta Publishers (Shanghai, 1935), 214.

5. A man was allowed only one real wife, although he could have numerous concubines. Ting-lang assumes that his father did not tell his new father-in-law that he had a wife. Mr. Hu would not have given him his daughter, because if he had known, the girl would have had to be a concubine.

6. This man occurs as a "gentleman bandit" in dramas like *T'ien yo yen* and *Chin i kui.*

7. The date refers to Chinese months, not to our months.

8. Famous poet (712-770 A.D.).

9. On the 5th day of the month.

10. Refers to the folktale *Swan Maiden* (Eberhard, *Typen*, No. 34).

11. On the 15th day.

12. On the ninth day.

13. On the first day; reference to the Meng Chiang tale (*Typen*, no. 210).

14. Nine sets of nine days.

15. *Ting-hsien yang-ko hsüan,* I, 335-362.

16. Ho Feng-ju and Alide Eberhard, *50 Pekinger Kinderspiele.*

17. *Pei-p'ing ko-yao chi,* II, 88.

18. *Shan-tung ko-yao chi,* II, 114.

19. *K'ai-feng ko-yao,* 124.

20. *Min-su,* No. 83, 39 f.

21. According to *Miao-hsiang shih ts'ung-hua,* I, 4a-b.

22. *Chien-hu chi,* part 3, chap. III, 10a-b.

23. See, in addition, *Chien-hu chi,* part 7, chap. III, 12b.

24. A Sung poem of Buddhist type can be found in *Taishô-Tripitaka,* XC, 704a.

25. First attestation in *T'ai-p'ing kuang-chi,* VII, 90. 9a, according to *Kao-seng chuan.*

26. Text from the Sung period in *Yeh-k'o ts'ung-shu,* XVIII, 6b-7a.

27. *Hai-tse-men-ti ko-sheng,* 147.

28. *Chê-tung Chin-shu ko-yao,* I, 84.

29. Chao Yüan-jen, *Kuang-hsi Yao-ko chi-yin,* 56 ff.

30. *Hai-tse-men-ti ko-sheng,* 87.

31. Ibid., 196.

32. *K'ai-feng ko-yao,* 117.

33. Ku Chieh-kang, *Meng-chiang-nü ku-shih yen-chiu,* II, 62 ff.

34. Ku Chieh-kang, *op. cit.*

35. *Shih yüeh hua-t'ai ko.*

36. Chu-lin Publishers, Hsin-chu, 1962.

37. *Erh-shih pu sung mei hsin-ko.*

38. *Pei-p'ing ko-yao chi,* II, 49.

39. The original Chinese texts were deposited in the Berlin Anthropological Museum and were unfortunately destroyed during World War II.

CHAPTER 13A

1. "Pekinger Sprichwörter. Gesammelt von Ho Feng-ju," *Baessler-Archiv* XXIV (1941), 1-43.

2. Chu Chieh-fan, the greatest Chinese authority on proverbs, in his *Chung-kuo yen-yü lun* (Taipei, 1965), discusses local differences in proverbs, but mainly stresses deviations due to differences in dialects (275-280).

3. Chu Chieh-fan, loc. cit., p. 452. See discussion below.

4. Chu published a series of articles, a draft of a new book on social values expressed in Chinese proverbs, in the Taipei daily newspaper *Hsin-sheng pao,* 1967.

5. *Die amtliche Sammlung chinesischer Rechtsgewohnheiten* (Bergen-Enkheim, 1965-66), 3 vols.

CHAPTER 13B

1. The largest collection seems to have been made by Chu Chieh-fan, who has also published an excellent analysis of Chinese proverbs in his *Chung-kuo yen-yü luh,* (Taipei, 1965), 741 pp.

2. Eduard Kroker, *Die amtliche Sammlung chinesischer Rechtsgewohnheiten,* 3 vols. (Frankfurt, 1965).

3. Author Shih Nai-an, 16th century; but the common editions represent versions of the novel which are hardly earlier than the 17th century. We used a Hong Kong edition, Kwong Chi Book Co., 1966, in 71 chapters. — I want to express my thanks to Mr. Chang Ju-hsiu who excerpted the proverbs from the text and prepared punch cards for me on which he noted the names and character of the speakers and the way in which the proverb was used. A grant from the Institute of International Studies, University of California, Berkeley, allowed me to make use of Mr. Chang's talents and time.

4. Author Ching-kuan-tse, a pseudonym, (Shanghai, 1929), 140. This novel is not a literary masterpiece but represents modern entertainment literature. I selected this novel because it was one of those which I read recently. — Another novel of similar type, *Ch'ing-hua* by Hu Chi-chen, (Shanghai, 1925), 104. contains only three proverbs. This novel is, however, more strongly influenced by Western models than the other one.

5. Represents a classical novel of the eighteenth century.

6. A 1919 detective story, *Hung fen ch'ai* (author Yin-nien-sheng, a pseudonym; Shanghai, 1919), which has six proverbs, gives only one proverb without an introduction. It uses three times the phrase "This is truly," once "This is called," and once "The people of old (times) said so well." This story has about one proverb per 6,000 words (six proverbs on 98 pages).

7. "Pekinger Sprichwörter," gessamelt von Ho Feng-ju, bearbeitet von W. Eberhard, *Baessler-Archiv* XXIV (1941), 1-43.

8. I want to express my thanks to Miss L. Kremer who typed this article. A grant from the Institute of International Studies, Berkeley, allowed me to make use of Miss Kremer's time.

CHAPTER 14

1. See also my "Topics and Moral Values in Chinese Temple Decorations," *Journal of the American Oriental Society* LXXXVII (March, 1967), 22-32.

2. A. Conrady, *Das älteste Dokument zur chinesischen Kunstge-schichte, T'ien-wen* (Leipzig, 1931).

3. A. Bulling, "Die Kunst der Totenspiele in der östlichen Han-Zeit," *Oriens Extremus* III (1956), 28-56.

4. It might be mentioned that the same representations occur as moving scenes, operated by a small motor, in temples at the time of the New Year's festival or at the great temple ceremonies (*chiao*). The pictures are also found on the three-to-five-story buildings which are constructed out of paper and bamboo in open places of Taiwanese towns on the occasion of the *chiao* ceremonies (personally witnessed in Chung-li, Taiwan, November 26, 1967). I have even come across such pictures on tomb structures and in private houses.

CHAPTER 15

1. My main text comes from Lung-shan temple in Taipei. I found the same text in Chieh-hsiu-kung, Taipei, on March 21, 1964, and in the only temple in Wu-she in T'ai-chung on April 9, 1964.

2. On August 17, 1935, as the oracle text and as a manuscript book.

3. In *Ching-mei-en i-yü,* p. 12a (edition: *Shuo-k'u*), and in *Chin-ku ch'i-kuan,* story No. 27. Text 74 is attested for the mid-19th century in Kiangsu (*Hsiang-yin lou pin t'an,* II, 5b). Thus far the earliest texts known to me are in the *Keng-szu pien* III, 8a-b, a text written in the 15th century. One of these quotations has a slightly different wording.

4. *Mo-yü-lu,* chap. I, p. 15a (edition: *Pi-chi hsiao-shuo ta-kuan*).

5. *K'ang yo chi-hsing,* chap. XIII, p. 4b (edition: *Pi-chi hsiao-shuo ta-kuan*).

6. My main text is from T'ien-hou-kung in Taipei. I found the same series in Yü-nü-kung in Kuan-tu, Taipei, on March 26, 1964; in Chiu-fen near Keelung in Taiwan on March 23, 1964; on the Shih-t'ou-shan near Hsin-chu in Taiwan on March 15, 1964; in Ming-fo-kung in Nan-kang near Taipei, on March 18, 1964; in Ling-yüan szu in Sung-shan, Taiwan, on March 25, 1964; in a small temple without a name near Pa-li, near Taipei, March 27, 1964; in Ti-tsang en in Hsin-chuang near Taipei, March 28, 1964; and in a small temple near Ching-mei near Taipei, April 4, 1964. The same oracle is used also in the Ma-tsu temple in Shih-lin (Aug. 15, 1967), the San-fu shan-yeh temple and the Ma-tsu temple, both in Chin-shan (Sept. 9, 1967), and a temple near Hsin-tien (Oct. 21, 1967).

7. Found in Tung-ho ch'an-szu in Taipei, March 19, 1964.

8. Seen in a Kuan-yin temple in Asakusa park in Tokyo, August 2, 1937.

9. In the Chinese temple in Weaverville, California, 1963.

10. In Shang-ti miao in Marysville, California, 1962. The founder came from Hsin-hui in Kuangtung province. The Wu-tang shan is a well known cult center, especially for the god Chen-wu, who has already been mentioned above.

11. Collected in Wu-chou, September 6, 1937. I have no better information about the deity Hua-kuang ta-ti. The novel *Nan-yo chi,* chap. V, mentions a certain Hua-kuang t'ien-wang, who was taken prisoner by Chen-wu (see Liu Ts'un-yan, *Buddhist and Taoist Influences,* I, 157). This is a Buddhist deity who is captured by a god which is usually designated as Taoistic. A Hua-kuang fo is also known elsewhere (see H. Doré, *Recherches sur les superstitions en Chine,* VI, 13). I don't know whether Hua-kuang ta-ti is identical with one of these two Buddhist gods.

12. Collected in Li-chiao-miao in Taipei, March 12, 1964.

13. Collected on March 24, 1964 in Ch'ing-shui yen in Tan-shui, Taiwan; on March 22, 1964 in Kuan-yin Temple in Tan-shui; on April 2, 1964 in Chih-nan-kung in Mu-shan near Taipei; and in Pao-an-kung in Taipei, March 19, 1964. The 19th century *Li-yüan ts'ung-hua* (XIII, 4a-b) quotes 2 oracles, one supposedly dated 1679, which differ from all sets known to me. In San Francisco, I found a Hou-wang oracle set with 100 oracles, again differing from all others. A Canton ballad, printed before 1840, *Chen-tsung Mei Li cheng Hua,* part 1, quotes the 36th oracle of a set also not otherwise known. All these sets have 7 words per line. There are some texts with only 5 words per line. The oldest is in a 1594 edition of the collection *Pao-kung an* (stories 8 and 68: I owe the reference to Prof. W. Bauer). But I found in Taiwan four different sets with 5-word poems: the Tsu-shih oracle in the Ch'ing-shui temple in San-hsia (Oct. 8, 1967) and the same temple in Tan-shui (March 22, 1964); the T'ien-huang oracle, a set of only 24 oracles (a temple on Chungking North road, Taipei; Aug. 24, 1967); a set of 32 oracles in the Yüan-kuang temple on Shih-t'ou shan, Hsin-chu (Aug. 13, 1967); a set in the Chu-shun General temple in Wan-hua, Taipei (Nov. 12, 1967) with a total of 28 oracles. A 5-word set of the Hsien-ku goddess on Mt. T'ai-i in Hopei (quoted in the drama *Yin p'ai chi*) is closely related to a line in the 27th oracle of the Kuan-ti set. Thus, there seems to be a relation between some 5-word and some 7-word sets. Equally, the 48th oracle of the 60 oracle set of Lü-tsu (seen in the Chih-nan kung, Mu-shan, Taiwan on Aug. 19, 1967) is identical with the 63rd oracle of the 100 oracle Kuan-tsi set, indicating that the same oracles may occur in sets of different length.

CHAPTER 16

1. A description of the character of the sample is found in Wolfram Eberhard and Alide Eberhard, *Family Planning in a Taiwanese Town,* Center of Chinese Studies, University of California, 1961, mimeo. Only Taiwan-born couples are included; immigrants are excluded.

2. A description of the content and reliability of the genealogy is found in Wolfram Eberhard, *Social Mobility in Traditional China* (Leiden, 1962). Data on couples born after 1900 were excluded, as well as data on persons born before 1600.

3. The total in this column is slightly larger than our selection, because in some cases the information on either the husband or the wife was incomplete for our selection.

4. Mr. R. Feinbaum calculated the significance of all auspicious and inauspicious marriages mentioned in Tables 1-4. Only this one is significant at the .05 level. I want to thank Mr. Feinbaum for his assistance.

CHAPTER 17

1. More than twenty years after this short note was written, Professor Schuyler Cammann published a detailed analysis of this collection, which in the meantime had grown considerably. His book, *Substance and Symbol in Chinese Toggles* (Philadelphia: University of Philadelphia Press, 1962), is certainly the last word on the Bieber Collection, and will remain the standard work on toggles. Nevertheless, my brief remarks may still be of some interest. For further literature, see Schuyler Cammann, "Toggles and Toggle-Wearing," *Southwestern Journal of Anthropology* XVI (1960), 463-75.

2. *Li-chi, Nei-tse,* in *Li Gi, Das Buch der Sitte,* trans. Richard Wilhelm (Jena, 1930), 305.

3. Cammann, *Substance and Symbol,* 18.

4. Toggles of value are mentioned in a drama *Ch'iu-chiang* (see *Hsi-ch'ü hsüan,* V, 78), and in a moralistic 19th-century text, the *T'ai-shang pao-fa t'u-shuo,* II, 55a.

5. *Archeological Research in Indo-China* (Stockholm, 1947), plate No. 77.

6. *Hsi-yo-chi* (*The Journey to the West*) is a Ming dynasty novel by Wu Ch'eng-en.

7. See Henri Doré, *Recherches sur les superstitions en Chine,* XVI, chap. IX, 521, and fig. 153.

8. *Yü-chih-t'ang t'an-hui,* a late Ming dynasty encyclopedia by Hsü Ying-ch'iu, chap. XII, 15b.

9. See Yao I-chih, *Hu-nan ch'ang-pen t'i-yao* (*Abstracts of Ballads from Hunan*) (Canton, 1929); 98, also W. Eberhard *Typen chinesischer Volksmärchen* (Helsinki, 1937), 216. Other sources consulted in the preparation of this essay include *Chung-hsing yü-wu-lu* (late Sung dynasty, author unknown), *Ho-lin yü-lu* (by Lo Ta-ching, Sung dynasty), *Hou-Han-shu* (by Fan Yeh, late Han dynasty), *Hsü I-chien-chih* (by Chin Ku-chih), and *Meng-chai pi-t'an* (by Cheng Ching-wang, Sung dynasty).

CHAPTER 18

1. I am obliged to Mr. Hsü kuo-san who excerpted the nicknames from the above-mentioned newspaper series.

2. Although there are today personal names consisting of a single word, people feel uncomfortable with them and apply different methods to extend the name to two words, if they do not try to avoid the use of the name altogether.

3. *Hsin-sheng pao* 53/1/10. In this and the following numbers, 53 refers to the 53rd year of the Republic, i.e., to 1964, the next number to the month, the last one to the day. In every case, the name is found in the so-called *"fu-k'an,"* the "additional page," in which the series of articles was published.

(4)53/2/9.
(5)53/5/5. "Old" is a term of endearment; it does not always indicate age.
(6)53/5/12.
(7)53/5/22.
(8)53/5/26; for women 53/2/8.
(9)53/3/21.
(10)53/6/19.
(11)53/4/8.
(12)53/6/19.
(13)53/4/26.
(14)53/5/4.
(15)53/1/10.
(16)53/1/31.
(17)53/4/26.
(18)53/4/26.

(19)53/4/26.
(20)53/5/23.
(21)53/1/17.
(22)53/5/13.
(23)53/5/2.
(24)53/5/8.
(25)53/6/19.
(26)53/5/18.
(27)53/5/18.
(28)53/1/1.
(29)53/1/31.
(30)53/1/1.
(31)53/1/1.
(32)53/5/4.
(33)53/4/12.
(34)53/2/16.
(35)53/6/21; he is called by his Chinese name "Small Cat King".
(36)53/2/9,
(37)53/4/25.
(38)53/5/18.
(39)53/5/17.
(40)53/4/26.
(41)53/1/31.
(42)53/1/18.
(43)53/4/25.
(44)53/4/26.
(45)53/1/1.
(46)53/4/18.
(47)53/4/18.
(48)53/3/21.
(49)53/1/31 and 53/3/18.
(50)53/1/27.
(51)53/5/24.
(52)53/1/2.
(53)53/2/10.
(54)53/2/8.
(55)53/1/10.
(56)53/5/2.
(57)53/5/24.
(58)53/1/17.
(59)both 53/6/15.
(60)53/5/26.

(61)53/4/26.

(62)53/1/31.

(63) as it appeared to me when I read a similar column of the *Hsin-sheng pao*
about the problems with family names published in 1965.

(64)53/5/26.

CHAPTER 19

1. Published in *Tung-fang Tsa-chih* XX, No. 23-24.

2. *Fêtes et Chansons anciennes de la Chine.* (Paris, 1919).

3. Compare H. Maspero, *Bull. Ec. Franc. Extr. Or.* (1919), 67 f.

4. See F. Jäger, "Über chinesische Miaotse-Alben," *Ostasiatishe Zeitschrift* N.F. IV, 266 f.

5. The album illustrations have not been reproduced here; on the very
similar role of the sash in ancient Chinese marriage ritual, see Marcel Granet
in *T'oung Pao* XII, 519 ff.

6. Compare with the analysis of Chêkiang bullfighting above, chap. I,
sec. 5.

CHAPTER 20

1. The Ainu on Karafuto have not yet been brought together in such
settlements, and they are fewer in number than those living on Hokkaido.

2. I undertook the trip together with my friend Dr. H. Zachert
(Matsumoto, Japan). The Japanese also had the same policy of resettling
aborigines in Taiwan. The place of the old settlement is often still
recognizable and well-known to the tribes.

3. The one old man (with his wife) seems to have been a leader in the
community even back around 1920, because I once saw a photograph, taken
by a British teacher around 1920, which showed exactly the same couple,
though naturally much younger than in 1937.

4. The 'beard-lifter' is a stick of wood similar to those wooden sticks
we use to stir coffee in cafeterias. Its function is to lift the beard
(moustache) so as to keep the beard clean of any food or drink. In Chinese

opera, the male actors wear long moustaches, and before speaking or eating, they lift the moustache by hand. The Ainu custom seems to be of similar character.

CHAPTER 21

1. See, for example, W. Ruben, *Die 25 Erzählungen des Daemons,* FF Communications No. 133 (Helsinki, 1944); also his "Das Märchen vom bösen Bruder," *Monumenta Serica* VII (Peking, 1942),   No. ½, and "Ende Gut, alles Gut," *Belleten* no. 25 (Ankara, 1943), 113-155; compare my review in *Revue de la Faculté de Langues* III (Ankara, 1945), no. 2, 227-228.

2. Julius Eisenstädter, *Elementargedanke und Übertragungstheorie in der Völkerkunde* (Stuttgart, 1912).

3. See W. Eberhard and P. N. Boratav, *Typen türkischer Volksmärchen* (Wiesbaden, 1953).

4. *Op. cit.,* Type No. 126; our text was collected in Mersin and Yildizeli.

5. See W. Eberhard, *Typen Chinesischer Volksmärchen*, FF Communications No. 120 (Helsinki, 1936), Type No. 125; our text comes from Chêkiang and Kuangtung provinces. Cf., A. Aarne No 461; K. Seki, *Types of Japanese Folktales,* No. 202 and 203; H. Ikeda, *A Type and Motiv Index*, p. 135, Type 460B. The earliest allusion is in the *Hsi-yo chi,* chapters 99 and 49. The tale is also reported from non-Chinese tribes in Yünnan (*Yün-nan ko-tsu min-chien ku-shih hsüan,* p. 30-34).

6. *Typen türkischer Volksmärchen,* No. 124, 125, 126, 127.

7. *Op. cit.,* No. 58, 173, 175, 182, 190, 258.

8. "Taxes cannot be collected from the sun; a written thing cannot be undone."

9. *Typen türkischer Volksmärchen,* No. 126; text from Ankara-Hasanoğlan.

10. *Loc. cit.,* text from Mersin.

11. *Loc. cit.,* text from Konya.

12. *Loc. cit.,* text from Zonguldak.

13. *Loc. cit.,* text from Mersin.

14. See Hans Schmidt and Paul Kahle, *Volkserzählungen aus Palästina* (Göttingen, 1918), 244-47.

15. See Leo Frobenius, *Atlantis* I (Jena, 1921), 272-74.

16. N.P. Andreyev, *Die Legende vom Räuber Madej,* FF Communications No. 69 (Helsinki, 1927).

17. *Typen türkischer Volksmärchen,* No. 67, 114, 123, 133, 135, 253, 351.

18. *Op. cit.,* No. 56, 57.

19. This theme also occurs as a variant of the Chinese tale; see *Typen chinesischer Volksmärchen,* 184.

20. *Typen türkischer Volksmärchen,* No. 127; occurs in Ankara, Kastamonu, Sivas, Amasya.

21. *Op. cit.,* No. 125, occurring in Anatolia and Thracia.

22. On the relationship between the folktale and the novel, see W. Eberhard, *Volksmärchen aus Südost-China,* FF Communications, No. 128 (Helsinki, 1941), 151-58.

23. *Typen chinesischer Volksmärchen,* No. 28; this folktale is also found in the Near East!

24. But normally the method of curing a girl's disease is the main theme of this folktale, just as it is in the Near East.

25. This takes place on the second day of the second Chinese month; see, for example, *Yen-ching sui-shih chi,* 17a.

26. See, for example, L. de Saussure, *Origines,* 168, 354, 589, and de Visser, *The Dragon in China and Japan,* 88; according to de Visser, this motif is comparatively new and is connected with Indian ideas (op. cit., 107).

27. *Typen türkischer Volksmärchen,* No. 123, from the Turkish population in Adakale (Rumania).

28. See *Volksmärchen aus Südost-China,* 151ff.; *Revue de la Faculté de Langues* III (Ankara, 1944), no. 2, 199-200; an extensive analysis of this novel can be found in my *Die chinesische Novelle des 17.-19. Jahrhunderts, eine soziologische Untersuchung* (Ascona, 1948), 120-53.

29. See J.J.L. Duyvendak, "The True Dates of the Chinese Maritime Expeditions in the Early Fifteenth Century," *T'oung Pao* XXXIV, 341-412; the importance of these late commercial connections from the migration of cultural traits from the West to the East, especially in the field of folktales, has never been properly stressed.

30. G. Ecke and Demiéville, *The Twin Pagodas of Zayton* (Cambridge, Mass., 1935), and G. Ecke, "Atlantes and Caryatides in Chinese Architecture," *Bulletin of the Catholic University,* no. 7, (Peking,1930), 63-102; A.K. Coomaraswamy, "Hindu Sculptures at Zayton," *Ostasiatische Zeitschrift* N.V N.F. IX (Berlin, 1933), 5-11.

CHAPTER 22

1. The basic material for this problem is collected in a publication of W. Eberhard and P.N. Boratav, *Typen türkischer Volksmärchen* (Wiesbaden, 1953).

2. The special version used here is published in the journal *Min-su* No. 108, (Sun Yat-sen University, Canton), 37-42, from Tung-wan, province of Kwangtung.

3. See *Typen türkischer Volksmärchen,* No. 89.

4. Variants in W. Eberhard, *Typen chinesischer Volksmärchen,* FF Communications, No. 120 (Helsinki, 1937), No. 31. The tale is also reported from Yünnan province (Sung Chê, *Yün-nan min-chien ku-shih,* pp. 66-76) und from Taiwanese aborigines (Linguis. Res. Center, Tai-hoku University, *The Myths and Traditions of the Formosan Native Tribes,* (1935), pp. 145-50).

5. Another example has been published in the journal *Sinologica,* I (1947), 144-151; see chap. 21.

6. The material has been studied in W. Eberhard, *Volksmärchen aus Südost-China,* FF Communications, No. 128 (Helsinki, 1941), 56-61.

7. Some examples for this Persian influence may suffice: *a.* A man sells a pearl in Canton, in a Persian shop (*Ch'uan-ch'i =T'ai-p'ing kuang-chi,* chap. XXXIV, 3, 17a). *b.* A Persian, named Mu Chao-szu, knows medicines (*Pei-meng so-yen = T'P'KCh* [VII,98] 42a). *c.* The native chief of Wan-an-chou in South Kwangtung used to capture Persian ships and sell the sailors as slaves; therefore around Wan-an-chou one finds Persian slaves everywhere (*T'ang ta-ho shang-tung-cheng-chuan = Tripitaka* LI, 991a). *d.* A monk planned to go to India aboard a Persian ship in 672 (*Ta-T'ang Hsi-yü ch'iu-fa kao-seng chuan,* II = *Tripitaka* LI,   7c). *e.* In the autumn of 759, Persians attacked Canton and tried to sack the city (*Tzu-chih t'ung-chien = Bulletin of Chinese Studies.* IV, 196). *f.* For further detailed information see *Fu-jen hsüeh-chih* XV, 95-118; *Bulletin of Chinese Studies* IVa, 196 f., and V. 76 f.

8. This happened in 1357-1366 (*Monumenta Serica* III, 611-27).

9. *Min-su,* No. 108, 38 f.

10. Already, A. Rémusat, *Histoire de la ville de Khotan* (1820), 169, has remarked that Chinese *po-li* (= glass) corresponds to Uigurian and Mongolian *bolur* and Persian *billur.* The classical word for 'crystal,' however, is *liu-li,* also used for 'glassware'. *Liu-li* is mentioned often in post-Christian texts (See *Bull. Mus. Far East. Antiq.* X, 9 ff.; further, cf.,*Wei-lüeh = Commentary to San-kuo Wei-chih* XXX; *Wei-shu* CII; *T'P'KCh* XIX, 236. 8b, and 197, XV, 37a; *Han-shu,* 28b, 17b; *Shih-shuo hsin-yü,* XXV = 285, and XXX = 320; *Chin-shu,* XLX = 1198a; *San-kuo Wu-chih,* IV, 5a and VIII, 4a; *Chin-shu,* XLV = 1206c; E. Chavannes, *500 Contes,* No. 9). Popular etymology explains the first part of this word meaning 'fluid,' leaving the other part unexplained. Attempts have been made to compare *liu-li* with skr. *vaidûrya,* but it seems equally possible to identify *liu-li* (ancient: *liôg-ljie*) with *billur.*

As for Irano-Chinese connections, some jokes should be mentioned: *a.* An old man with a grayish beard has a wife and a concubine. The concubine pulls all the white, his wife all the dark hair out of his beard, so that he becomes beardless. This joke appears in Aesop (W. Wienert, *Typen der griechisch-römischen Fabel,* FF Communications, No. 56, p. 129), then in Buddhist Chinese texts (E. Chavannes, *500 Contes,* III, 247-248, 516), and also in later popular literature (*Mo-k'o hui-hsi,* VI, 2a). *b.* The well-known joke that a man with a beard is asked whether he keeps his beard above or below the blankets, and he becomes sleepless because he cannot stop thinking about it, was already known in eleventh century China (*T'ieh-wei-shan ts'ung-t'an=Hsiao-hsiao-lu,* VI, 12b). c. A man bets that he can get another man's shoes. He throws his hat on the roof of a house. In order to get it back, the other man steps on the first man's shoulders, after having left off his shoes. When he is on the roof, the first man steals the shoes (*Tse-pu-yü,* XXII, 8a-b; eighteenth century). The same joke is told in present-day Anatolia. This list could easily be continued.

11. In some of his articles and books on Indian tales W. Ruben seems to have in mind such a sociological analysis of tales (see, for instance, his *Die 25 Erzählungen des Daemons,* FF Communications, No. 133; Helsinki, 1944). But in other studies (for instance, "Ende Gut, alles Gut, ein Märchen bei Indern, Türken, Boccaccio, Shakespeare," *Belleten* No. 25 [Ankara, 1943],113-55) he seems to be mainly interested in comparisons.

12. W. Eberhard, *Typen chinesischer Volksmärchen,* 243-245, and *Volksmärchen aus Südost-China* (Helsinki, 1941), 206-209. Cf., A. Aarne, no. 1641; K. Seki, *Types of Japanese Folktales,* no. 254. The earliest allusion to the tale is in the *Hsi-yo chi,* chapters 44-46.

13. W. Eberhard and P. N. Boratav, *Typen türkischer Volksmärchen,* No. 311.

14. The corresponding Near Eastern tale (*Typen türkischer Volksmärchen,* No. 274) also has the element of a fake oracle. It is only a short tale. Th. Zachariae (*Kleine Schriften zur indischen Philologie,* (Bonn, 1920), 138-145) gives European versions of the main tale, as well as Indian forms. He believes that the Indian form is the original one. This might be so, but our Chinese tale did not reach China by way of Buddhist priests or early Indian merchants, like most Indian tales, but in a form much nearer to the Near Eastern one and apparently much later.

15. One version is reported from Korea. Korea is an interesting area, for in many respects it seems to belong to the Southeastern Chinese circle. But on the other hand, Near Eastern tales might have reached Korea also directly; e.g., the Ordos Mongols are under strong Persian influence (see my review of Mostaert's *Folklore Ordos* in *JAOS* LXX (1950), 110). The Polyphemus tale, e.g., occurs only in Korea and the Near East, not in China, so far as we know. The Korean tale goes as follows: Seafarers reach a foreign country which is inhabited by giants. The giants catch them and keep them in a house which is closed with a stone. They eat one by one the first fifty fat sailors. The remaining few sailors, one day when the giants are drunk,

find some women whose husbands have already been killed. On the advice of the women they kill the sleeping giants, and with the help of some silk cloth they manage to descend to their ship from the cliff where the house is (*T'ai-p'ing kuang-chi,* XXXVIII, 481. 58a). The Turkish corresponding tale is: Seven friends emigrate and stay overnight in a caravansary. By and by, six are killed and eaten by Tepegöz. The last one takes a lance in the night and puts it first into a fire, then into Tepegöz's only eye. Tepegöz closes the entrance of his cave with a stone. The hero dresses in the hides of two sheep and escapes. Tepegöz cries for help, but when the others of his kind arrive, our hero is already in safety (*Ülkü,* 3rd ser., No. 23 (Ankara, 1948),28-29; collected in Bogazliyan). Other versions and texts are given in *Typen türkischer Volksmärchen,* No. 146. Tepegöz means a man with a single eye at the top of his head. The similarity to the text in Homer's *Odyssey* is quite striking. But F.M. Köprülü (in his translation of W. Barthold, *Islam Medeniyeti Tarihi* (Istanbul, 1940), 235) is of the opinion that no connection exists. The Korean tale leaves out several important details. Some of them, such as herding of sheep by the giants, could be ascribed to the different culture, but not all. No similar tales are known to me between Korea and the Near East. Merely to point out that one-eyed men play a role in Mongolian stories (*Yüan-ch'ao pi-shih,* I, 3b = E. Haenisch, *Geheime Geschichte der Mongolen,* p.1: an ancestor of Chinggiz Khan had only one eye) proves nothing.

16. It belongs to Type No. 56 in *Typen türkischer Volksmärchen.*

17. *Typen chinesischer Volksmärchen,* 245-247, and *Volksmärchen aus Südost-China,* 209-212. Cf., K. Seki, *Types of Japanese Folktales,* nos. 253 and 257.

18. *Typen türkischer Volksmärchen,* No. 351.

19. *Yü-chih-t'ang t'an-hui,* XXXII, 1a.

20. The hare is a symbol of the moon (see J.J.M. de Groot, *Religious System,* I, 200; R. Wilhelm, *Chinesische Volksmärchen,* No. 19; *Ts'an-t'ung-ch'i,* X= *Isis* LIII, 234; *T'ai-p'ing yü-lan,* 907, 2b). He spits his offspring out of his mouth (*Yu-yang tsa-tsu,* XVI, 2 = B. Laufer, *The Cormorant,* p. 255; *Lun-heng,* III, 6 = A. Forke, *Mitt. d. Sem. f. Or. Spr.,* Abt. 1, (1907), 100; *Po-wu-chih,* IV, 1a). In Central China he is regarded as the earth-god, and no one eats or kills him (commentary to *Erh-ya* = Schlegel, *Uranographic chinoise,* 167). Pregnant women should avoid seeing a hare (*Lung-heng,* II, 1 = A. Forke, *Mitt. d. Sem. f. Or. Spr.,* Abt. 1, (1906),320-21; *Po-wu-chih*

and other texts, quoted in *Yü Ch'ü-yüan pi-chi*, II, 116). In modern China the hare is also a symbol for homosexuals. (*Hsieh-to* I, 5a-b and *Li-yüan ts'ung-hua* XXI, 4b).

21. Here another tale should be mentioned, which is somewhat dubious since it is known to me in only one Chinese text, (*Min-su*, No. 44, 14-16, published by the Sun Yat-sen University in Canton, probably from Canton), whereas it is a very well known Near Eastern tale (*Typen türkischer Volksmärchen*, No. 157). The Chinese source usually contains good material, but on the other hand the Near Eastern parallel belongs to the very small group of tales translated into European languages and therefore the possibility that some young Chinese student has read this tale and simply retold it remains open. The Chinese tale goes as follows: (1) A widow with three unmarried daughters has only one hen which produces the nourishment for all of them (Near East: three daughters and a hen). (2) When the hen disappears, the mother sends one daughter to search for it. A robber meets her, and kills her when she refuses to marry him (Near East: A seller of household articles kidnaps a daughter and asks her to eat human meat. He kills her when she refuses). (3) The same thing happens to the second daughter. (4) The third daughter marries the man and lives with him (Near East: She gives the meat to a cat. The man, a sorcerer, is deceived. They marry). (5) She sees that her husband has a medicine which resurrects the dead. (Near East: She finds the corpses of her sisters). (6) When he is absent, she revives her sisters with the medicine (Near East: She does it with a whip). (7) She puts one of her sisters into a bag and asks the bandit to bring it to her mother; then follows the second sister. (8) When the bandit is absent, she makes a straw figure of a girl and levants with all the bandit's gold and the hen. The bandit is killed when he tries to bring her back another day. (The end differs very much in different versions; sometimes she just runs away. The motif of a straw figure occurs in other tales). It should be remarked that the version which is translated (Fr. Giese, *Türkische Märchen*, Jena, 1925, 90-92) does not have the motif of the hen and differs from the Chinese text.

BIBLIOGRAPHY

Traditional Chinese books are listed under the title; modern Chinese books and articles under the name of the author. For Chinese characters see the Appendix. All Chinese books marked * are scheduled to be reprinted in Taipei 1970, by the Folklore Books Co., Ltd.

1. *Adult Education Quarterly.* Peking, 1933.

2. Andreyev, N.P. *Die Legende vom Räuber Madej.* Folklore Fellows Communications no. 69. Helsinki, 1927.

3. Barthold, W. *Islam Medeneyeti Tarihi* (History of Islamic Civilization). Translated by Fuad Köprülü. Istanbul, 1940.

4. *Biographical Dictionary,* see H.A. Giles, *A Chinese Biographical Dictionary.* London, 1898.

5. Bishop, C.W. "The Ritual Bullfight." *China Journal* 1: 630-37.

6. Bourne, Henry. *Antiquitates Vulgares.* London, 1725.

7. Brand-Ellis. *Observations on Popular Antiquities.* London, 1770.

8. *Bulletin of Chinese Studies.* Cheng-tu.

9. *Bulletin of the Institute of Ethnology, Academia Sinica.* Nankang, Taipei.

10. *Bulletin of the Museum of Far Eastern Antiquities.* Stockholm.

11. Bulling, A. "Die Kunst der Totenspiele in der östlichen Han-Zeit." *Oriens Extremus 3* (1956): 28-56.

12. Burkhardt, V.R. *Chinese Creeds and Customs.* Taipei reprint 1961 (Three volumes in one).

13. Burgess, J. St. *The Guilds of Peking.* New York, 1928.

14. Burne, Charlotte. *The Handbook of Folklore.* London, 1914.

15. Cammann, Schuyler. "Toggles and Toggle-wearing." *Southwestern Journal of Anthropology* 16 (1960): 463-75.

16. _____ *Substance and Symbol in Chinese Toggles.* Philadelphia, 1962.

17. *Chan-huang p'ao.* Drama. Author unknown.

18. *Ch'ang ch'eng chi.* Drama. Author unknown. 17th century?

19. Chang Chih-chin. *Hu-chou ko-yao* (Songs from Hu-chou).

20. *Ch'ang pan p'o.* Drama. Author unknown.

21. Chao Yüan-jen. *Kuang-hsi yao-ko chi-yin* (Yao Songs from Kuang-hsi). Academia Sinica, Institute of Phil.-History, Monographs, Series A, vol. 1, Peking 1930.

22. Chavannes, E. *Mémoires historiques de Se-ma Ts'ien.* Paris 1895-1905.

23. _____ *Le T'ai Chan.* Paris, 1910.

24. _____ *Quinc Cent Contes et Apologues,* Paris 1910.

25. *Chê-tung Chin-shu ko-yao* (Songs from the Chin-hua Area in East Chekiang).

26. *Ch'en T'uan Kao wo.* Drama by Ma Chih-yüan. 14th century?

27. Ch'en Yüan-chu, *T'ai-shan ko-yao chi* (Collection of Songs from T'ai-shan).*

28. *Cheng tung chi.* Hunanese folk drama. Modern.

29. *Chi-ku-lu.* Author Sih-ma Kuang. Sung period.

30. *Chi-kung huo-fo.* Author unknown. Popular novel. (also called: *Chi-kung chuan*).

31. *Ch'i-lin ko.* Drama. Author Li Yüan-yü. Middle Ming period.

32. *Chi-shen lu.* Author Hsü Hsüan. Sung period. (quoted in *T'P'KCh*).

33. *Chien-hu chi.* Author Ch'u Hsüeh-chia (Edition *Pi-chi hsiao-shuo ta-kuan*).

34. Ch'ien Nan-yang. *Mi-shih* (History of the Riddle).*

35. _____, *Min-su chiu-wen* (Folklore from Ancient Sources).

36. *Chien tan chi.* Drama. Author Hsieh T'ien-jui.

37. *Ch'ien-tse wen* (The Thousand Character Text). Textbook for children.

38. *Ch'ien-yen-t'ang chin-shih-wen pa-wei* (Colophons on Inscriptions on Metal and Stone). Author Ch'ien Ta-yin.

39. *Ch'ih lung hsü.* Drama. Author Chu Yün-ts'ung. 17th century.

40. *Ch'ih-pei ou-t'an.* Author Wang Shih-chen. Late Ming period. Edition Ta-ta, Shanghai, 1934. 2 volumes.

41. *Ch'ih sung chi.* Drama. Author unknown.

42. *Chin-hua hsien-chih* (Gazetteer of Chin-hua). Edition Chin-hua 1934 in 8 volumes.

43. *Chin i kui.* Drama. Author supposedly Chu Hui.

44. *Chin-ku ch'i kuan.* Collection of short-stories, probably by Feng Meng-lung. Early 17th century.

45. *Chin-p'ing mei.* Novel. Author unknown.

46. *Chin-shu* (Chin Dynastic History). Author Fan Ch'iao and others. T'ang period. K'ai-ming edition. Shanghai.

47. *Chin-yang kung.* Drama. Author unknown.

48. *Chin-yün hsien-chih* (Chin-yün Gazetteer).

49. *China-Dienst.* Periodical. Shanghai.

50. *Ch'ing-hua.* Novel by Hu Chi-chen. Shanghai, 1925.

51. *Ch'ing-kang hsiao.* Drama. Author Tsou Yü-ch'ing. Ming period.

52. *Ching-mei en i-yü.* Author Mao Hsiang. Manchu period (*Shuo-K'u* edition).

53. Ch'ing-shui. *Hai-lung-wang-ti nü-erh* (The Daughter of the Sea Dragon King).*

54. *Ch'iu chiang.* Drama. Author unknown.

55. Ch'iu Chün. *Ch'ing-ko ch'ang-ta* (Love Songs in Antiphony).*

56. *Ch'iu ju yüan.* Drama. Author unknown.

57. Chiu-tse. *Jen-hsiung p'o* (The Bear Woman).

58. Chou Chen-ho. *Su-chou feng-su* (Customs in Su-chou). Canton, 1928.

59. *Chou-li* (Rites of Chou). Author unknown. (Translated by E. Biot. *Le Tcheou Li, ou Rites,* Paris, 1841).

60. Choe Sang-su. *Annual Customs of Korea.* (Korean Folklore Studies Series, no. 3). Seoul, 1960.

61. Chu Chieh-fan. *Chung-kuo yen-yü lun* (Discussions on Chinese Proverbs). Taipei, 1965.

62. *Ch'ü-hai tsung-mu t'i-yao.* Peking, 1959. 3 volumes.

63. *Chü-ting kuan-hua.* Drama. Author unknown. (cf., W. Grube. *Volkskunde.* p. 134.)

64. *Ch'uan-ch'i.* Author P'ei Hsing. T'ang period. (quoted in *T'P'KCh*).

65. *Chuang-tse.* Author supposedly Chuang Chou. Late Chou period. (Translated by R. Wilhelm. *Dschuang Dsi.* Jena, 1923).

66. *Ch'ün hsing fu.* Drama. Author unknown.

67. *Ch'ün hsing hui.* Drama. Author unknown.

68. *Ch'un-ming yü-lu.* Author Sun Ch'eng-tsê. Manchu period.

69. *Ch'un-tsai-t'ang pi—chi.* Author Yü Yüeh. 19th century. Shanghai, 1934.

70. Chung Ching-wen, *Min-chien i-wen ts'ung-hua* (On Folk Literature).*

71. _____, *Lang T'ung ch'ing-ko* (Love Songs of the Lang and T'ung).*

72. _____, *Ch'u-ts'ih-chung-ti shen-hua ho chuan-shuo* (On Mythology and Tradition in the Elegies of Ch'u).*

73. _____, *Yin-Ou min-chien ku-shih hsing-shih-piao* (Some Types of Indo-European Folktales).*

74. _____, *Lao-hu wai-p'o ku-shih chi* (Collection of Folktales about the Tiger-Grandmother).

75. _____, *Chung-kuo min-t'an hsing-shih piao* (Survey of the Types of Chinese Folk Narratives).

76. *Chung-hsing yü wu lu.* Author unknown. Sung period. (Edition *Pi-chi hsiao-shuo ta-kuan*).

77. *Chung-hua ch'üan-kuo feng-su chih.* Author Hu P'u-an. Shanghai, 1935. 4 volumes.

78. *Chung-kuo jen-ming ta-ts'ih tien* (Cyclopedia of Chinese Biographical Names). Shanghai, 1921.

79. *Chung-kuo ti-fang hsi-ch'ü chi-ch'eng.* Peking, 1959.

80. Conrady, A. and E. Erkes. *Das älteste Dokument zur chinesischen Kunstgeschichte, T'ien-Wen, die "Himmelsfragen" des Küh Yüan.* Leipzig, 1931.

81. Coomaraswamy, A.K. "Hindu Sculpture at Zayton." *Ostasiatische Zeitschrift*, N.F. 9 (1933).

82. Doré, H. *Recherches sur les superstitions en Chine.* Shanghai, 1911 ff.

83. Duyvendak, J.J.L. "The True Dates of the Chinese Maritime Expeditions in the Early 15th Century." *T'oung Pao* 34: 341-412.

84. Eberhard, Wolfram. *Die chinesische Novelle des 17.-19. Jahrhunderts, eine soziologische Untersuchung.* Ascona, 1948.

85. ———. "Eine neue Arbeitshypothese über den Aufbau der frühchinesischen Kulturen. *Tagungsberichte der Gesellschaft für Völkerkunde.* Leipzig, 1937.

86. ———, "Early Chinese Cultures and their Development; a new Working Hypothesis." *Annual Report of the Smithsonian Institution,* 1937.

87. ———, *Typen chinesischer Volksmärchen.* Folklore Fellows Communications no. 120. Helsinki, 1936.

88. ———. *Volksmärchen aus Südost-China.* Folklore Fellows Communications no. 128. Helsinki, 1941.

89. ———. *Erzählungsgut aus Südost-China.* Berlin, 1966.

90. ———. *Folktales of China.* Chicago, 1965.

91. ———. *Lokalkulturen im alten China* (vol. 1 = Supplement to *T'oung Pao* 37. Leiden, 1943; vol. 2= *Monumenta Serica 3.* Peking, 1943.

92. ———. *Local Cultures of South and East China.* Leiden, 1968.

93. ———. *Kultur und Siedlung der Randvölker Chinas.* Leiden, 1942 (Supplement to *T'oung Pao* 36).

94. ———. *Social Mobility in Traditional China.* Leiden, 1962.

95. ———. *Settlement and Social Change in Asia.* Hong Kong, 1967.

96. ———. *Guilt and Sin in Traditional China.* Berkeley, 1967.

97. ———. "Topics and Moral Values in Chinese Temple Decorations." *Journal of the American Oriental Society* 87 (1967): 22-23.

98. ———. "Pekinger Sprichwörter, gesammelt von Ho Feng-ju." *Baessler-Archiv* 24 (1941).

99. _____. and Alide Eberhard. "Family Planning in a Taiwanese Town" in *Settlement and Social Change in Asia.* Hong Kong, 1967.

100. _____. and Pertev N. Boratav. *Typen türkischer Volksmärchen.* Wiesbaden, 1953.

101. Ecke, G. "Atlantes and Caryatides in Chinese Architecture." *Bulletin of the Catholic University,* no. 7, pp. 63-102. Peking, 1930.

102. _____. and P. Demiéville. *The Twin Pagodas of Zayton.* Cambridge, 1935.

103. Eisenstädter, Julius, *Elementargedanke und Übertragungstheorie in der Völkerkunde.* Stuttgart, 1912.

104. *Erh-shih lu.* Author Lo Yün. 19th century. (Edition *Pi-chi hsiao-shuo ta-kuan*).

105. *Erh-shih pu sung mei hsin-ko.* Anonymous Taiwanese folk ballad. Hsin-chu, Taiwan.

106. *Erh-ya.* Author unknown. Pre-Han period. Edition *Shih-san ching.* Shanghai.

107. *Fa-yüan chu-lin.* Author Monk Tao-shih. T'ang period. Edition Sih-pu ts'ung-k'an. Shanghai.

108. *Fan Wen-cheng-kung chi.* Author Fan Chung-yen. 11th century.

109. *Feng-shen pang* (also:*Feng-shen yen-i*). Folk novel. Author unknown. 17th century. (Partial translation by W. Grube. *Feng-shen yen-i, die Metamorphosen der Götter.* Leiden, 1912).

110. *Feng-su t'ung-i.* Author Ying Shao. 2nd century.

111. *Feng yün hui.* Drama. Author Li Yü. 17th century.

112. *Folklore Studies* (later: *Asian Folklore Studies*). Periodical.

113. Frobenius, Leo. *Atlantis.* Jena, 1921.

114. *Fu-jen hsüeh-chih.* Periodical. Catholic University: Peking.

115. Granet, M. *Danses et légendes de la Chine ancienne*. Paris, 1926.

116. _____, *Fêtes et chansons anciennes de la Chine*. Paris, 1919.

117. de Groot, J.J.M. *Religious System of China*. Leiden, 1892-1910. 6 volumes.

118. Grube, W. *Pekinger Volkskunde* (Veröffentlichungen des Königlichen Museums für Völkerkunde 7, no. 1-4 Berlin).

119. _____, *Chinesische Schattenspiele*. München, 1915.

120. Gulik, R.H. van. *Sexual Life in Ancient China*. Leiden, 1961.

121. *Hai-tse-men-ti ko-sheng* (Children's Songs). Author Huang Chao-nien.*

122. *Han Fei-tse*. Author Han Fei. 3rd century. B.C.

123. *Han kung ch'iu*. Drama. Author Ma Chih-yüan. 14th century.

124. *Han-shu* (Dynastic History of Han). Author Pan Ku and others. First century A.D. K'ai-ming edition.

125. *Historical Annual*. Periodical.

126. Ho Feng-ju and Alide Eberhard. "Fünfzig Pekinger Kinderspiele." *Sinica,* 1937.

127. *Ho-lin yü-lu*. Author Lo Ta-ching. Sung period. Edition *Pi-chi hsiao-shuo ta-kuan*.

128. *Hou Han-shu* (Dynasty History of Later Han). Author Fan Yeh and others. 5th century. Edition K'ai-ming.

129. *Hou-tê lu*. Author Li Yüan-kang. Sung period. (Edition *Pi-chi hsiao-shuo ta-kuan*).

130. *Hsi-ch'ü hsüan*. Peking, 1959. 5 volumes.

131. *Hsi-hsiang chi*. Opera. Author Wang Shih-fu. Ming period.

132. *Hsi yu chi*. Author probably Wu Ch'eng-en. Late Ming period.

133. *Hsiang lin chien.* Drama. Author Yao Tse-i. Ming period.

134. *Hsiang-nang chi.* Drama. Author Ch'in Jui. Ming period.

135. *Hsiang-yin-lou pin-t'an.* Author Lu Ch'ang-ch'un. Manchu period. (Edition *Pi-chi hsiao-shuo ta-kuan*).

136. Hsiao, K.Ch. *Rural China; Imperial Control in the 19th Century.* Seattle, 1960.

137. *Hsiao fang niu.* Comedy. Author unknown.

138. Hsiao Han. *Yang-chou-ti chuan-shuo* (Folktales from Yang-chou).*

139. *Hsiao-hsiao lu.* Anonymous. 19th century.

140. *Hsiao-T'ang ch'u-chien chuan.* Folk novel.

141. *Hsiao tou-p'eng.* Author Tseng Yen-tung. Early 19th century. Shang-hai: Ta-ta Press.

142. *Hsiao-ts'ang-shan-fang wen-chi.* Author Yüan Mei. 18th century.

143. Hsieh Yün-sheng. *Min-ko chia-chi* (First Collection of Songs from Fukien).*

144. _____, *T'ai-wan ch'ing-ko chi* (Collection of Love Songs from Formosa).*

145. *Hsin-sheng pao* (or:*T'ai-wan Hsin-sheng pao*). Newspaper. Taipei.

146. *Hsü Ch'i-hsieh-chi.* Author Wu Chün. Liang period (Quoted in *Yü-chih t'ang*).

147. *Hsü I-chien chih.* Author Chin Yü-chih. Mongol period (Edition *Pi-chi hsiao-shuo ta-kuan*).

148. *Hsü Wen-ch'ang chi.* Author Hsü Wei. Ming period.

149. Hsüan-pao. *T'ien-lo nü* (The Snail Woman).

150. *Hsüeh Jen-kui jung-kui ku-li.* Drama. Author Chang Kuo-pin. 14th century.

151. *Hsüeh Ting-shan cheng hsi.* Folk novel. Author unknown.

152. *Hu fu chi.* Drama. Author Chang Feng-i. Ming period.

153. Hu Shih. *Pai-hua wen-hsüeh shih.* Peking.

154. *Hu Ti Pang yen.* Shadow play, quoted from W. Grube, *Schattenspiele.*

155. *Hua-yüeh chih* (Chronicle of Mt. Hua). Author Li Jung. Manchu period.

156. *Hua Yün tai chien.* Folk play from Canton. No author known. Modern.

157. *Huai-nan tse.* Author Liu An. 2nd century B.C.

158. Hummel, A.W. *Eminent Chinese of the Ch'ing Period.* Washington, 1943.

159. *Hung-fen ch'i.* Novel by Yin-nien-sheng. Shanghai, 1919.

160. *Hung i kuan.* Drama. Author unknown.

161. *Hung-lou meng.* Classical novel. 18th century.

162. *I feng shu.* Drama. Author Ting Yü. 17th century?

163. *I p'eng hsüeh.* Drama. Author Li Yüan-yü. 17th century.

164. *I-wen lei-chü.* Author Ou-yang Hsün. T'ang period.

165. *Isis.* Periodical.

166. *JAOS, Journal of the American Oriental Society.* Periodical.

167. Jäger, Fr., "Über chinesische Miaotse-Alben." *Ostasiatische Zeitschrift,* N.F. 4: 266 ff.

168. Janse, O. *Archeological Research in Indo-China.* Stockholm, 1947.

169. *Journal of Chinese Folklore.* Periodical. Canton, 1936.

169a. *Journey to the West,* see *Hsi yo chi.*

170. *Ju shih kuan.* Drama. Author Wu Yü-kang. Early 17th century.

171. *Ju-lin wai-shih.* Novel by Wu Min-hsien. 18th century. Shanghai, 1936.

172. Jung Chao-tsu, *Mi-hsin yü chuan-shuo* (Superstition and Tradition). Canton.*

173. *K'ai-chan yüeh-k'an.* Periodical. Hangchou (July 1931).

174. *K'ang-yo chi-hsing.* Author Yao Jung. 19th century. (Edition *Pi-chi hsiao-shuo ta-kuan*).

175. *Kao seng chuan.* Author Yü Hsiao-ching. T'ang period (quoted in *T'P'KCh*).

176. *Kao Wang chin piao.* Folk play from Hunan Province. Modern.

177. *Ko-yao chou-k'an.* Periodical. Peking, 1922.

178. Kroker, Eduard, *Die amtliche Sammlung chinesischer Rechtsgewohnheiten.* Bergen-Enkheim 1965. 3 volumes.

179. Ku Chieh-kang, *Meng-chiang-nü ku-shih yen-chiu chi* (Studies on the Tale of the Meng Chiang). Canton. 3 volumes.*

180. Ku Chieh-kang, *Su-Yüeh-ti hun-sang* (Marriage and Mourning Customs from Su-chou and Canton). Canton.*

181. ———, *Miao-feng shan* (Mt. Miao-feng and its Cult). Canton.*

182. *Kua-ts'ang chin-shih chih.* Author Li Yü-sun. Around 1800.

183. *Kuan P'an-p'an.* Drama. Author Hou K'o-chung. 14th century.

184. *Kui-lin feng-t'u chi.* Author Mo Hsiu-fu. T'ang period. (quoted in *Yüeh-hsi*).

185. *K'un-hsüeh chi-wen.* Author Wang Ying-lin. Sung period.

186. Kuo Mo-jo. *Chung-kuo ku-tao shê-hui shih* (History of Ancient Chinese Society). Shanghai, 1930.

187. Laufer, B. *The Domestication of the Cormorant in China and Japan* (Chicago: Field Museum Publication no. 300). Chicago, 1930.

188. Levy, H.S. and Ryooji Sasaki. *Unsung Hero. The Late Nagao Ryûzô. Conversations.* Yokohama, 1967.

189. *Li-chi* (Book of Rites). Authors unknown. Han period. (Translation see R. Wilhelm. *Li Gi, das Buch der Sitte.* Jena, 1930).

190. *Li-sao.* Poem, attributed to Ch'ü Yüan. 3rd century B.C.

191. *Li-tai pi-chi hsiao-shuo hsüan.* Section: Ming Dynasty. Hong Kong. No date.

192. *Lieh-hsien chuan.* Author supposedly Liu Hsiang. Supposedly first century B.C.

193. *Lien-huan t'ao.* Drama. Author unknown.

194. (*Hsien-shun*) *Lin-an chih* (Gazetteer of Lin-an). Late Sung period.

195. Lin Pe-lu, *Min-su-hsüeh lun-wen-chi* (Collection of Essays on Folklore). Canton.

196. *Liu Hsiu tsou-kuo.* Folk play from Ting-hsien (Hopei). Modern.

197. Liu Ta-po. *Ku-shih ti t'an-tse* (Types of Folktales). Canton.

198. Liu Ts'un-yan, *Buddhist and Taoist Influences on Chinese Novels.* Volume 1: *The Authorship of the Feng Shen Yen I.* Wiesbaden, 1962.

199. Liu Wan-chang. *Kuang-chou mi-yü* (Riddles from Canton). Canton.*

200. _____. *Kuang-chou min-chien ku-shih* (Folktales from Canton). Canton.*

201. _____. *Kuang-chou erh-ko chia-chi* (First Collection of Children's Songs from Canton). Canton.*

202. Lou Tse-k'uang, *Ch'iao-nü ho kai-niang ti ku-shih* (Stories about the Clever and the Stupid Girl). Canton.

203. _____, *Chung-kuo hsin-nien fêng-su chih* (Chinese New Year's Customs).

204. _____. *Yüeh-kuang-kuang ko-chi* (Collection of Moonlight Songs).

205. _____. *Shao-hsing ku-shih* (Folktales from Shao-hsing).*

206. _____. *Hsi-Ts'ang lien-ko* (Tibetan Love Songs).

207. Lou Tse-lun. *Chu Ying-t'ai* (Stories about Chu Ying-t'ai).

208. *Lu Pan ching.* Author supposedly Lu Pan. Probably written in Ming period.

209. *Lu-shui t'ing tsa-chih.* Author Hsing-te. Manchu period. (Edition *Pi-chi hsiao-shuo ta-kuan*).

210. *Lun-heng.* Author Wang Ch'ung. First century A.D. (Translated by A. Forke, *Lun-heng,* Leipzig und Berlin 1907-1911).

211. *Lun-yü* (Analects). Chou period (Translation R. Wilhelm, *Kung Futse, Gespräche.* Jena, 1923).

212. Mabuchi, T. "Spiritual Dominance of the Sister." *Ryukuan Culture and Society.* Honolulu, 1964.

213. *Mai lun t'ing.* Drama. Author Li Yüan-yü. 17th century?

214. Matignon, J.J. *La Chine hermétique.* Paris 1936.

215. *Mê Ti.* Authors unknown. Chou period. (Translation A. Forke. *Mê Ti.* Berlin, 1922).

216. *Mélanges chinois et bouddhiques.* Periodical. Bruxelles.

217. *Meng-chai pi-t'an.* Author Yeh Meng-te. Sung period. (Edition *Pi-chi hsiao-shuo ta-kuan*).

218. *Meng Chiang-nü hsün-fu.* Folk play from Anhui Province. Modern.

219. *Meng-liang-lu.* Author Wu Tse-mu. Sung period. (Edition *Pi-chi hsiao-shuo ta-kuan*).

220. *Meng Liang tao-ku.* Drama. Author unknown.

221. *Miao-hsiang-shih ts'ung-hua.* Author: Chang P'ei-jen. 19th century. (Edition *Pi-chi hsiao-shuo ta-kuan*).

222. *Min-chien yüeh-k'an.* Periodical. Hangchou.

223. *Min-su (chou-k'an).* Periodical. Canton.

224. *Ming-chai hsiao-shih.* Author Chu Mei-hsiang. Manchu period. (Edition *Pi-chi hsiao-shuo ta-kuan*).

225. *Mo-k'o hui-hsi.* Author P'eng Sheng. Sung period. (Edition *Pi-chi hsiao-shuo ta-kuan*).

226. *Mo-yü-lu.* Author Mao Hsiang-lin. Manchu period. (Edition *Pi-chi hsiao-shuo ta-kuan*).

227. *Monumenta Serica.* Periodical.

228. Mostaert, A. *Folklore Ordos.* Peking, 1947.

229. Nagao Ryûzô. *A Record of Chinese Customs.* Tokyo, 1940 ff.

230. *Nan-ching hsüeh-pao.* (Nanking Journal). Periodical.

231. *Nan-yo chi.* Novel. Author unknown.

232. *Nao hua-teng.* Drama. Author unknown. Early 17th century?

233. Nivison, D. *Confucianism in Action.* New York, 1959.

234. *Pa-hsien ch'ing-shou.* Play. Modern.

235. *Pai-men-lou.* Drama. Unknown Author.

236. *Pai-shê chuan.* Folk novel. Author unknown.

237. *Pai-sui kua-shuai.* Folk play from Kiangsu Province. Modern.

238. *Pai-sui yüan.* Drama. Author unknown. Around 17th century.

239. *Pai ts'ao p'o.* Folk play from Ting-hsien (Hopei Province).

240. *P'an-t'ao hui.* Drama. Author unknown. 17th century?

241. *P'ang Chüan yeh tsou Ma-ling-tao.* Drama. Author unknown.

242. *Pao-ch'uan chi.* Drama. Author unknown. 17th century?

243. *Pao-kung an.* Folk novel. 16th century?

244. *Pei Ch'i-shu* (Dynastic Annals of Northern Ch'i Dynasty). Author Li Po-yao and others. T'ang period. (Edition K'ai-ming).

245. *Pei-meng so-yen.* Author Sun Kuang-hsien. Sung period (quoted in *T'P'KCh*).

246. *Pei-p'ing ko-yao* (Songs from Peking).

247. Po Ch'i-ming. *Ho-nan mi-yü* (Riddles from Honan). Canton.*

248. *Po-hu-t'ung.* Author Pan Ku and others. First century A.D. (Edition *Sih-pu ts'ung-k'an.* Shanghai).

249. *P'o Hung-chou.* Folk play from Shantung Province. Modern.

250. Po Shou-i. *K'ai-feng ko-yao chi* (Collection of Songs from K'ai-feng). Canton.*

251. *Po-wu chih.* Author supposedly Chang Hua. 4th century.

252. Rémusat, A. *Histoire de la ville de Khotan.* Paris, 1820.

253. *Revue de la Faculté des Languages.* Ankara Üniversitesi: Ankara.

254. Ruben, W. "Ende gut, alles gut: ein Märchen bei Indern, Türken, Bocaccio und Shakespeare." *Belleten* (Ankara), no. 25 (1943), pp. 113-55.

255. _____. "Das Märchen vom bösen Bruder." *Monumenta Serica* 7 (1942), no. 1.

256. _____ *Die 25 Erzählungen des Dämons. Folklore Fellows* Communications no. 133. Helsinki, 1944.

257. Rudolph, W., "Bull Grappling on Early Chinese Reliefs." *Archeology* 3 (1960).

258. *San-fu huang-t'u.* Author unknown. Pre-T'ang period. (Quoted in *T'P'YL*).

259. *San-hsia wu-i.* Folk novel. Author unknown.

260. *San hsing chao.* Drama. Author unknown. 17th century?

261. *San-hu hsia-shan.* Folk play. Author unknown.

262. *San-kuo chih* (Dynastic History of the Three Kingdoms). Author Ch'en Shou and others. Chin period. (quoted as *San-kuo Wei-chih; San-kuo Wu-chih, San-kuo Shu-chih*) (Edition *T'u-shu chi-ch'eng*).

263. *San-kuo chih yen-i.* Novel. Ming period.

264. *San-to sho.* Drama. Author unknown.

265. de Saussure, L. *Les Origines de l'astronomie chinoise.* Paris, 1930.

266. Schlegel, G. *Uranographie chinoise.* Leiden, 1875. 2 volumes.

267. _____. *La prostitution en Chine.* Rouen, 1886.

268. Schmidt, H., and P. Kahle. *Volkserzählungen aus Palästina.* Göttingen, 1918.

269. *Shan-hai ching.* Authors unknown. Han period.

270. *Shan-tung ko-yao chi* (Songs from Shantung Province).

271. *Shang t'ien-t'ai.* Drama. Author unknown.

272. *Shih-chi.* Author Sih-ma Ch'ien and others. First century B.C. (Translated by E. Chavennes. *Memoires historiques).*

273. *Shih-ching* (Book of Songs). Author unknown. Chou period.

274. Shih Fang. *Tou niu* (Bullfighting).

275. *Shih-mo chien-hua.* Author Chao Hsien. 1580.

276. *Shih-shuo hsin-yü.* Author Liu I-ch'ing. Liang period.

277. *Shih-yüeh hua-t'ai ko.* Modern Taiwanese folk ballad. Hsin-chu.

278. *Shui-ching chu.* Author Li Tao-yüan. 6th century.

279. *Shuang ch'ui chi.* Drama. Author Fan Hsi-chê. 17th century?

280. *Shuang jui-chi.* Drama. Author Fan Hsi-chê (*see* 279).

281. *Shuang-pao en.* Drama. Author unknown. 17th century?

282. *Shui-en ch'i-chün.* Local play from Anui Province. Modern.

283. *Shui-hu chuan.* Classical novel.

284. *Shuo-wen (chieh-tse).* Author supposedly Hsü Shen. Han period.

285. *Sih-liang-ch'i.* Drama. Author unknown. 17th century?

286. *Sinica.* Periodical. Frankfurt.

287. *Sinologica.* Periodical. Basel.

288. *Sou-shen chi.* Author supposedly Kan Pao. Pre-T'ang period.

289. Stübel, H. *Die Hsia-min of Tse-mu shan.* Academia Sinica, Institute of Social Sciences, Monography no. 6. Nanking, 1932.

290. *Sui Fan Shu.* Drama. Author Kao Wen-hsiu.

291. *Sui-shu* (Dynastic History of Sui). Authors Wei Cheng and others. T'ang period. Edition K'ai-ming.

292. *Sui-T'ang yen-i.* Folk novel. Author unknown.

293. *Ta-T'ang hsi-yü ch'iu-fa kao-seng chuan.* (Quoted in *Taishô Tripitaka*).

294. *Ta Wang Ying.* Local play from Canton Province. Modern.

295. *T'ai-pei-hsien, Chung-ho-shê-ch'ü-chih yen-chiu.* (Study of the Chung-ho Area in Taipei District). Anonymous B.A. thesis. (Manuscript). National Taiwan University (1951).

296. *T'ai-p'ing kuang-chi.* Compiler Li Fang. 10th century. (Edition *Pi-chi hsiao-shuo ta-kuan*).

297. *T'ai-p'ing yü-lan.* Compiler Li Fang. 10th century. (Sih-pu ts'ung-k'an Edition).

298. *T'ai-shang pao-fa t'u-shuo.* Editor Huang Chen-yüan. 1903.

299. *Taishô Tripitaka* (Buddhist Canon in the Edition of the Taishô Period). Tokyo.

300. *T'ai-wan feng-t'u.* Folkloristic Supplement to the *Kung-lun pao.* Newspaper. Taipei 1948-1954.

301. *T'an-hua chi.* Drama. Author Tu Lung 16th century.

302. *Tang jen pei.* Drama. Author Ch'iu Yüan.

303. *T'ao-en meng-i.* Author Chang Tai. Ming time (Edition *Shuo-k'u*).

304. *T'ieh-wei-shan ts'ung-t'an.* Author Ts'ao T'ao. Sung period. (Edition *Shuo-k'u*).

305. *T'ien-shui kuan.* Drama. Author unknown.

306. *T'ien-sui-ko.* Drama. Author unknown.

306a. T'ien-wen (*see* A. Conrady).

307. *T'ien yo yen.* Drama. Author Chang Ta-fu. 17th century.

308. *Ting-hsien yang-ko hsüan.* (Selected Plantation Songs of Ting-hsien). Peking, 1933. 2 volumes.

309. *T'o-nang ying.* Drama. Author Hsü Yang-hui. Ming period.

310. *T'ou T'ang chi.* Drama. Author unknown.

311. *T'oung Pao.* Periodical. Leiden.

311a. *T'P'KCh* see *T'ai-p'ing kuang-chi.*

311b. *T'P'YL* see *T'ai-p'ing yü-lan.*

312. Trippner, J. "Das Lied von Ma Wu-ko." *Folklore Studies* 17 (1951).

313. *Ts'an t'ung ch'i.* Author unknown. Pre-T'ang period.

314. *Tse pu yü.* Author Yüan Mei. 18th century. Shanghai, 1932. 2 volumes.

315. *Tse-li Wan-pao* (Independent Evening Paper). Taipei.

316. *Tso-chuan.* Compiler supposedly Tso-ch'iu Ming. Chou period.

317. Ts'ui Tai-yang. *Ch'u-min hsin-li yü ko-chung shê-hui-chih-tu-ti ch'i -yüan* (Primitive Psychology and the Origin of Social Institutions). Canton.

318. *T'u-hua chien-wen chih.* Author Kuo Jo-hsü.

319. *T'u-shu chi-ch'eng.* Encyclopedia. 18th century.

320. *Tung-fang tsa-chih* (*Eastern Miscellany*). Periodical. Shanghai and Taipei.

321. *Tung-Han yen-i.* Folk novel. Author unknown.

322. *Tung-p'o Chih-lin.* Author supposedly Su Tung-p'o. Sung period. (Edition *Pi-chi hsiao-shuo ta-kuan*).

323. *Tung-p'o shih.* Collected poems of Su Tung-p'o. Sung period.

324. *Tzu-chih t'ung-chien.* Author Ou-yang Hsiu. 11th century.

325. *Ülkü.* Publication of the People's House. Ankara.

326. van Gennep, A. *Le Folklore.* Paris.

327. Visser, J.de. *The Dragon in China and Japan.* Amsterdam, 1913.

328. *Wan pi.* Drama. Author Wang Tse-chung. Ming period.

329. Wang Chü-hou. *Ning-po mi-yü* (Riddles from Ningpo). Canton.*

330. Wang I-chih. *Wu-ko i-chi* (Second Collection of Songs from Su-chou). Canton.*

331. *Wei-lüeh.* Author Yü Huan. 3rd century. (Quoted in *San-kuo chih*).

332. Wei Ying-ch'i. *Fu-chou ko-yao chia-chi* (First Collection of Songs from Fu-chou).*

333. _____, *Fu-chien san-shen k'ao* (On the Three Deities in Fukien). Canton.*

334. *Der Weltkreis.* Periodical. Berlin.

335. *Wen-jou hsiang.* Modern novel by Ching-kuan-tse. Shanghai, 1929.

336. Wienert, W. *Typen der griechisch-römischen Fabel.* Folklore Fellows Communications no. 56. Helsinki.

337. Wilhelm, R. *Chinesische Volksmärchen.* Jena, 1914.

338. Wright, A.R. *English Folklore.* London, 1927.

339. *Wu-chou fu-chih* (Gazetteer of Wu-chou, Kuanghsi). (quoted in *Yüeh-hsi*).

340. *Wu-hua tung.* Drama. Author unknown.

341. *Wu-lin chiu-shih.* Author Chou Mi. Sung period. (Edition *Pi-chi hsiao-shuo ta-kuan*).

342. Wu Tsao-t'ing. *Ch'üan-chou min-chien chuan-shuo* (Folktales from Ch'üan-chou). Canton.*

343. Yang Ch'eng-shih. *Min-su-hsüeh wen-t'i ko* (Folklore Questions). Canton.*

344. *Yang-chia chiang.* Folk novel. Author unknown.

345. *Yao-ch'ang chi.* Drama. Manchu period?

346. Yao I-chih. *Hu-nan ch'ang-pen t'i-yao* (Summaries of Ballads from Hunan). Canton, 1929.*

347. *Yeh-k'o ts'ung-shu.* Author Wang Mao. Sung period. (Edition *Pi-chi hsiao-shuo ta-kuan*).

348. *Yeh-kuang chu.* Drama. Author Wang Wei-hsin. Ming period.

349. Yeh Tê-chün. *Huai-an ko-yao* (Songs from Huai-an). Canton.*

350. *Yo Fei chuan.* Folk novel. Author unknown.

351. *Yü-chih t'ang t'an-wei.* Author Hsü Ying-ch'iu. 16th century. (Edition *Pi-chi hsiao-shuo ta-kuan*).

352. *Yü Ch'ü-yüan pi-chi.* Author Yü Yüeh. 19th century. Shanghai, 1934. 2 volumes.

353. *Yü-hu ch'ing-hua.* Author Wen-yung. Sung period. (Edition *Pi-chi hsiao-shuo ta-kuan*).

354. *Yu-yang tsa-tsu.* Author Tuan Ch'eng-shih. T'ang period.

355. *Yüan-ch'ao pi-shih.* Author unknown. 14th century.

356. *Yüeh-hsi ts'ung-tsai.* Compiler Wang Sen. 17th century. (Edition *Pi-chi hsiao-shuo ta-kuan*).

357. *Yün-ho hsien-chih* (Gazetteer of Yün-ho, Chêkiang Province).

358. *Yung-hsien chai pi-chi.* Author Ch'en Ch'i-yüan. Manchu period. (Edition *Pi-chi hsiao-shuo ta-kuan*).

359. Zacharias, Th. *Kleine Schriften zur indischen Philologie.* Bonn, 1920.

360. *Zeitschrift du deutschen morgenländischen Gesellschaft.* Periodical.

361. *Zeitschrift für Ethnologie* Periodical. Berlin.

8. 中國文化研究彙刊。 9. 民族學研究所集刊.

17. 斬黃袍。 18. 長城記。 19. 湖州歌謠.張之金.

20. 長坂坡。 21. 廣西猺歌記音. 15. 浙東金華歌謠.

16. 陳博高卧。 27. 台山歌謠集.陳元柱. 28. 征東記.

29. 稽古錄.司馬光. 30. 濟公活佛.濟公傳. 31. 鹿其鹿秦閣.

32. 稽神錄。 33. 堅瓠集.筆記小說大觀. 34. 謎史,

錢南揚. 35. 民俗舊聞. 36. 劍丹記. 37. 千字文。

38. 潛研堂金石題尾.錢大昕. 39. 赤龍鬚. 40. 池北

偶談. 41. 赤松記. 42. 金華縣志. 43. 錦衣歸.

44. 今古奇觀. 45. 金瓶梅. 46. 晉書. 47. 晉陽宮.

48. 縉雲縣志. 50. 情話.胡寄塵. 51. 青銅嘯.

52. 影梅庵憶語. 53. 海龍王的女兒.清水. 54. 秋江.

55. 情歌唱答.兵峻. 56. 求如願. 57. 人熊婆.

58. 蘇州風俗.周振鶴. 59. 周禮. 61. 中國諺語論.

朱介凡. 62. 曲海總目提要. 63. 舉鼎觀畫. 64. 傳奇.

65. 莊子. 66. 羣星輔. 67. 羣星會. 68. 春明(夢)餘錄.

69. 春在堂筆記. 70. 民間藝文叢話.鍾敬文.

71. 狼獐情歌. 72. 楚辭中的神話和傳說. 73. 印歐民

間故事型式表. 74. 老虎外婆故事集. 75. 中國民談

型式表. 76. 中興禦侮錄. 77. 中華全國風俗志.

78. 中國人名大辭典. 79. 中國地方戲曲集成. 104. 耳食錄.

105. 二十步送妹新歌. 106. 爾雅. 107. 法園珠林.

108. 范文正公集. 109. 封神榜.封神演義. 110. 風俗通義.

113. 風雲會. 114. 輔仁學誌. 121. 孩子們的歌聲. 黃紹年. 122. 韓非子. 123. 漢宮秋. 124. (前)漢書. 125. 史學年報. 127. 鶴林玉露. 128. 後漢書. 129. 厚德錄. 131. 戲曲選. 131. 西廂記. 132. 西遊記. 133. 祥麟見. 134. 香襄記. 135. 香飲樓賓談. 137. 小放牛. 138. 楊州的傳說. 蕭漢. 139. 笑笑錄. 140. 小唐出奸傳. 141. 小笠棚. 142. 小倉山房文集. 143. 閩歌甲集. 謝雲聲. 144. 台灣情歌集. 145. 台灣新生報. 146. 續齊諧記. 147. 續夷堅志. 148. 徐文長集. 149. 田螺女. 150. 薛仁貴榮歸故里. 151. 薛丁山征西. 152. 虎符記. 153. 白話文學史. 胡適. 156. 華嶽志. 156. 花云帶箭. 157. 淮南子. 159. 紅粉菱. 列年生. 160. 紅電閣. 161. 紅樓夢. 162. 一封書. 163. 一捧雪. 164. 藝文類聚. 170. 如是觀. 171. 儒林外史. 172. 迷信與傳說. 容肇祖. 173. 開展月刊. 174. 康輶紀行. 125. 高僧傳. 176. 高旺進表. 177. 歌謠週刊. 179. 孟姜女故事研究集. 顧頡剛. 180. 薊粵的婚喪. 181. 妙峰山. 182. 括蒼金石志. 183. 闞眄盷. 184. 桂林風土記. 185. 困學記聞. 186. 中國古代社會史. 189. 禮記. 190. 離騷. 191. 歷代筆記小說選. 192. 列仙傳. 153. 連環套. 194. 咸淳臨安志. 195. 民俗學論文集. 196. 劉秀走國. 197. 故事的鐘子. 198. 廣州謎語. 劉萬章. 200. 廣州民間故事. 201. 廣州兒歌甲集. 202. 巧女和呆娘的故事. 婁子匡. 203. 中國新年風俗志. 204. 月光光歌集. 205. 紹興故事. 206. 西藏戀歌. 207. 朱英台. 婁子倫. 218. 魯班經. 219. 淥水亭雜識. 210. 論衡. 211. 論語.

214. 埋輪亭。 215. 墨耀。 216. 蒙齋筆談。 217. 孟姜女考夫。 219. 夢梁錄。 220. 孟良盜骨。 221. 妙香室叢話。 222. 民間月刊。 223. 民俗週刊。 224. 明齋小識。 225. 墨客揮犀。 226. 墨餘錄。 227. 支那民俗誌,永尾龍造。 230. 南京學報。 231. 南遊記。 232. 鬧花燈。 233. 人仙慶壽。 235. 白門樓。 236. 白蛇傳。 237. 白歲掛帥。 238. 白歲園。 239. 白草坡。 240. 蟠桃會。 241. 龐涓夜走馬陵道。 242. 寶劍記。 243. 包公案。 244. 北齊書。 245. 北夢瑣言。 246. 北平歌謠。 247. 河南謎語,白啟明。 248. 白虎通。 249. 破洪州。 250. 開封歌謠集,白壽彝。 251. 博物志。 258. 三輔皇圖。 259. 三俠五義。 260. 三星照。 261. 三虎下山。 262. 三國志（魏志、吳志、蜀志）。 263. 三國志演義。 264. 三多朔。 269. 山海經。 270. 山東歌謠集。 271. 上天台。 272. 史記。 273. 詩經。 274. 鬥牛。 275. 石墨鐫華。 276. 世說新語。 277. 十月花胎歌。 278. 水經注。 279. 雙鎖記。 280. 雙瑞記。 281. 雙報恩。 282. 水淹七軍。 283. 水滸傳。 284. 說文解字。 285. 杞梁妻。 288. 搜神記。 290. 薛范叔。 291. 隋書。 292. 隋唐演義。 293. 大唐西域求法高僧傳。 294. 打玉英。 295. 台北縣中和社區之研究。 296. 太平廣記。 297. 太平御覽。 298. 太上寶法圖說。 299. 大正大藏經。 300. 台灣風土（公論報）。 301. 疊花記。 302. 黨人碑。 303. 陶庵夢憶。 304. 金錢圍山叢談。 305. 天水關。 306. 天燈閑。 306a. 天問。 307. 天有眼。 308. 定縣秧歌選。 309. 脫囊穎。 310. 投唐記。 311. 迪報。 313. 參通契。 314. 子不語。 315. 自立晚報。 316. 左傳。 317. 初民心理與各種社會制度起源,崔載陽。 318. 圖畫見聞誌。 319. 圖書集成。 320. 東方雜誌。 341. 東漢演義。 342. 東坡志林。 343. 東坡詩。 344. 資治通鑑。 348. 完璧。 349. 寧波諺語，王鞠侯。 330. 吳歌乙集，王翼之。 331. 魏晷。 332. 福州歌謠甲集，魏應騏。 333. 福建三神考。 335. 溫柔鄉，靜觀子。 337. 梧州府志。 340. 天花洞。 341. 武林舊事。 342. 泉州民間傳說，吳藻汀。 343. 民俗學問題格，楊成志。 344. 楊家將。 345. 瑤媧記。 346. 湖南唱本提要，姚逸之。 347. 野客叢書。 348. 夜光珠。 349. 淮南歌謠。 350. 岳飛傳。 351. 玉芝堂談薈。 352. 俞曲園筆記。 353. 玉壺清話。 354. 酉陽雜俎。 355. 元朝秘史。 356. 粵西叢載。 357. 雲和縣志。 358. 庸閒齋筆記。

Written by 蔡文輝

INDEX